Certain Hope *for Uncertain Times!*

A Positive View
of End-Time Events

LOWELL LUNDSTROM

LOWELL
LUNDSTROM
Ministries, Inc.
Sisseton, SD 57262

Lowell Lundstrom Ministries, Inc.
Sisseton, South Dakota 57262

CERTAIN HOPE FOR UNCERTAIN TIMES
formerly published as What's Coming Next

Certain Hope for Uncertain Times!

Table of Contents

Preface   5
1. A New World Is Coming!   8
2. The Key Questions   15
3. The Cycle of Sorrows   26
4. The Coming Persecution   34
5. The First Signal of the Last Days   47
6. The Sign of the Star of David   60
7. Sensual Signs of the Last Days   72
8. The Apostate Church   87
9. The Rise and Fall of Russia!   105
10. The Coming Antichrist   124
11. The Great Tribulation   141
12. The Great Tribulation—Part II   154
13. The Great Escape   167
14. The Judgment Seat of Christ   180
15. When Christ Returns to Reign!   193
16. The Coming 1,000 Years
    of Peace and Prosperity   202
17. The Millennium—Part II   216
18. The Final Cleansing of the Earth   233
19. The Great White Throne Judgment   248
20. Superlife!   263
21. Superworld!   280
22. The Super-Universe!   298
23. Living Now So It Counts
    Later—Part I   322
24. Living Now So It Counts
    Later—Part II   344

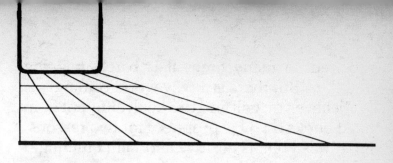

Preface

I believe this book will change your life. Modern day "prophets" from every walk of life predict that we are living in the last days of this planet.

Scientists, military strategists, sociologists, political leaders and clergymen are all warning us that we are only 18 minutes away from Doomsday. This is how short a time it takes for 100-megaton Russian missiles to reach the heartland of North America. Of course, the United States would retaliate, and within hours the world would be reduced to a radioactive pile of rubble.

But wait! Even though we are living in the last days of human government, I believe that for God's people, the best days are ahead. This world, like an old suit, has been patched up and repaired so many times it is barely hanging together. But there is a new world coming!

I believe you will find this book different from most books on Bible prophecy for two reasons. First, this book is positive and faith building. I read every major book on Bible prophecy while researching this book, and honestly, I became depressed. Page after page, chapter after chapter, was filled with gloom and doom, and I felt smothered with depressing facts.

Recently, I explained the problem of Bible prophecy to one of my associates. I said, "There are many facts that reveal we are living in the last days, but within themselves, these facts are dead. They do not produce spiritual life. Only God's word, as it applies to our daily lives in a living practical way, produces life and hope for the future."

Second, this book is simple and easy to understand. I have studied prophecy for nearly 25 years, and each author I have read has a different idea on how end-time events will unfold.

One of my friends mentioned that his Bible study group had discussed the possibility of studying prophecy. They finally gave up on the idea because they thought the subject was too speculative and would cause many arguments.

As I studied the scriptures and the many great prophetic books that have been written on prophecy, I almost shelved this project. It seemed there were just too many different points of view. How could I possibly set forth the chronological order of coming prophetic events without creating more speculation?

Then one day the Holy Spirit impressed me to study what Jesus said on the subject. *Suddenly, I made a miraculous discovery.* IN THE THREE GOSPELS OF MATTHEW, MARK AND LUKE, JESUS SETS FORTH THE SERIES OF COMING EVENTS IN A SIMPLE, EASY-TO-UNDERSTAND ORDER. The disciples were not theologians. They were common people (as most of us are) who required a clear step-by-step lesson in prophecy, and Jesus did not disappoint them. I will share His outline with you in the coming chapters of this book.

Now, you may find some truths in these chapters that are not directly related to Bible prophecy. These inclusions are intentional. I added them to feed your soul. Paul the apostle said, *"The letter killeth, but the spirit giveth life"* (2 Corinthians 3:6). Dead letter facts and statistics will kill your soul, but inspired spiritual truth will feed it.

A friend of mine, who is an avid reader, often commented when finishing a book, "It was a good read." I hope you'll say the same when you finish this book with one addition, "It was a good feed."

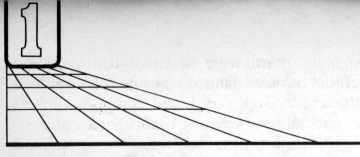

A New World Is Coming !

The future of our world is something like a good news-bad news joke: The bad news is that this world is headed for a great tribulation that will destroy one-half the earth's population and end in Armageddon. The good news is this planet has a grand and glorious future.

Christianity is actually a futuristic religion. Christians believe in:
* A new birth
* A new life-style
* A new set of moral values
* A new world leader
* A new government
* A new heaven
* A new earth
* A new life after death

8

This list could go on and on, but it is easy to see that *Christians are the only bona fide futurists in the world.*

The reason why Christians are optimistic about the future is that we have faith in Jesus Christ. We believe He is the Son of the living God. We also believe He is the greatest prophet ever born.

If you are not a committed Christian, hear me out. Of all the prophets ever born, Jesus Christ is the only one who ever rose from the dead. Buddha, Mohammed, Confucius, the gurus, etc., all died and remained dead—*but Jesus rose alive from the tomb!*

Examine the Evidence

If you doubt the fact of the resurrection, please examine the evidence. The chief priests remembered that Jesus had declared that He would rise again. They didn't believe Him, but to make certain that His followers did not steal His body and spread rumors that He had risen, they placed a guard of soldiers around the tomb to protect it from thieves. They even placed the seal of Caesar on the stone. This meant that if anyone tampered with the grave, they would be accountable to the Emperor himself. The situation was simply this: *if they could make certain the body of Jesus remained in the tomb until the fourth day—the Christian church would be no more.*

But they could just as well have tried to seal the grave with Scotch tape. On that third morning there was a great quaking and the stone rolled away, not so that Jesus could get out, but so that everyone could look in and see the empty place where His body had been.

Jesus Christ appeared alive unto His disciples for 40 days. He showed Himself alive with so many infallible proofs that even doubting Thomas, who would not believe until he had touched the nail prints in the Savior's hands and touched the spear scar in His side, met Jesus alive and was convinced and cried, *"My Lord and my God"* (John 20:28).

Finally, on the day of our Savior's ascension into heaven, Jesus met with His band of about 500 followers on the Mount of Olives. While they looked on, He was taken up into heaven (see 1 Corinthians 15:6).

Who is Jesus Christ?

Before I share the prophecies of Jesus Christ with you, it is important for you to come to some kind of conclusion as to who Jesus really is. Was He a lunatic, a liar, a legend, or the Lord? If you approach His prophetic teachings with doubt, you will not receive the impact of His message.

DO YOU THINK JESUS WAS A LUNATIC? As you read the New Testament, do you get the impression that Jesus was some sort of religious weirdo? Jesus was such a practical teacher that *"the common people heard him gladly"* (Mark 12:37). Jesus attracted down-to-earth fishermen like Peter and Andrew. He was admired by fiery-tempered men like James and John. Jesus even persuaded Matthew, a tax agent of Caesar, to follow Him.

If Jesus had been a wild-eyed mystic, if He had expressed Himself with the disjointed phrases and "off-the-wall" comments that so many cult leaders do today, He would never have succeeded with the people who followed Him then and now. Jesus was not a lunatic.

WAS JESUS A LIAR? Hardly. Jesus spoke the truth so fearlessly the religious leaders would tremble in terror when He taught. His exposé of their hypocrisy offended their pride and made them so angry they eventually killed Him. They crucified Jesus because the truth He proclaimed exposed them as the hypocrites they were. Jesus was not a liar.

IS JESUS A LEGEND? Is He only the product of men's imaginations? Did Matthew, Mark, Luke, John, Peter and Paul dream up this man? The truth is that Jesus Christ actually lived on earth. Secular, non-christian historians include Him in their writings of history. Tacitus and Pliny, the Roman historians, mention Jesus, but Josephus, the Jewish chronologer, says the

11

most. You can be confident that Jesus actually did exist in time and space.

But there is another fact to keep in mind. Nearly all of the apostles gave their lives for Jesus Christ. Judas betrayed Jesus and later threw down the payoff money and cried, *"I have sinned in that I have betrayed...innocent blood"* (Matthew 27:4). John the apostle was exiled for his testimony, finally set free and later died of old age. But according to history, the rest of the apostles were martyred for their testimony about Jesus Christ.

My question is, if Jesus was only a story they had made up, if He was only a legend of their creation, would these practical, hard-working family men have died for their own lies? Never! About the time that they were faced with cruci-fixion, when the eight-inch spikes were to be driven through their hands, they would have renounced their words and admitted their lies.

But they denied nothing because they had told the truth. They had seen Jesus with their own eyes. They had been with Him as He healed the sick, cast out evil spirits, stilled the storm, and fed the multitudes with a little boy's lunch. *They had even seen Him raise the dead back to life!* They had seen Jesus die and they watched the soldiers drive the spear into His side. They were His witnesses because they had seen Jesus alive after His resurrection.

So most of the apostles of Jesus Christ willingly gave their lives for their testimony because they were convinced *beyond all doubt THAT JESUS CHRIST WAS THE SON OF THE LIVING GOD.*

Remember, a man might die for another man's lie, but he seldom will for his own. If the disciples had heard of Jesus Christ second-handedly, they might have been deceived into believing. But they had seen the resurrected Christ with their own eyes, they had held Him with their own hands, they had eaten meals with Jesus after His resurrection and there wasn't even a slim chance they were wrong.

SO IF JESUS WAS NOT A LUNATIC, LIAR OR LEGEND, THEN HE MUST BE THE LORD, THE SON OF THE LIVING GOD!

Now, you might not be able to believe this statement yet, but can you at least agree that Jesus Christ was a good, honest and miraculous man? Even though this is not enough to save you, it helps to establish the credibility of the prophecies of Jesus.

Gospels Tell Our Future

Because of His resurrection, I believe Jesus Christ is the greatest prophet ever born. Remember, anyone can preach religion but rising from the dead is most difficult. The disciples asked Jesus to give them an outline of the future, and this is what I am going to share with you in the coming chapters.

As I mentioned in the introduction, *I was surprised to discover that Jesus gave His disciples a simple step-by-step outline of the future.* His outline is recorded by three of the Gospel writers, Matthew, Mark and Luke. The Bible says that by the mouth of two or three witnesses shall every word be established, so as you read these prophecies in triplicate, I hope it will give you confidence and hope for the future.

Many revolutionary changes are taking place in our world today, but one thing is true – Christians have a grand and glorious future. This is why we are futurists. I can tell you now that your future with Jesus Christ is more wonderful than anything that you could ever imagine.

Let me share with you the two key questions about the future in the next chapter.

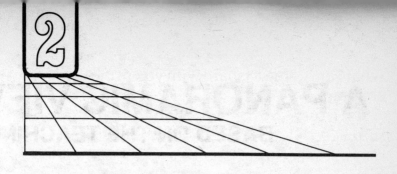

The Key Questions

If you could ask Jesus Christ about the future, you would probably inquire:

1. Lord, what will be the sign of Your coming?
2. When will be the end of the world?

Peter, James and John asked Jesus these very questions when He taught on the Mount of Olives.

Earlier that day Jesus had prophesied the coming destruction of the beautiful Jewish temple. It had taken King Herod more than 40 years to build this marvelous structure. The disciples were alarmed when Jesus said the temple would be destroyed. Here is the account from all three gospels. Please read these scriptures carefully because they are the strength of this prophetic book. So many authors bounce around, expounding on prophecies here and there, but *my aim is to share the coming prophetic*

A PANORAMIC VIEW
BASED ON THE TEACHINGS

Jesus Christ's
death, resurrection
and ascension
to the Father's
right hand
in Heaven

> **True believers caught up**
> **to be with Jesus Christ**
> Matt. 24:42-51; Mark 13:32-37;
> Luke 21:34-37; 1 Thes. 4:16-18;
> 1 Cor. 15:51,52

(TIME LINE)

SIGNS OF THE LAST DAYS

Deceivers will come in His name, deceiving many
    Matt. 24:4,5; Mark 13:5,6; Luke 21:8; 1 Tim. 4:1

Nations will run their cycle of wars, rumors of wars, famines, pestilences and earthquakes
    Matt. 24:6; Mark 13:8; Luke 21:9-11

A great persecution of believers is coming
    Matt. 24:9-13; Mark 13:9, 11-14; Luke 21:12-19

The Jews return to their homeland and repossess Jerusalem
    Matt. 24:32-35; Mark 13:28-31; Luke 21:29-33; Ezek. 37:21,22

The sign of Noah's day—gross immorality and a concern with material things
    Matt. 24:37-42; Luke 17:26,27

The sign of Lot's day—gross homosexuality
    Luke 17:28-37

The rise of Soviet Russia to power
    Ezek. 38 and 39 (Ancient maps show "Land of Magog" is Soviet Russia)

When the Gospel is preached in all the world, the end time begins
    Matt. 24:14; Mark 13:10

Anti-Christ rises to power—recognized by true Christians
    Matt. 24:15-20; Mark 13:14-18; 2 Thes. 2:1-12; I John 2:18,22

OF THE FUTURE
OF JESUS CHRIST

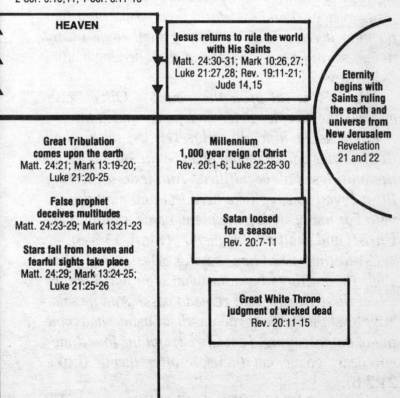

The Judgment Seat of Christ
and Marriage Supper
of the Lamb
2 Cor. 5:10,11; 1 Cor. 3:11-15

HEAVEN

**Jesus returns to rule the world
with His Saints**
Matt. 24:30-31; Mark 10:26,27;
Luke 21:27,28; Rev. 19:11-21;
Jude 14,15

**Eternity
begins with
Saints ruling
the earth and
universe from
New Jerusalem**
Revelation
21 and 22

**Great Tribulation
comes upon the earth**
Matt. 24:21; Mark 13:19-20;
Luke 21:20-25

**False prophet
deceives multitudes**
Matt. 24:23-29; Mark 13:21-23

**Stars fall from heaven and
fearful sights take place**
Matt. 24:29; Mark 13:24-25;
Luke 21:25-26

**Millennium
1,000 year reign of Christ**
Rev. 20:1-6; Luke 22:28-30

**Satan loosed
for a season**
Rev. 20:7-11

**Great White Throne
judgment of wicked dead**
Rev. 20:11-15

events *(as much as possible)* IN THE EXACT CHRONOLOGICAL ORDER *Jesus gave them.*

Deceivers will come in Jesus' name deceiving many

"And as he sat upon the mount of Olives, the disciples came unto him privately, saying, Tell us, when shall these things be? and what shall be the sign of thy coming, and of the end of the world? And Jesus answered and said unto them, Take heed that no man deceive you. For many shall come in my name, saying I am Christ; and shall deceive many" (Matthew 24:3-5).

"And as he sat upon the mount of Olives, over against the temple, Peter and James and John and Andrew asked him privately, Tell us, when shall these things be? and what shall be the sign when all these things shall be fulfilled? And Jesus answering them began to say, Take heed lest any man deceive you: For many shall come in my name, saying, I am Christ; and shall deceive many" (Mark 13:3-6).

"And they asked him, saying, Master, but when shall these things be? and what sign will there be when these things shall come to pass? And he said, Take heed that ye be not deceived: for many shall come in my name, saying, I am Christ; and the time draweth near: go ye not therefore after them" (Luke 21:7,8).

Notice: ALL THREE WRITERS report the same inquiry and answer.

The Rise of False Doctrines

The question is, when Jesus says deceivers will come in His name saying they are the Christ and deceiving many, is Jesus referring to false teaching or false Christs? I believe the answer is both. However, I think He is primarily referring to deceivers who will come in His name, using His reputation and favor to peddle their false doctrines. Paul the apostle says, *"Now the Spirit speaketh expressly, that in the latter times some shall depart from the faith, giving heed to seducing spirits, and doctrines of devils; Speaking lies in hypocrisy; having their conscience seared with a hot iron"* (1 Timothy 4:1,2).

Jesus realized that after He returned to heaven that false teachers would come in His name deceiving many. Paul and the other apostles had to deal with this problem even in their days. Wherever Paul preached, the false Jewish teachers would follow him, instructing the new Gentile converts to be circumcised. *"And certain men which came down from Judea taught the brethren, and said, Except ye be circumcised after the manner of Moses, ye cannot be saved. When therefore Paul and Barnabas had no small dissension and disputation with them"* (Acts 15:1,2).

However, the high church council of elders decided that circumcision was unnecessary for salvation. *"But there rose up certain of the sect of*

19

the Pharisees which believed, saying, That it was needful to circumcise them, and to command them to keep the law of Moses" (Acts 15:5).

These false teachers followed Paul everywhere and gave him a terrible time. They were so bad that Paul says, "I have fought with beasts at Ephesus" (1 Corinthians 15:32). Jesus said the first order of prophetic events would be the rise of false teachers and deceivers: "For wheresoever the carcass is, there will the eagles be gathered together" (Matthew 24:28).

Just as you need to protect your body from disease, you must also protect your faith in God from error. Germs kill, and lies will destroy your relationship with God.

Truth Or Error?

The questions arise, How can you tell truth from error? and, How can you identify the true Christian religions from the false?

Most false religions have a book of writings they reverence to be as inspired as the Bible. They build their doctrine on their leader's theories rather than on the Word of God. But Paul the apostle said to the Galatian Christians, "I marvel that ye are so soon removed from him that called you into the grace of Christ unto another gospel: Which is not another; but there be some that trouble you, and would pervert the gospel of Christ. But though we, or an angel from heaven, preach any other gospel unto you than that which we have preached unto you, let him be accursed" (Galatians 1:6-8).

So the Apostle Paul says that any so-called "gospel message" that doesn't agree with the Bible is false. *The Bible as we have it today is the final authority in matters of faith.*

I know many false teachers will tell of visions, dreams and revelations, but if the illuminations they have received do not square with God's Word, they are wrong. When someone brings up a book other than the Bible and gives reverence to it as inspired—look out!

The Apostle John wrote the Revelation of Jesus Christ as God gave it to him. I believe God meant it to be the last book in the Bible. John wrote, *"If any man shall add unto these things, God shall add unto him the plagues that are written in this book: And if any man shall take away from the words of the book of this prophecy, God shall take away his part out of the book of life, and out of the holy city, and from the things which are written in this book"* (Revelation 22:18,19).

There is only one Revelation from God that is the final authority on matters of Christian faith—the Holy Bible. If anyone starts quoting other books—beware! They are treading on thin ice.

The second thing I have noticed about false teachers is that they are confused about the person of Jesus Christ. In the days of John the

21

apostle, the false teachers were already multiplying. This is why John wrote, *"Every spirit the confesseth not that Jesus Christ is come in the flesh is not of God"* (1 John 4:3).

It is always good to ask religious teachers these two questions: "Do you believe that Jesus Christ is the Son of the Living God? Do you believe He died for the sins of the world and literally rose again from the dead?"

Most cults and false doctrines do not recognize Jesus Christ as Lord. They deny that He is truly the Son of God in a way unique and separate from the rest of us.

False teachers also have the wrong spirit. John the apostle said, *"But ye have an unction from the Holy One, and ye know all things"* (1 John 2:20). By this John meant that you can detect the "spirit of false doctrine" by the Holy Spirit who dwells in you. Truth feels right—error feels wrong. If you feel something in your inner spirit that is not right, it is your spiritual "early warning" system telling you that a lie is on its way— that error is coming your direction.

John also said, *"Hereby know we the spirit of truth, and the spirit of error. Beloved, let us love one another: for love is of God; and every one that loveth is born of God, and knoweth God. He that loveth not knoweth not God; for God is love"* (1 John 4:6-8).

Down through the past 25 years of ministry I have noticed that false teachers do not have much love for the body of believers. They speak critically of the true church of born-again believers as if they are above it. John said when someone begins to attack devoted Christians, it is a giveaway that he is in the wrong.

False teaching usually comes wrapped in a package called *"Deeper Spiritual Truth."* I like to study new things about God, but when someone comes saying, "This is it! I have a new revelation of what you need," I move very carefully. It is possible that God may be trying to teach me something deeper or it could be Satan trying to deceive me with something deadly.

Paul the apostle says, *"For the time will come when they will not endure sound doctrine; but after their own lusts shall they heap to themselves teachers, having itching ears; And they shall turn away their ears from the truth, and shall be turned unto fables"* (2 Timothy 4:3,4).

There is something seductive about a spiritual lie. It allows you to remain as you are while offering you the benefit of a "New Truth." Error also appeals to your ego—it gives you the "heady" feeling of being one of the chosen ones or one with "insight and wisdom."

Know Your Bible

Jesus Christ said that many deceivers would come in His name. This would be the first of all coming events and will continue until He returns. This is why it is so important for you to study the Bible regularly.

I have heard that the FBI teaches their agents to detect counterfeit money not by studying the counterfeit—but the genuine. The more you learn about Jesus Christ from the Bible, the stronger you will be when the counterfeit Christian comes your way.

Jesus said, *"Beware of false prophets, which come to you in sheep's clothing, but inwardly they are ravening wolves. Ye shall know them by their fruits. Do men gather grapes of thorns, or figs of thistles? Even so every good tree bringeth forth good fruit; but a corrupt tree bringeth forth evil fruit. A good tree cannot bring forth evil fruit, neither can a corrupt tree bring forth good fruit. Every tree that bringeth not forth good fruit is hewn down, and cast into the fire. Wherefore by their fruits ye shall know them.*

"Not every one that saith unto me, Lord, Lord, shall enter into the kingdom of heaven; but he that doeth the will of my Father which is in heaven. Many will say to me in that day, Lord, Lord, have we not prophesied in thy name? and in thy name have cast out devils? and in thy name done many wonderful works? And then will I profess unto them, I never knew you: depart from me, ye that work iniquity" (Matthew 7:15-23).

Do Not Be Deceived

Beware of deceivers! Jesus said to check out the teacher's life. Carefully observe whether or not he or she is really living for God. One of the signs of the last days is the increase of lies being promoted in the name of truth. Jesus said, *"When the Son of man cometh, shall he find faith on the earth?"* (Luke 18:8). In other words, in the last days people will teach a "faith" that will be so watered down and changed around, it will hardly be Christian at all.

So watch the life of the one who teaches you about God. If his life is not holy, get away from him as quickly as you can before you get entangled in his web of error. Beware of men who have "charisma" without character.

When it comes to your body, you don't want anyone tampering with it unless he is a doctor of great reputation. If possible you want a proven specialist. They may charge a little more in the beginning, but because they have specialized knowledge, they may be able to help you get well quicker and end up costing you less.

Use the same caution when it comes to matters of your soul. You want to consult the writings of proven men and women of God before you depart on any new faith teaching.

"Beware of deceivers!" Jesus said. "They will come in my name and deceive many."

The Cycle of Sorrows

The second major division of prophetic events, according to Jesus Christ, would be *the cycle* of wars, rumors of wars, famines, pestilences and earthquakes in many places.

"And ye shall hear of wars and rumors of wars: see that ye be not troubled: for all these things must come to pass, but the end is not yet. For nation shall rise against nation, and kingdom against kingdom: and there shall be famines, and pestilences, and earthquakes in divers places. All these are the beginning of sorrows" (Matthew 24:6-8).

"And when ye shall hear of wars and rumors of wars, be ye not troubled: for such things must needs be; but the end shall not be yet. For nation shall rise against nation, and kingdom against kingdom: and there shall be earthquakes in divers places, and there shall be famines and troubles: these are the beginnings of sorrows" (Mark 13:7,8).

"And he said, Take heed that ye be not deceived: for many shall come in my name, saying, I am Christ; and the time draweth near: go ye not therefore after them. But when ye shall hear of wars and commotions, be not terrified: for these things must first come to pass; but the end is not by and by. Then said he unto them, Nation shall rise against nation, and kingdom against kingdom: And great earthquakes shall be in divers places, and famines, and pestilences; and fearful sights and great signs shall there be from heaven" (Luke 21:8-11).

Again you notice that all three writers, Matthew, Mark and Luke recorded almost the same words of Jesus. The only reason why the narratives vary at all is that each writer recorded what he remembered. It's just like asking three witnesses to describe a car accident. Each will tell a slightly different story of the same accident. The truth is the same, but the words are different.

A Cycle, Not a Sign

There's something you should take note of concerning this second sign: When the calamity of war arises, or pestilences, famines or earthquakes, Jesus knew that people would panic and many would say, "The end of the world is come!" But Jesus taught that these events were only a cycle of sorrows, and at the conclusion of this teaching he said, *"But the end is not yet"*

(Matthew 24:6); *"But the end shall not be yet"* (Mark 13:7); *"But the end is not by and by"* (Luke 21:9).

Unbelievers have become skeptical of "Bible-believing" Christians because it seems that each time a great war or natural disaster has taken place, preachers and teachers point to this passage of scripture and say, "See! The Bible says this is a sign we are reaching the end of the world." It is very easy to do. I know because I have done it too. However, if you are going to interpret the words of Jesus correctly, *these events are part of a cycle more than a specific sign.* There have been wars, rumors of wars, famines, pestilences and earthquakes for the past 2,000 years.

Yet, I believe these events will increase in frequency as the last days approach. Just think, during World War II there were over 43 million casualties. Then communism took over much of the world and leaders of state like Stalin, Khrushchev and Mao Tse-tung destroyed millions in their efforts to stay in power. It is estimated that Stalin killed 50 million; Khrushchev, 30 million; and according to the *Guinness Book of Records*, Mao Tse-tung put 100 million Chinese to their deaths. This is nearly one-half of the population of the United States, or five times the population of Canada.

The Power of Nuclear Warfare

Today the world stands at the threshold of destruction. For the first time in the history of mankind, nations have enough nuclear bombs and weapons to destroy all life on this planet. (The United States and Russia have more than 50,000 nuclear devices.) Take a moment to study this sketch.

DESTRUCTION OF A 25-MEGATON BOMB
DETONATED ABOVE GROUND

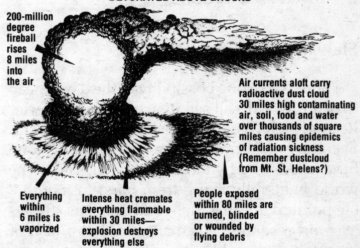

200-million degree fireball rises 8 miles into the air

Air currents aloft carry radioactive dust cloud 30 miles high contaminating air, soil, food and water over thousands of square miles causing epidemics of radiation sickness (Remember dustcloud from Mt. St. Helens?)

Everything within 6 miles is vaporized

Intense heat cremates everything flammable within 30 miles— explosion destroys everything else

People exposed within 80 miles are burned, blinded or wounded by flying debris

However, the Russians have armed many of their 1,400 ICBM's (missiles) with 100-megaton warheads. This sketch shows only the damage from a 25-megaton warhead. It is reported that if just one 100-megaton warhead exploded over the state of Ohio, every living creature in the state would perish. People standing as far away as 300 miles looking in the direction of the blast would have their eyes melted in their sockets. No wonder Jesus said, "All these are the beginning of sorrows."

Remember, the Russians have 1,400 long-range missiles aimed at the heartland of North America. This is why we are only 18 minutes away from total destruction. If it weren't for the protection of God, this world would have destroyed itself by now.

Starvation Threatens Many

There is a strong possibility in the days ahead that the world will see its worst famines ever. Recently Orville Freeman, who was the U.S. Secretary of Agriculture under Presidents John F. Kennedy and Lyndon B. Johnson, said, "The world is literally living from hand to mouth." He pointed out that the world only has 40 days of grain reserves. Freeman said that a rash of crop failures could trigger a panic as reserve stocks are exhausted.

He also said, "I'm not all doom and gloom. This is just a question of realism. I don't think we have to go into massive famine. But when prices get high, poor people can't afford to eat very well.

We took these pictures in North Africa, where a famine had devastated these people. It could happen in North America too.

"Now I know that's not a very pleasant thought, and if that's gloom and doom, so be it. This is the most important single problem we face—except perhaps for the big bomb."

Freeman also pointed out, "It is estimated that 500 million human beings perished from malnutrition and starvation between 1972 and 1973. This could happen again at almost any time for, as matters now stand, reserve stocks are not adequate to meet a major shortfall in production."

These sobering words warn us that the world is at the brink of a frightening famine. We're only 40 days from a food panic.

According to Orville Freeman, world farmland production is dropping. Consider this with the fact that the world population will double from 4.5 billion persons to 8 billion by the year 2000, fewer than 20 years from now. It is plain to see that world famine is in our immediate future on a scale never imagined before.

Earthquakes

From reports available, the frequency of earthquakes is increasing. It is reported that the number of earthquakes per decade has approximately doubled in each of the past ten years. But we must remember that the wars, famines and earthquakes and pestilences are a cycle of sorrows that is leading up to the last days.

Dr. George Wald, the Nobel Prize-winning scientist from Harvard University, has said, "I think human life is threatened as never before in the history of this planet. Not just by one peril, but by many perils that are all working together and coming to a head at about the same time, and that time lies very close to the year 2000. I am one of those scientists who finds it hard to see how the human race is to bring itself much past the year 2000."

Keep Looking Up

It might be good to keep Dr. Wald's quote in mind as you continue reading this book. Many prophetic events are coming together that tell us the end is near. But Jesus said, *"Let not your heart be troubled: ye believe in God, believe also in me"* (John 14:1).

God has everything under control. The whole world is in His hands. But the cycle of sorrows has about run its course. In the next chapter I will tell you about the coming worldwide persecution of the saints.

The Coming Persecution

True believers in Jesus Christ have always suffered persecution. It is a fact that more Christians are being persecuted for their faith today than ever before. Think of the Christians in Russia, China, Poland and in many other Iron Curtain countries. We should also remember the many in the Muslim and Hindu countries who must worship secretly for fear of reprisals.

However, according to the chronological order of events set forth by Jesus Christ in the Gospels, this persecution of true believers will spread until it is worldwide, including the United States and Canada. Note that Jesus said, *"Ye shall be hated of ALL nations for my name's sake"* (Matthew 24:9). Before I comment on this series of events, I want you to read the scriptures for yourself. Note that Mark and Luke quote Jesus almost exactly.

"Then shall they deliver you up to be afflicted, and shall kill you: and ye shall be hated of all nations for my name's sake. And then shall many be offended, and shall betray one another, and shall hate one another. And many false prophets shall rise, and shall deceive many. And because iniquity shall abound, the love of many shall wax cold. But he that shall endure unto the end, the same shall be saved" (Matthew 24:9-13).

"But take heed to yourselves: for they shall deliver you up to councils; and in the synagogues ye shall be beaten: and ye shall be brought before rulers and kings for my sake, for a testimony against them. And the gospel must first be published among all nations. But when they shall lead you, and deliver you up, take no thought beforehand what ye shall speak, neither do ye premeditate: but whatsoever shall be given you in that hour, that speak ye: for it is not ye that speak, but the Holy Ghost. Now the brother shall betray the brother to death, and the father the son; and children shall rise up against their parents, and shall cause them to be put to death. And ye shall be hated of all men for my name's sake: but he that shall endure unto the end, the same shall be saved" (Mark 13:9-13).

"But before all these, they shall lay their hands on you, and persecute you, delivering you up to the synagogues, and into prisons, being brought before

kings and rulers for my name's sake. And it shall turn to you for a testimony. Settle it therefore in your hearts, not to meditate before what ye shall answer: For I will give you a mouth and wisdom, which all your adversaries shall not be able to gainsay nor resist. And ye shall be betrayed both by parents, and brethren, and kinsfolks, and friends; and some of you shall they cause to be put to death. And ye shall be hated of all men for my name's sake. But there shall not an hair of your head perish. In your patience possess ye your souls" (Luke 21:12-19).

Persecution is Coming

For many years I have felt in my inner spirit that a great persecution is going to come to believers in North America. I am more convinced of it now than ever. (If you are a student of Bible prophecy, do not confuse the words "persecution" and "tribulation." I'll deal with the tribulation period later, but here I am speaking of persecution.)

The United States and Canada are rapidly changing. The Judeo-Christian ethic, or concept of right and wrong, that we inherited from our forefathers is being abandoned. The Bible and its truths of absolute morality have been thrown out of our schools and shunned by many segments of our society.

On a Sunday morning in America there are 40 million people in church, but with a popula-

36

tion of 230 million plus, this means there are 190 million who are not in church. This is why I have had such a great burden for the television ministry. It is the one force that can bring the gospel message into 98 percent of the American homes so families can hear God's Word just as if they were attending a crusade service.

America Has Forsaken God

When the Supreme Court ruled that mandatory prayer was illegal (technically it is still legal for a teacher to read the Bible aloud in the classroom to her students for literature or history), the forces of humanism and atheism used this decision to pressure superintendents, principals and teachers to dump Bible reading and prayer from the classrooms. Even baccalaureate services, assembly programs featuring ministers, priests or rabbis as guest speakers have been discontinued. The reaction of school administrators is, "We must maintain separation of church and state," which means, "We cannot allow any religion in our schools."

Lawrence Welk was one of America's top band leaders for fifty years. He is a patriot as well as a family man. He says that the Supreme Court's decision on prayer was the most tragic decision in the history of this nation. I agree, for this tipped the scales in favor of the anti-

God forces that are seeking to destroy the Judeo-Christian faith that made America great.

George Washington said, "The basis of freedom is law, the basis of law is morality, the basis of morality is religion and the basis of religion is the Bible." God's Word and the teaching of right from wrong is the foundation of a strong nation.

I believe that history will show that America's decline in power and influence began when we threw God out of our public schools.

But the end is not yet. The result of this decision is that millions have lost their Judeo-Christian heritage. They don't even know right from wrong. A survey was taken in a large public school in Chicago and most students could only quote three of the ten commandments. It is no wonder that we are becoming a lawless people and that serious crimes have risen nearly 200 percent in the past ten years.

The final results of forsaking God will be seen in the years ahead. Most of the leaders in government and communications today had their concepts of morality seasoned by the Judeo-Christian ethic as taught by the Bible. But when the millions of young men and women, who have been raised in godless homes, come to power—look out!

I believe the words of Jesus are true. Persecution of Christians in North America will take place so suddenly that hardly anyone will believe it is happening. But the wheels of persecution are in motion today. The 190 million persons not in church on Sunday morning have a different set of values than our forefathers and when it comes their turn to run the show, believers beware!

An Eye Opener

There's something else that is almost as frightening to me. In surveys of audiences I have conducted across the United States and Canada during the past five years I have discovered that only one in ten professing Christians read the Bible and pray ten minutes a day. No wonder the church is powerless and unable to change the course of government. Jesus said, *"Ye are the salt of the earth: but if the salt have lost his savour* [or flavor], *wherewith shall it be salted? it is thenceforth good for nothing, but to be cast out, and to be trodden under foot of men"* (Matthew 5:13).

So when the forces of humanism and atheism get into power, they will quickly separate the salt from the sludge. A great persecution is going to sweep over this land, and most Christians will be unprepared. Millions wille be suddenly swept away from the true faith.

How to Prepare Yourself

If you hope to protect your family and loved ones from the apostasy and denial of Jesus Christ, you must begin by preparing *NOW*.

Here's what you must do:

1. Study the Bible regularly. *"Faith cometh by hearing, and hearing by the word of God"* (Romans 10:17).

2. Encourage the members of your family to study the scriptures. During Hitler's persecution of the Christians in World War II, it was reported that the traditional mainline denominational Christians stood stronger for their faith than many of the evangelical and fundamental Christians. The reason given is that the Lutherans and Catholic catechisms gave young people a better foundation than the average fundamental or evangelical church offered.

3. Another important step to take in preparing for the coming persecution is to learn the relationship between faith and suffering.

Suffering Saints

Today there are some false teachers saying that if you truly believe in God you won't suffer; that you can *claim* your deliverance. This may sound good but it simply does not square with the scriptures. This "deliverance gospel" sounds terrific in countries like the United States and Canada where the laws of our land protect us, but there are precious Bible-believing saints suffering in many places throughout the world today. To say they don't have faith in God is nearly blasphemy.

The Apostle Peter wrote his first letter to the suffering saints scattered throughout Asia Minor. He said,

"Blessed be the God and Father of our Lord Jesus Christ, which according to his abundant mercy hath begotten us again unto a lively hope by the resurrection of Jesus Christ from the dead, To an inheritance incorruptible, and undefiled, and that fadeth not away, reserved in heaven for you, Who are kept by the power of God through faith unto salvation ready to be revealed in the last time. Wherein ye greatly rejoice, though now for a season, if need be, ye are in heaviness through manifold temptations: That the trial of your faith, being much more precious than of gold that perisheth, though it be tried with fire, might be found unto praise and honor and glory at the appearing of Jesus Christ" (1 Peter 1:3-7).

"Beloved, think it not strange concerning the fiery trial which is to try you, as though some strange thing happened unto you: But rejoice, inasmuch as ye are partakers of Christ's sufferings; that, when his glory shall be revealed, ye may be glad also with exceeding joy" (1 Peter 4:12,13).

"Wherefore, let them that suffer according to the will of God commit the keeping of their souls to him in well doing, as unto a faithful Creator" (1 Peter 4:19).

Heroes of Faith Also Suffered

The writer to the Hebrew Christians listed many of the heroes of faith in Hebrews 11. He mentions Abel, Noah, Abraham, Moses and Samson. Then he writes, *"And others had trial of cruel mockings and scourgings, yea, moreover of bonds and imprisonment: They were stoned, they were sawn asunder* [this means that many of the faithful had their bodies sawn into pieces], *were tempted, were slain with the sword: they wandered about in sheepskins and goatskins; being destitute, afflicted, tormented;*

"(Of whom the world was not worthy:) they wandered in deserts, and in mountains, and in dens and caves of the earth. And THESE ALL, HAVING OBTAINED A GOOD REPORT THROUGH FAITH" (Hebrews 11:36-39).

The Bible says that these who suffered all had a good reputation of faith. Somehow there is an effort today by a few "faith teachers" to separate faith from suffering. The error of this teaching is that it implies if you are suffering, you don't have faith or you'd be delivered.

Recently I visited an elderly woman who was dying of stomach cancer. I encouraged her to look forward to her visit to heaven. I read from Revelation 21 about the Holy City.

The pastor who accompanied me then related a terribly unfortunate experience he had had with a man who prayed for a little girl who was dying of cancer.

Instead of showing compassion for the child and her relatives in the hospital room, he berated them for their lack of faith and said, "If you had faith in God, this girl wouldn't be suffering." After his reprimand the child and her parents were simply crushed. The man prayed for the girl, but she died a few days later. However, the parents and relatives must live with the pain of his mistaken words for the rest of their lives.

Now, don't interpret my remarks to mean that I do not believe in miracles or healing or deliverance. Do not assume that I am making a negative confession because I am willing to face the reality of death.

Actually, if the man believed the girl should be healed, he should have asked the unbelievers present to step out of the room for a moment while he prayed just as Jesus did when He raised Jairus' daughter from the dead (see Mark 5:40).

Suffering is Part of God's Plan

The Bible says of Jesus, *"Who in the days of his flesh, when he had offered up prayers and supplications with strong crying and tears unto him that was able to save him from death, and was heard in that he feared; THOUGH HE WERE A SON, YET LEARNED HE OBEDIENCE BY THE THINGS WHICH HE SUFFERED; And being made perfect, he became the author of eternal salvation unto all them that obey him"* (Hebrews 5:7-9).

We can learn a lot about suffering from the Apostle Paul. In reviewing his experiences and defending his apostolic position, he writes, *"Are they ministers of Christ? (I speak as a fool) I am more; in labors more abundant, in stripes above measure, in prisons more frequent, in deaths oft. Of the Jews five times received I forty stripes save one. Thrice was I beaten with rods, once was I stoned, thrice I suffered shipwreck, a night and a day I have been in the deep; In journeyings often, in perils of waters, in perils of robbers, in perils by mine own countrymen, in perils by the heathen, in perils in the city, in perils in the wilderness, in perils in the sea, in perils among false brethren; In weariness and painfulness, in watchings often, in hunger and thirst, in fastings often, in cold and nakedness. Beside those things that are without, that which cometh upon me daily, the care of all the churches"* (2 Corinthians 11:23-28).

I believe without question that the persecution our fellow Christians are experiencing throughout the world in the Communist and Muslim countries is going to come to North America. It will happen as Jesus said, we will be *"hated of all nations for my name's sake"* (Matthew 10:22). You had better have your theology in order before it happens. I believe when persecution comes, the saints will experience many miracles of deliverance—but many will suffer too!

The important thing for you to do is begin preparing today. If you wait until you have to go to prison or face a firing squad, it will be too late. You need to study God's Word so your faith will be stronger than your fears.

His Grace is Sufficient

There's also another truth that should be brought out here: GOD'S GRACE WILL BE SUFFICIENT FOR YOU IN THE HOUR OF TRIAL. It is easy to become afraid and tremble at the thought of persecution. But Jesus said, *"Settle it therefore in your hearts, not to meditate before what ye shall answer: For I will give you a mouth and wisdom, which all your adversaries shall not be able to gainsay nor resist"* (Luke 21:14,15). (In other words, He will give us special grace and power.)

His next words of encouragement are really

special. In one breath He says, *"Some of you shall they...put to death...but there shall not an hair of your head perish"* (Luke 21:16,18). What a glorious paradox. Jesus said they may kill you, but not a hair of your head will be lost. Wow! Just as Jesus walked with Shadrach, Meshach and Abednego in the midst of the fiery furnace and protected them, Jesus will walk with you (see Daniel 3).

Jesus says, *"These things I have spoken unto you, that in me ye might have peace. In the world ye shall have tribulation: but be of good cheer; I have overcome the world"* (John 16:33).

5

The First Signal of the Last Days

Sir Isaac Newton (1642-1727) was a committed Christian as well as an innovative scientist. He would alternate reading his Bible with his experiments. Today modern science reveres this man as one of the pioneers of discovery.

Sir Isaac Newton said, "About the time of the end, a body of men will be raised up who will turn their attention to the prophecies (of the Bible) and insist on their literal interpretation, in the midst of much clamour and opposition."

Today there is much uncertainty about the future and many are returning to the scriptures just as Newton foretold. In fact, Jesus encouraged us to watch for the fulfillment of Bible prophecies because they would reveal when He was about to return. He said, *"And when these things begin to come to pass, then look up, and lift up your heads; for your redemption draweth nigh"* (Luke 21:28). In other words, Jesus said, when the prophecies that Sir Isaac Newton mentioned begin to come to pass, then prepare yourself, for the end has come.

I really believe God has opened these prophecies to His people to help prepare them for the last days. God told the Prophet Daniel, *"For the words [of the prophecies] are closed up and sealed till the time of the end. Many shall be purified, and made white, and tried; but the wicked shall do wickedly: and none of the wicked shall understand; but the wise shall understand"* (Daniel 12:9,10).

In the study of our Savior's prophetic message from the Mount of Olives, Jesus has given us three general signs of His return.

1. Many deceivers will come in His name.
2. Nations will run their "cycle of sorrows." There will be an increasing number of wars, famines, pestilences and earthquakes.
3. True Christians throughout the United States and Canada will experience a great persecution similar to that of other believers around the world.

The Last Days Are Here

Jesus gives us a specific sign that signals the last days. He says, *"And this gospel of the kingdom*

48

shall be preached in all the world for a witness unto all nations; and then shall the end come" (Matthew 24:14).

"And the gospel must first be published among all nations" (Mark 13:10).

So finally Jesus gives us a specific sign. This sign has been fulfilled before us and tells us with certainty that we have reached the last days. *The gospel has gone around the world!*

Notice that Jesus did not say that all nations would be converted, but He did say that all nations would be presented with the opportunity to accept or reject the gospel. Even in Jesus' day, many of the villages where He appeared were not converted, but He had been there and given them God's Word. The same is true today. Nations like Red China, Russia and many Muslim, Buddhist and Hindu countries have had Christian missionaries for years.

Recently, in the Chicago *Tribune*, I read an article stating that the American Bible Society says the Bible has been translated into 1,647 languages. This means that every major tribe and people on earth have the gospel in their own language. Pope Paul visited Jerusalem in 1967, following the six-day war between the Arabs and Jews. The Israelis had regained possession of the city of Jerusalem, and the Pope, realizing its prophetic importance, sent telegrams to the heads of state of all countries; to presidents, kings, queens; to parliaments and governments. He stated, "In this generation the Christian message has gone around the world. *This marks the end of an era.*"

What the Pope perceived in Bible prophecy you will see if you take a look; *The Christian message has gone around the world and this means the last days have begun.*

Bondage Versus Freedom

Looking back, it's really amazing that Jesus was so successful in bringing His message to the world. Who would have thought that this humble carpenter with his rag-tag group of misfits, castaways and rejects would have shaken the world?

Jesus never wrote a book, never established a university, never raised an army (in the kill-or-be-killed sense of the word) or passed an ordinance...yet His message has affected more people for good on this planet than has the message of any other man in history. (It is true that Mohammed has many followers today, but his message has not been able to raise the life-style of the millions of Muslims who follow his teachings. Muslim women live in great bondage and Muslims are intolerant of people who do not embrace their faith. Many Muslim countries forbid the preaching of the gospel of Jesus Christ. Historians agree that it was the

Christian Reformation that brought about "the great enlightenment" that gave birth to modern science, literature, government and art. I have traveled around the world visiting "Christian" and "nonchristian" nations and there is no comparison to the freedom enjoyed by Christian nations of the West compared to the bondage and persecution of the East. I have visited these countries and the masses of people are still running the same goat trails that their fathers did 5,000 years ago.) Most of the creative medicine, art, government and business has come from the West. This is not to say that there are not poor and illiterate people living in "Christian" countries, but it is nothing compared to nonchristian countries. There is a redemptive lift that new converts experience when they commit their lives to Jesus Christ, and this freedom is reflected in our culture.

Guarantees of the Gospel

I believe the gospel of Jesus Christ is successful because it provides people with the three major requirements for happiness.
1. Everyone needs someone to love. (Christ provides the greatest love. Through Him we have a personal relationship with a loving God.)
2. Everyone needs something to live for. (What greater cause is there to live for than

helping your family and friends to find eternal life and happiness through Jesus Christ?)

3. Everyone needs something to look forward to. (Is there any future better than the one Jesus offers His saints in heaven?)

And there is one other reality that Jesus guarantees that the other religions cannot—the assurance of a resurrection from the dead. Remember, Mohammed and Buddha as well as all the other founders of religions in the world are dead. *Jesus Christ is the only living leader of a world religion in the world today.*

I've said it many times, "Anyone can dream up a religion and win converts, but rising from the dead is the hard part." *If a religious teacher cannot conquer death, how can he claim to be in the same "class" as Jesus Christ.* How can a corpse declare the way to eternal life? There are dozens of religions floating around today, and each offers some enlightenment, but WHO HAS THE ULTIMATE TRUTH? I would say THE RELIGIOUS LEADER WHO IS IMMORTAL AND CAN PROVE IT BY CONQUERING DEATH. It's like the old joke of two men who were commenting on the power of Christian religion. One man asked the other, "How could we start another religion like Christianity?" His friend replied, "All you have to do is be crucified and rise from the dead on the third day."

Don't ever make the mistake of equating Jesus Christ with Buddha or Mohammed; these religious leaders were only good men. JESUS IS GOD. When you examine the religious leaders of the world, you will see that Jesus Christ is the only one who has conquered death. Buddha was cremated and his ashes thrown into a riverbed. Mohammed is a corpse in a tomb. But Jesus Christ is alive and at the right hand of God in heaven!

What Jesus Can Do For You

Christians have the only living leader! All others are dead or will be soon. This makes the Christian faith unique. But lest you think Christianity is only "pie-in-the-sky-when-you-die-by-and-by," consider what Jesus Christ will do for you now.

Jesus said, *"The Spirit of the Lord is upon me, because he hath anointed me to preach the gospel to the poor; he hath sent me to heal the brokenhearted, to preach deliverance to the captives, and recovering of sight to the blind, to set at liberty them that are bruised"* (Luke 4:18).

Let's take a careful look at what Jesus Christ does for you.

I. JESUS CAME TO PREACH THE GOSPEL TO THE POOR. The poor have often been forgotten, but Jesus made them His first priority. Jesus was called a friend of sinners (see Luke

15:2). His disciples were common men, called ignorant and unlearned by the intellectuals of their day (see Acts 4:13). But Jesus made a team out of them by molding them into dedicated disciples. They turned their world upside down (see Acts 17:6).

Every poor man who trusts in Jesus becomes rich beyond belief. Have you ever considered all that Jesus will do for you? Count the many blessings that come to you as a result of your commitment to Jesus Christ.

Jesus offers you FREEDOM FROM GUILT. Because He died for the sins of the world and has risen from the dead, you can have peace with God.

Jesus offers you FELLOWSHIP WITH GOD! Because He is God and yet man, Jesus is able to bring you into God's presence and bring God's presence into you. Instead of feeling as if God is a million miles away, He can be closer to you than the breath in your mouth.

Jesus offers you Christian FRIENDS. There is a fellowship of believers that is greater than any association in the world. They will pray for you and help you grow in God. They will lift you up when you fall and comfort you when you're heartbroken.

Jesus offers you a Christian FAMILY. When you consider that nearly one in two marriages split up today, it's great to know that Christ will strengthen your marriage so your family will endure. The cliche is true, "The family that *prays together stays together*."

Jesus offers you FREEDOM FROM BONDAGE. Have you ever stopped to consider how much time and money unbelievers spend on liquor, gambling, drugs and tobacco in an effort to be happy? Jesus gives you such inner joy that these enslaving counterfeit enjoyments lose their appeal. Jesus also will deliver you from any addiction.

Jesus offers you FINANCIAL SECURITY. When you make Jesus the Lord of your life, including your money, scores of Bible promises go into effect, all declaring that "...*my God shall supply all your need...*" (Philippians 4:19).

Jesus offers you a FIRE IN YOUR SOUL! I've traveled around the world for the past 25 years, and the most excited, fulfilled people I've ever met are committed Christians. John the Baptist said, "*I...baptize you with water...he shall baptize you with the Holy Ghost, and with fire*" (Matthew 3:11).

Jesus offers you a FUTURE IN HEAVEN! He extends to us the same promise that He made to the thief who was crucified with Him, "...*verily I say unto thee, Today shalt thou be with me in paradise*" (Luke 23:43).

II. JESUS CAME TO HEAL THE BROKEN-HEARTED. The longer you live the more heartaches and heartbreaks you will experience. The question is, "Who can heal your broken heart?" When death claims your loved one, when sickness destroys your chances to live actively again, when unforeseen events strike and maim your soul, who can heal your heart and put it back together again?

I grieve for the many broken people whose hearts have been shattered by tragedy. Thank God, Jesus is the heart-mender! The God who created you knows how to "put you back together again."

You may feel that you'll never know joy and gladness again, but I can assure you that what Christ has done for others—He'll do for you!

Recently I read in the news that one of the world's richest men went into hiding after the death of his wife. He became a recluse. His grief had driven him to a "living death." If he could only experience the love of God in Christ, if he could only feel the moving of the Holy Spirit in his life, he could be happy and whole again. But he dwells in darkness, haunted by grief.

Jesus wants to heal your broken heart. He will minister unto you in a very personal way if you will invite Him in to heal your wounded soul. Otherwise, you will die one day at a time.

III. JESUS CAME TO RESTORE YOUR HEALTH. I believe that Jesus heals people today just as He did when He walked in Galilee.

Jesus commissioned His disciples to lay hands on the sick and they would recover (see Mark 16:18).

I don't know why God doesn't heal everyone. This has been a mystery to me and everyone else who has ever prayed for the sick. However, I know God heals many who believe, and I am determined to believe Him for His healing power rather than doubt His ability or willingness. Someone once said, "People seldom believe in miracles until they need one." If you need a miracle, remember God loves you and wants to help you today.

Jesus healed the sick when He walked this earth. His apostles and disciples healed the sick. This is to be part of the ministry of the church today. James writes, *"Is any sick among you? let him call for the elders of the church; and let them pray over him, anointing him with oil in the name of the Lord: And the prayer of faith shall save the sick, and the Lord shall raise him up..."* (James 5:14,15).

If Jesus were with you in person this moment, He would reach out, touch you and you would be healed. I believe if you will reach out to Him in faith, God will work a miracle for you.

IV. JESUS CAME TO LIBERATE THE BRUISED. A bruise is often worse than a break. It is much sorer and the pain often lasts longer.

Jesus said that it is impossible to live in this world without getting bruised (see Matthew

18:7). Painful experiences are all part of life. But what do you do when someone cuts you so deeply with their words or deeds that you cannot recover?

I've seen wives beaten by bullish husbands until they are completely crushed. I've seen husbands worn down by nagging wives until they have lost their self-respect. I've seen children with inferiority complexes caused by their parents' verbal assaults.

I have been haunted by this letter from the first day I read it.

"My father severely beat my two-year-old sister with a golf club. When I visited her in the hospital, the doctor let me hold her bruised little body before she died. I could hardly recognize her. How can a loving and merciful God allow a baby to suffer like that?"

I cannot imagine a father destroying his child in such a way. Who but Jesus could ever heal the emotional bruises of the sister who saw this happen?

A newspaper article recently carried the story of a man who, despondent over the rape and murder of his wife, tried to take his own life. He had left a suicide note explaining that ever since he lost his wife, things never had been right. He said, "I can't get over the situation and I can't do right by myself and my five kids. This is the only thing I know to do."

You and I should deal softly with people because we never know when someone is hurting inside. You can never tell when they have reached the point of giving up. The Bible says of Jesus, *"A bruised reed shall he not break, and smoking flax shall he not quench"* (Matthew 12:20). Jesus will help you when you're almost burned out. Jesus will sustain you when you're almost broken. Jesus is a wonderful Savior who wants to meet your personal needs and heal your hurts today.

The reason why the gospel of Jesus Christ has been so successful is that Jesus does wonderful things for His followers and He wants to do wonderful things for you.

Because the gospel has gone around the world fulfilling Matthew 24:14, we know we have reached the last days. Jesus Christ is coming very soon—but wait, I'm getting ahead of my story—there are even greater signs of His soon return. You'll find the next chapter very interesting.

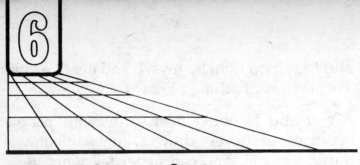

The Sign of the Star of David

Israel is God's timepiece. When King Frederick the Great asked his court preacher to prove the Bible was true, the minister replied, "The Jew."

He was correct.

Whenever you want to know what time it is, prophetically speaking, all you have to do is look at Israel. From the beginning God chose to reveal Himself to the world through the Jewish people.

Through the Jews God gave us the Ten Commandments.

Through the Jews God gave us the prophets.

Through the Jews God gave us the Savior.

Through the Jews God gave us the New Testament.

Through the Jews God gave us the apostles.

Jesus said through the Jews you will know when we have reached the last days. Let us continue our study in the same pattern as we began this book. Follow the chronological order of prophecy in triplicate as the writers recorded it.

The Budding of the Fig Tree

"Now learn a parable of the fig tree; When his branch is yet tender, and putteth forth leaves, ye know that summer is nigh: So likewise ye, when ye shall see all these things, know that it is near, even at the doors. Verily I say unto you, This generation shall not pass, till all these things be fulfilled. Heaven and earth shall pass away, but my words shall not pass away. But of that day and hour knoweth no man, no, not the angels of heaven, but my Father only" (Matthew 24:32-36).

"Now learn a parable of the fig tree; When her branch is yet tender, and putteth forth leaves, ye know that summer is near: So ye in like manner, when ye shall see these things come to pass, know that it is nigh, even at the doors. Verily I say unto you, that this generation shall not pass, till all these things be done. Heaven and earth shall pass away: but my words shall not pass away" (Mark 13:28-31).

"And he spake to them a parable; Behold the fig tree, and all the trees; When they now shoot forth, ye see and know of your own selves that summer is now nigh at hand. So likewise ye, when ye see these things *come to pass, know ye that the kingdom of God is nigh at hand. Verily I say unto you, This generation shall not pass away, till all be fulfilled. Heaven and earth shall pass away: but my words shall not pass away"* (Luke 21:29-33).

The fig tree is the national symbol of Israel. Jesus said the budding of the fig tree (the return of the Jews to their homeland) would be a clear sign that we have reached the last generation.

The question arises, "When did the nation of Israel bud forth into existence?" Modern-day Israel became a nation in April 1948. Jesus said the generation that witnesses the regathering of Israel will not die until all of the end-time prophecies are fulfilled.

This means that you and I are living in the last generation.

Do not make the mistake of saying that I am setting a date for His return. I am not. For Jesus clearly stated, *"But of that day and hour knoweth no man, no, not the angels of heaven, but my Father only"* (Matthew 24:36). But even though we do not know the day and hour, we do know the general time frame of His return. This is why Jesus told us to look for the sign of the fig tree.

No one really knows when summer actually arrives (even though we set a date on our calendars). We have general signs of the coming of summer and then one day it just happens. You can feel it in your bones. In the same way

we will know we have reached the last days—
the prophetic signs of "summer" tell us to
prepare and then one day the time is here.

The return of the Jews to their promised land,
the renewed Jewish state, is a greater prophetic
sign than you realize.

Israel's Rebellion

Remember, approximately 500 years before
Christ came, the Jews lost their independence.
When Jesus came, with His miracle powers,
they wanted to make Him King so He would
free them from the Romans. But Jesus came first
to free men and women from sin. After He has
set up His kingdom within us spiritually, we
will be qualified to rule. When the church is
completed, Christ will return in power.

Jesus tried to persuade the nation of Israel to
repent but they refused. Finally, after the death
and resurrection of Christ, the Jews rebelled
against Rome and 80,000 soldiers were sent to
conquer them.

In the awful siege that followed, approximately one million inhabitants of Jerusalem
died. In the year A.D. 70 Titus carried thousands
away into bondage. Earlier Jesus had wept over
Jerusalem, saying, *"If you, even you, had only
known on this day what would bring you peace—but
now it is hidden from your eyes. The days will come*

upon you when your enemies will build an embankment against you and encircle you and hem you in on every side. They will dash you to the ground, you and the children within your walls. They will not leave one stone on another, because you did not recognize the time of God's coming to you" (Luke 19:42-44, NIV). The King James Version says, *"Because thou knewest not the time of thy visitation"* (Luke 19:44).

Jesus grieved over what was going to happen to Jerusalem. He saw Roman armies with their battering rams and catapults, and He saw the soldiers raping, killing and dashing the little children against the stones.

What caused the Jews to rebel against God? It was the religious leadership. Something unusual follows our Savior's tearful prophecy of doom. Immediately following, the Bible says, *"And he went into the temple, and began to cast out them that sold therein, and them that bought; Saying unto them, It is written, My house is the house of prayer: but ye have made it a den of thieves. And he taught daily in the temple. But the chief priests and the scribes and the chief of the people sought to destroy him. And could not find what they might do: for all the people were very attentive to hear him"* (Luke 19:45-48).

Jesus was so disturbed by the impending Judgment of God that was coming on Jerusalem, it stirred Him to attack the cause of the evil—the mercenary religious leaders. He threw them out of the temple. His righteous indignation prompted His civil disobedience.

A Lukewarm Gospel

Today the root cause of the evil in our land is a corrupt religious system. Very few preach repentance and holiness as a way of life. Consequently, the gospel is watered down until no one wants it. A lukewarm message produces carnal Christians who neither love God nor fear sin. Such a message becomes weak and ineffective. God help us!

The Prophet Jeremiah said of the ministers of his day, *"For the pastors are become brutish, and have not sought the Lord: therefore they shall not prosper, and all their flocks shall be scattered"* (Jeremiah 10:21). The prophet said the great sin of pastors in his day was prayerlessness.

"Many pastors have destroyed my vineyard, they have trodden my portion under foot, they have made my pleasant portion a desolate wilderness" (Jeremiah 12:10).

I believe the only way a nation can be saved from the ravages of sin and the wrath of God is by spiritual renewal. Pray that God will raise up fearless men of God who will preach and pray and call their congregations to repentance.

A Warning

If Jesus wept over Jerusalem, He really must be weeping over our cities today. When General Carlos Romulo, from the Philippines, was about to return home after World War II, he made a farewell statement that read:

"I'm going home, America, farewell. For 17 years I've enjoyed your hospitality. I have visited every one of your states. I can say I know you well. I admire and love America.

"What I have to say in parting is both a tribute and a warning. Never forget, America, that yours is a spiritual country. Yes, I know you are a practical people, and like others, I've marveled at your skyscrapers, and your arsenals.

"But underlying everything else is the fact that America began as a God-loving, God-fearing and God-worshiping people. It is this spirit that makes America invincible.

"May God keep you always and may you always keep God."

The Great Migration

The Jewish people failed to keep God, so they were carried away. From A.D. 70 until the late 1800s they were driven from country to country.

But something happened in the early 1900s that signaled a shift in events. The Jews began to migrate back to Palestine, the land of their forefathers. They felt an "inner prompting" to return home.

Many of them purchased barren, worthless wasteland from the Arabs and began to till it. Soon the deserts began to blossom and kibbutzim (communal farms) began to spring up throughout the land. But the Arabs became jealous and wanted their lands returned even though the Jews had paid for them. Then militant Jews began to arrive, and there was such a great civil strife between the Arabs and the Jews that the British were given a mandate by the League of Nations to keep peace in the land. This continued throughout the 1930s.

A Fight for Freedom

Then Hitler rose to power with his "Jewish solution" of gas chambers and firing squads. Jews began to flee to Palestine in greater numbers than ever. The book and movie *Exodus* tells their desperate plight and flight to freedom.

While thousands fled to Palestine, other millions died in awful places like Auschwitz and Dachau.

After World War II, when the nations of the world found out how much the Jews had suffered, the United Nations voted to make Palestine a homeland for them. As soon as the British mandate ended, and their soldiers pulled out, Israel declared to the world that it had become a nation. This small number of Jews defended themselves against great numbers of Arabs who attacked as soon as the British soldiers left. But the Arabs were not successful. The Jewish patriots held their ground and miraculously survived.

The fig tree had budded!

Times of the Gentiles

There is another prophecy you should be aware of in Luke 21:24. Jesus said, *"And they [the Jewish people] shall fall by the edge of the sword, and shall be led away captive into all nations."*

This prophecy was literally fulfilled in A.D. 70 when Titus, the Roman, destroyed Jerusalem and carried the Jews away. In Egypt the slave markets were so glutted with Jewish slaves that a man wasn't selling even for as much as a horse.

Then notice this: Jesus said, *"And Jerusalem shall be trodden down of the Gentiles, until the times of the Gentiles be fulfilled"* (Luke 21:24).

Jesus said that when the Jewish people recover the Holy City of Jerusalem, it will signal the completion of the "times of the Gentiles."

Prophecy teachers are unanimous as to the interpretation of the phrase "times of the Gentiles."

1. It refers to the time of the church age when God turned to the Gentiles to bring out a people for Himself, or
2. It refers to the years when Gentile nations rule the earth.

Either interpretation does not lessen the impact because Jesus is saying, "When the Jews get back the old city of Jerusalem, you will know that the church age and the time of the Gentile leadership in the world is coming to an end."

During the famous Six-Day War of June 1967 Israel regained possession of Jerusalem. I believe this clearly signaled the beginning of the end.

These are truly momentous days. When Israel became a nation, one Christian woman gathered her children around her, sat them down and said, "Children, today is the most important day since the birth of Jesus Christ." Then she explained the prophecy of the fig tree that I have shared with you in this chapter.

A Prophecy Fulfilled

I'll never forget when the Jews and Arabs were fighting the 1967 war. My wife, Connie, and I were conducting a church crusade in Sidney, Montana. Reports of the fighting were carried on all the major radio networks. I had a small transistor radio, and finally at 3 a.m.

Praying at the Wailing Wall within the old city of Jerusalem is a cherished heritage of the Jews even today.

What a privilege to preach Christ while overlooking Jerusalem from the Mount of Olives. Here Jesus Christ will return to begin His earthly reign.

We invite you to join the Lundstroms for our next special Tour of the Holy Land. Please mark and return the coupon at the back of this book.

reporters at the scene of battle confirmed that the Israelis were in possession of the old city of Jerusalem.

It was a moment I'll never forget—cold chills ran up and down my spine because in my lifetime God had fulfilled one of the greatest Bible prophecies: *"Jerusalem shall be trodden down of the Gentiles, UNTIL the times of the Gentiles be fulfilled"* (Luke 21:24).

The Beginning of the End

Today, after 2,500 years, their flag with the star of David is unfurled over the Holy City.

This signals the beginning of the end. It underscores the fact that we are living in the last generation.

Whatever we do for the Lord, we must do quickly.

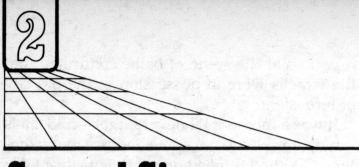

Sensual Signs of the Last Days

Carefully study the statistics below for a few seconds. They are what I call sensual signs of the last days.

In the United States today:

* One in two marriages ends in divorce.
* One in six babies born is illegitimate.
* One million babies are aborted each year.
* Two out of three teen-age brides are pregnant.
* More than 500,000 children are born illegitimately each year.
* More than one million persons will contract gonorrhea this year, according to the National Health Center in Atlanta, Georgia. Other estimates run as high as 2.5 million.
* An estimated 20 million people suffer from incurable Herpes Syphillis.

* More than 1.5 million young people are living together without being married.
* An estimated 40 million children are not living with one of their original parents.

Today's Crumbling Families

Jesus said one of the great signs of the last days would be gross immorality and the breakup of the family. He said, *"But as the days of Noah were, so shall also the coming of the Son of man be. For as in the days that were before the flood they were eating and drinking, marrying and giving in marriage, until the day that Noah entered into the ark, And knew not until the flood came, and took them all away; so shall also the coming of the Son of man be.*

"Then shall two be in the field; the one shall be taken, and the other left. Two women shall be grinding at the mill; the one shall be taken, and the other left.

"Watch therefore: for ye know not what hour your Lord doth come" (Matthew 24:37-42).

History shows that when people lose their true purpose in life, their passions drive them to ruin. This was true in Noah's day and in the days of ancient Greece and Rome, and it is true today.

The Bible explains what happened before the deluge—*"When men began to increase in number on the earth and daughters were born to them, the sons of God saw that the daughters of men were beautiful, and they married any of them they chose.*

"Then the Lord said, 'My Spirit will not contend [or strive] with man forever, for he is mortal; his days will be a hundred and twenty years'" (Genesis 6:1-3, NIV).

The Holy Spirit was convicting men of their immoral actions, and they refused to listen to the Lord. God finally had to close up shop. It is a fact that when the family crumbles, there is nothing left of society. It's all over.

Mankind's Pursuit of Pleasure

The same hedonistic spirit that seized Noah's world has seized ours.

* The top songs on the pop, country, rhythm and blues charts are filled with suggestive lyrics. One of the top tunes says, "There's nothin' left to talk about unless it's horizontally. Let's get physical."

I cannot imagine any singer singing such words or any recording company selling such records or any radio station playing them or anyone buying them—but sex sells and the Top Ten play list proves it.

What is worse, without even blushing, recording stars will sing these songs to millions watching TV!

* Filmmakers are flooding our theaters and TV screens with every variation of sex. Bed scenes, even among unmarried film characters, are common.

* Newsstands are choked with pornography. It is displayed in almost every major drugstore and bookstore in the nation. The newest craze is kiddie porn, showing children in suggestive poses and overt sexual acts.

It is no exaggeration to say we have sunk to the lowest level of immorality in the history of our nation. When this happened in Noah's day, God sent the flood. Jesus said that when it happens in our day, we should look for His return.

Divorce Wrecks Homes and Lives

The most shocking trend in divorce is among professing Christians. Even the clergy are jumping overboard. I recently counted 25 ministers and their wives, friends of mine, who have divorced to marry others. And they are doing this without any apparent remorse or repentance. One minister attended our Family Life Seminar to get counsel because his marriage was in trouble. His wife wanted to make a go of it, but he finally decided to divorce her and marry another woman.

This divorce took place while he was pastoring a church in the Midwest. After he remarried, the church asked him to continue as their minister—even though he had switched wives.

Someone has said evil goes through four steps.

* First, it shocks you.
* Then, you become accustomed to it.
* Soon, you embrace it.
* Finally, you defend it.

This is what is happening all over our nation. God says he hates divorce.

"You flood the Lord's altar with tears. You weep and wail because he no longer pays attention to your offerings or accepts them with pleasure from your hands. You ask, 'Why?' It is because the Lord is acting as the witness between you and the wife of your youth, because you have broken faith with her, though she is your partner, the wife of your marriage covenant.

"Has not the Lord made them one? In flesh and in spirit they are his. And why one? Because he was seeking godly offspring. So guard yourself in your spirit, and do not break faith with the wife of your youth.

"'I HATE DIVORCE,' says the Lord God of Israel, 'and I hate man's covering himself with violence as well as with his garment,' says the Lord Almighty.

"So guard yourself in your spirit, and do not break faith" (Malachi 2:13-16, NIV).

Your Marriage Needs Protection

With families disintegrating around us, every husband and wife must take steps to protect their marriage and their children from Satan's attacks.

When Moses was about to lead the people out of Egypt, the enemy said, *"I will pursue...I will divide...I will...destroy them"* (Exodus 15:9). This is still his plan of destruction today. Satan will pressure, divide and try to destroy your marriage. You must act wisely.

1. You must make a total commitment to Jesus Christ. This will bring the Holy Spirit into your life and will help strengthen you against Satanic attacks of discouragement and temptation.

2. You must devote time to Bible study and prayer. The average Christian home has TV turned on for five hours a day, yet spends only seven minutes a day reading (secular and/or spiritual material). Is it any wonder that so many Christians are weak and their marriages crumbling?

Job was a righteous man and prayed for his children constantly (see Job 1:5). Surround your children with prayer so that God will protect them from evil.

3. You need a Spirit-filled church home where a man of God preaches the Bible fearlessly and in great power.

With the devil walking about as a roaring lion, you need the protection of a dedicated body of believers. If you attend a compromising church that is spiritually cold, you will pay a great price for your error when your children are lost to the world and sin. I believe it is so important to have a good church home that, if possible financially, I would drive as far as 50 miles one way to make certain my family was raised in a warm spiritual atmosphere. Chances are there is a good Bible-preaching church near you—find it and support it faithfully with your presence and your gifts.

Guard Against Evil

I cannot emphasize strongly enough the danger of our immoral age. The Bible says, *"Now the Spirit speaketh expressly [emphatically], that in the latter times some shall depart from the faith, giving heed to seducing spirits, and doctrines of devils"* (1 Timothy 4:1).

I believe that evil spirits often draw people into acts of immorality. I have seen what appeared to be mature Christian men and women driven away into relationships that were unreasonably evil. They left beautiful, dedicated spouses to take up with new "partners" without values.

Stand guard over your prayer life and thought life. Jeremiah said, *"The heart is deceitful above all things, and desperately wicked: who can know it?"* (Jeremiah 17:9).

The biggest lie your heart ever tells you is that you can live a Christian life without faithfully studying God's Word and praying earnestly. Remember, Jesus couldn't-and you can't either!

LOOK AT WHAT SIN DID TO SATAN. In the beginning he was perfect. Because of his lovely perfection God exalted him to one of heaven's highest positions. But sin entered Satan's heart and he became evil. (See Ezekiel 28:11-15 and Isaiah 14:12-15.)

LOOK AT WHAT SIN DID TO DAVID, one of the best men who ever lived. The Bible says he was a man after God's own heart (1 Samuel 13:14). The Lord exalted David to the throne of Israel. But when sin crept into David's heart, he committed adultery with Bathsheba, the wife of Uriah the Hittite. When she became pregnant, David tried to get her husband drunk to cover his sin; when Uriah refused, David had him killed (2 Samuel 11).

Because of this, God said the sword would never depart from David's house (2 Samuel 12:10). Tragedy followed David for the rest of his life.

LOOK AT WHAT SIN DID TO SAMSON, the strongest man who ever lived. The Spirit of God enabled him to kill a thousand men single-handedly. But sin crept into his heart; he became involved with Delilah, a prostitute hired by the Philistines to corrupt Samson and discover the secret of his strength. When Samson finally broke his vow to God and told her all his heart, his strength went from him. His enemies dragged him to the ground, gouged out his eyes and made him their slave in Gaza. Samson had to pull the millstone as a beast (see Judges 13-16).

LOOK AT WHAT SIN DID TO SOLOMON, the wisest man who ever lived. His wisdom was so great that his proverbs are still in our Bible today. But sin crept into his heart and he became sensual. God commanded the kings of Israel not to multiply unto themselves horses, wives or gold (see Deuteronomy 17:16,17). But Solomon, yielding to the temptations of his position, multiplied horses and wives (2 Chronicles 9:25,28). The Bible says, *"And he had seven hundred wives, princesses, and three hundred concubines [lesser wives]...and his wives turned away his heart after other gods"* (1 Kings 11:3,4).

Can you imagine the emotional and physical energy it required for Solomon to manage 1,000 women? He also multiplied gold by the millions of dollars (see 1 Kings 10:16,17).

Here is a life-changing statement. May it sear its way into your heart. IF SIN DESTROYED GOD'S BEST, GOD'S STRONGEST, AND GOD'S WISEST, HOW DARE YOU MEDDLE WITH IT!

Increased Homosexual Activities

Another sensual sign of the last days is the rise of militant homosexuals. Jesus said, *"Likewise also as it was in the days of Lot* [If you read the story in Genesis 19, you will see that God destroyed Sodom and Gomorrah because of their sin of homosexuality]; *they did eat, they drank, they bought, they sold, they planted, they builded;*

"But the same day that Lot went out of Sodom it rained fire and brimstone from heaven, and destroyed them all.

"Even thus shall it be in the day when the Son of man is revealed.

"In that day, he which shall be upon the housetop, and his stuff in the house, let him not come down to take it away: and he that is in the field, let him not return back.

"Remember Lot's wife" (Luke 17:28-32).

Jesus said that just as it was in the days of Sodom, it will be at the time of His second coming.

* There are so many homosexuals living in San Francisco, that they have been able legally to force the schools to teach homosexuality as a "socially acceptable alternative life-style."

* Recently the governor of California appointed a lesbian judge.

* Well-known athletes, music and film stars now speak openly of their perverted life-styles.
* Homosexuals are now taking to the streets in growing numbers. In Minneapolis, Minnesota, they received legal permission to block off a main street and take over an entire area for their celebration.
* Homosexual plots are being written into film and TV. There is an effort to "normal-ize" their behavior even though the Bible says, *"Thou shalt not lie with mankind, as with womankind: it is abomination.*

"Neither shalt thou lie with any beast to defile thyself therewith: neither shall any woman stand before a beast to lie down thereto: it is confusion....

"For whosoever shall commit any of these abominations, even the souls that commit them shall be cut off from among their people.

"Therefore shall ye keep mine ordinance, that ye commit not any one of these abominable cus-toms, which were committed before you, and that ye defile not yourselves therein: I am the Lord your God" (Leviticus 18:22,23; 29,30).

The Bible says that in the days of Sodom and Gomorrah a great cry went up out of the city (Genesis 18:20). Have you ever wondered what caused the cry? The cry came from the innocent children whose mothers were out chasing women and whose fathers were out chasing men. The cry also came from the victims who were raped, beaten, robbed and killed in the darkened streets of the cities.

If you will read the story in Genesis 18 and 19, you will see that they were very militant. They surrounded Lot's house and demanded that the two angelic men be given into their hands. Remember, when homosexuals get into power they make demands in a militant manner. They are actually scaring councilmen into changing local ordinances in many cities.

Homosexuality Breeds Bondage and Danger

Homosexual behavior is deviant. God destroyed Sodom and Gomorrah because He was merciful. He did not want the suffering to continue.

Today there is fuzzy thinking in regards to homosexual behavior. But let's not forget, sex between the same sexes is sin!

* Biologically speaking, a man wasn't created to mate with the same sex. From the physical point of view, the homosexual act is confusion.

* Homosexuals do not reproduce, so they are actually a threat to the human race. If everyone lived as they do, the human race would die.

* Homosexuals are active in recruiting others. I read recently that the average number of new contacts are four or five a year.

I believe there are many young men and women who are vulnerable. Because of their psychological and emotional makeup they could become heterosexual (normal) or homosexual (abnormal) depending on what they are exposed to. This is why homosexual behavior is a danger to society. It persuades many young people who are undecided to choose in favor of the abnormal.

* Homosexuals want the full rights of normal citizens without realizing that if they want human rights they must act like normal humans.

God loves homosexuals and lesbians enough to command them to repent of their deviant behavior. He loves them too much to allow them to live in perversion.

It's strange how society calls them "gay" when they are anything but gay. Guilt, fear and anxiety are a way of life for them.

Hope for the Homosexual

The Bible says that homosexuals can be forgiven and set free. Paul said, *"Know ye not that the unrighteous shall not inherit the kingdom* of God? *Be not deceived: neither fornicators, nor idolaters, nor adulterers, nor effeminate, nor abusers of themselves with mankind,*

"Nor thieves, nor covetous, nor drunkards, nor revilers, nor extortioners, shall inherit the kingdom of God.

"AND SUCH WERE SOME OF YOU: but ye are washed, but ye are sanctified, but ye are justified in the name of the Lord Jesus, and by the Spirit of our God" (1 Corinthians 6:9-11).

Please note, Paul wrote to the Corinthian Christians about the effeminate and abusers of themselves with mankind. Then he goes on to state, *"And such were some of you."*

Some of these Christians had once been homosexual, but Jesus Christ had set them free! Praise God, there is hope for everyone, regardless of his or her condition!

Not only will the Lord deliver the homosexual, but He will keep the homosexual from falling into sin.

History reveals that the Roman emperors were grossly immoral. I read once that when a Caesar asked for a lover, his aide asked whom he preferred and the Emperor replied, "It doesn't matter, bring me a man or a woman."

Consider this immoral atmosphere as you read Paul's letter to the Philippian Christians. He writes, *"All the saints salute you, chiefly they that are of Caesar's household"* (Philippians 4:22).

Praise God! The Lord's grace kept His saints in the worst Sodomite situation of the day. They were "born-again" believers, washed in the blood of Jesus Christ.

Rely on the Lord

As we near the end of this age, immorality in the form of premarital sex, adultery, homosexuality, sadism/masochism and bestiality (having sex with animals) will increase. These are sensual signs of the last days.

If you will walk with God, totally committed to Jesus Christ, reading your Bible and praying regularly, you won't have to worry because *"Greater is he that is in you, than he that is in the world"* (1 John 4:4).

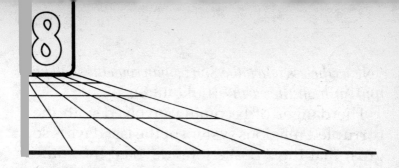

The Apostate Church

One of the dangers you and I must protect ourselves from during these last days is the Apostate Church. According to Webster's New Collegiate Dictionary, apostasy is the "renunciation of religious faith; the abandonment of previous loyalty; defection."

This abandonment of previous loyalty had already set in at the time the Bible was written. When Jesus appeared unto John the apostle and dictated letters to the seven churches of Asia Minor, He commanded five of them to repent. The falling away had already begun. Now, nearly 2,000 years later, the apostasy has spread until the true Church is a minority. As I mentioned in an earlier chapter, Jesus questioned whether or not there would be any true faith left on earth at the time He returns.

"Nevertheless when the Son of man cometh, shall he find faith on the earth" (Luke 18:8).

The danger of becoming involved with the corrupted religious system of the last days is so great that the Apostle John devoted the entire chapter of Revelation 17 to God's judgment upon this harlot church. This prostitute church is more than one denomination. It stands for many of the "professing" churches that have given up their standards of righteousness and "gone to bed" with the world.

The Bible says, *"One of the seven angels...came and said to me, 'Come, I will show you the punishment of the great prostitute, who sits on many waters.* [The "waters" refers to peoples of the world as explained in Revelation 17:15.] *With her kings of the earth were intoxicated with the wine of her adulteries"* (Revelation 17:1,2, NIV).

This corrupted religious system, this renegade Christian church, has failed to hold up the law of God. It has given kings, queens and world leaders a false sense of security. History has shown how men in power have bought off the church. Just recently I read that once a king and queen arranged for the church to annul the marriage of their daughter to a man she lived with for over a year. Their marriage broke up and the daughter wanted to be free to marry again. So the mother and father "arranged" it with the church.

Apostasy Rules the Antichrist

"Then the angel carried me away in the Spirit into a desert. There I saw a woman sitting on a scarlet beast that was covered with blasphemous names and had seven heads and ten horns.

"The woman was dressed in purple and scarlet, and was glittering with gold, precious stones and pearls. She held a golden cup in her hand, filled with abominable things and the filth of her adulteries. This title was on her forehead:

MYSTERY
BABYLON THE GREAT
THE MOTHER OF PROSTITUTES
AND OF THE ABOMINATIONS
OF THE EARTH"

(verses 4 and 5).

Remember, the word "babylon" means many. It comes from the time when God confused the people at the Tower of Babel by giving them different languages. They had to stop building the tower because they could not understand each other. So the title of the prostitute church reveals she is comprised of many different peoples and nations. She is very rich in material things (note the glittering gold, stones and pearls) but she is very corrupt.

"I saw that the woman was drunk with the blood of the saints, the blood of those who bore testimony to Jesus" (verse 6). Church history shows that it has always been the Apostate Christian church leaders who have persecuted the true Christian believers. This is why America was inhabited by the Puritans and Pilgrims. They fled the oppressive religious system of England to form colonies in America.

If you will study history, you will read about St. Bartholomew's massacre when Catholics decided to destroy everyone who was not committed to their faith. The fact is both Protestant and Catholic church leaders have put to death literally millions of true born-again Christians. Now I am not attacking a church denomination, but a corrupted system of apostate Christianity regardless of what name it goes by.

John the apostle goes into more detail about the relationship between the antichrist (the beast) and the Apostate Church in verses 7-14. Then in verse 15 he says, *"...the angel said to me, The waters you saw, where the prostitute sits, are peoples, multitudes, nations and languages. The beast and the ten horns you saw will hate the prostitute.* [Nonchristian leaders have a deep hatred for compromising clerics who use the loyalty of their church members as leverage upon political leaders.] *They will bring her to ruin and leave her naked; they will eat her flesh and burn her with fire. For God has put it into their hearts to accomplish his purpose by agreeing to give the beast their power to rule, until God's words are fulfilled. The woman you saw is the great city that rules over the kings of the earth"* (Revelation 17:15-18, NIV).

The antichrist will use the harlot church until he consolidates his power. Then he will turn on her and destroy her.

How to Find the Right Church

God's purpose in devoting an entire chapter of Revelation to this prostitute church is to keep you from becoming involved with this degraded form of Christianity. It is very important that you fellowship with true believers and not with those who have compromised Jesus Christ. I believe the church you attend with your family should:

1. Clearly set forth the Gospel of Jesus Christ—that Jesus is truly the Son of God, that He died for our sins, arose from the dead, ascended to the Father's right hand and is coming again.
2. Preach total commitment to Jesus Christ— that men need to be born again, that they should receive Jesus Christ into their hearts and lives. You should be able to

bring your friend to church and have confidence that he or she will hear a straightforward Christian message and have the opportunity to be converted.

3. Uphold standards of righteousness. *"For God hath not called us unto uncleanness, but unto holiness"* (1 Thessalonians 4:7).

   "Follow peace with all men, and holiness, without which no man shall see the Lord" (Hebrews 12:14). These standards of righteousness should especially apply to those in leadership positions in your church.

4. Allow you to sense the moving of the Holy Spirit in its midst. John writes, *"Beloved, believe not every spirit, but try the spirits whether they are of God: because many false prophets are gone out into the world.*

   "Hereby know ye the Spirit of God: Every spirit that confesseth that Jesus Christ is come in the flesh is of God: And every spirit that confesseth not that Jesus Christ is come in the flesh is not of God: and this is that spirit of antichrist, whereof ye have heard that it should come; and even now already it is in the world" (1 John 4:1-3).

When there is no freedom to clearly confess Christ and no freedom for people to be converted, John said the spirit of antichrist is present.

Fellowship With True Believers

If at all possible, you should fellowship with true believers. But be careful in making your decision. There are many Christian groups that are true to the Bible in many of their points of doctrine, but they have a "twist" in their spirit. Remember always that Jesus said, *"A new commandment I give unto you, That ye love one another; as I have loved you, that ye also love one another. By this shall all men know that ye are my disciples, if ye have love one to another"* (John 13:34,35).

If you visit a church or a group of believers and the air is tense with criticism of others, or you feel an air of suspicion, then you immediately know that this is not the place for you. Love is the proof of discipleship. Through the years I have made it a practice to listen with my "inner ear" to what is being said—even when it has been a new voice on the radio. After listening only a few moments I can usually tell if the person is right or wrong just by the spirit he projects. Jesus said, *"The sheep hear his voice: and he calleth his own sheep by name, and leadeth them out* [Note: the Lord will lead you out of a dead church.] *And when he putteth forth his own sheep, he goeth before them, and the sheep follow him: for they know his voice. And a stranger they will not follow, but will flee from him: for they know not the voice of strangers"* (John 10:3-4).

If you are reading God's word and praying as you should, you will have no problem deciding if a minister is a true man of God or a false shepherd. John says we can know the spirit of truth and the spirit of error (see 1 John 4:6). Truth feels right and the spirit is one of love. Error feels tense and the spirit is one of conflict. I am convinced that Christians would not be so confused if they would spend time in God's word and earnest prayer.

So, when you select a church, listen first to what is said. Make sure the minister is preaching the Gospel in a clear and committed way. And listen to "how" he is saying it. If he has love and his words feel right to your spirit, you know then he knows the shepherd of your soul.

The Wheat and the Weeds

Now, you might be in a situation where you cannot decide for yourself where you will attend church. I know wives and children often find themselves in this position. I believe Jesus gave this story for you.

"The kingdom of heaven is like a man who sowed good seed in his field. But while everyone was sleeping, his enemy came and sowed weeds among the wheat, and went away. When the wheat sprouted and formed heads, then the weeds also appeared.

"The owner's servants came to him and said, 'Sir,

94

didn't you sow good seed in your field? Where then did the weeds come from?'

"'An enemy did this,' he replied.

"The servants asked him, 'Do you want us to go and pull them up?'

"'No,' he answered, 'because while you are pulling the weeds, you may root up the wheat with them. Let both grow together until the harvest. At that time I will tell the harvesters: First collect the weeds and tie them in bundles to be burned, then gather the wheat and bring it into my barn.'

"Then he left the crowd and went into the house. His disciples came to him and said, 'Explain to us the parable of the weeds in the field.'

"He answered, 'The one who sowed the good seed is the Son of Man. The field is the world, and the good seed stands for the sons of the kingdom. The weeds are the sons of the evil one, and the enemy who sows them is the devil. The harvest is the end of the age, and the harvesters are angels.'

"As the weeds are pulled up and burned in the fire, so it will be at the end of the age. The Son of Man will send out his angels, and they will weed out of his kingdom everything that causes sin and all who do evil. They will throw them into the fiery furnace, where there will be weeping and gnashing of teeth. Then the righteous will shine like the sun in the kingdom of their Father. He who has ears, let him hear" (Matthew 13:24-30,36-43, NIV).

Separate Yourselves

As I have already mentioned, it is very important for you to separate yourself from weedy worldly churches that have corrupted the Gospel. You need to attend an "on fire" church where you can worship God in spirit and in truth. I cannot tell you which church to attend because there are "weedy churches" and "wheat churches" everywhere I go. In one city the church of a particular denomination will be alive and dedicated to evangelism, in the next city a church of the same affiliation will be dead and worldly. But for your own sake, and the sake of your children, you need to attend a lively church.

The Bible says, *"Do not be yoked together with unbelievers. For what do righteousness and wickedness have in common? Or what fellowship can light have with darkness? What harmony is there between Christ and Belial* [a false god]? *What does a believer have in common with an unbeliever? What agreement is there between the temple of God and idols? For we are the temple of the living God. As God has said: 'I will live with them and walk among them, and I will be their God, and they will be my people.'*

"Therefore come out from them and be separate,' says the Lord. *'Touch no unclean thing and I will receive you. I will be a Father to you, and you will be*

my sons and daughters,' says the Lord Almighty"
(2 Corinthians 6:14-18, NIV).

Do Not Remain in a Dead Church

One of the greatest tragedies I have seen repeated over and over throughout the 25 years of my ministry is that of committed Christians who have died spiritually because they chose to remain in a dead church. I know of one particular family whose daughters and sons have married, divorced and all but ruined their lives just because Dad and Mom thought more of their social obligations to a dead church than their spiritual obligation to God and their children.

I have often heard the argument, "I'm going to remain in my church and turn it back to God." I believe, after experiencing true conversion, it might be good to stay for a while and give your testimony but in all my 25 years of traveling across the United States and Canada, I have only seen members change the direction of their church only once or twice. It boils down to this: if the pastor of a church is not an enlightened man or if the church endorses a false doctrine or fails to stress personal commitment to Jesus Christ, it is almost impossible for an individual Christian (or a few) to turn the church around.

It doesn't work because the pastor and board members have their hands on the wheel; the members are just passengers in the car. Arthur

Bloomfield says, "The greatest weakness of all churches is their refusal to allow any machinery for self-cleansing. The doctrine of church loyalty means this: Be loyal to your church leaders whether they are right or wrong. To criticize an evil is considered equivalent to criticizing the church. If the church puts into its literature some false teaching, it must not be pointed out. No protest may be raised. Be loyal to your church!"*

I have often illustrated it this way. The reason many people remain in a dead church is because their parents or grandparents attended it. However, what would happen if your parents or grandparents liked a certain restaurant years ago, but today the food is cold and distasteful? Would you continue to eat at that restaurant? No! You would find a new one that served hot tasty food. If you will be faithful to your body, then be even more faithful to your soul. There comes a time when you must withdraw yourself or your soul will turn sour.

Jesus said, *"No one tears a patch from a new garment and sews it on an old one. If he does, he will have torn the new garment, and the patch from*

* Reprinted by permission
  from *All things New*
  by Arthur E. Bloomfield
  Published and copyrighted 1959
  Bethany House Publishers
  Minneapolis, MN 55438

the new will not match the old. And no one pours new wine into old wineskins. If he does, the new wine will burst the skins, the wine will run out and the wineskins will be ruined. No, new wine must be poured into new wineskins" (Luke 5:36-38, NIV).

Why Denominations Die

If you are wondering why denominations die, I believe it happens in our Bible colleges and seminaries. Churches die when bookworms replace the prophets of God.

Most denominations begin in the fire of revival when a small number of men and women experience God in a powerful way. They discover the truths of holiness, set strict standards and place much emphasis on Bible reading and prayer. Note the Reformation under Martin Luther and the Methodist awakening under John Wesley. There have been many other movements such as Presbyterian, Mennonite, Assemblies of God, Wesleyan, Christian and Missionary Alliance, Church of God, Open Bible, Foursquare, etc. I could name others but this gives you an idea. (Please note my mention of these is not to criticize these denominations, but only to cite examples. Throughout the years of my ministry I have worked with many people of God from these great churches.)

When these denominations and others begin, the first leaders are godly men and women.

They may not speak with refined English, but they know God and the Bible and they know how to pray. The first professors of Bible schools, preparing ministers for churches, are these "on-fire" uncompromising giants.

But after around 40 years, the oldtimers retire and replacements for the professors are sought. By this time the denomination has grown and become more sophisticated. The denomination now feels that its Bible colleges need accreditation. So they begin to seek for ministers with degrees behind their names rather than degrees of spiritual temperature in their hearts! I remember holding church meetings many years ago and living in the parsonages with pastors who were taking extra courses at the local college "to complete their degree." Some of these men were "on-fire" men, but others were only bookworms. Not once during an entire week would they join me in prayer and get on their knees to call on God. (Not that I needed to see them pray, but when a pastor and evangelist are working closely together, even living in the same house, you don't have to be of a critical nature to notice if a man is a praying man or not.)

Today, some of these men are in Bible colleges teaching future ministers how to preach. You can be sure these cold-hearted teachers are going to turn out cold-hearted ministers who will preach icy formalistic messages from their pulpits. *"Our God is a consuming fire"* (Deuteronomy 4:24). When a minister has God alive in his heart, his sermons will be ablaze with a holy fire. His words will also cause the hearts of his hearers to burn so they will say like the disciples on the road to Emmaus, *"Did not our heart[s] burn within us, while he talked with us by the way, and while he opened to us the scriptures?"* (Luke 24:32).

Every minister must understand as Paul did that God *"also made us able ministers of the new testament; not of the letter, but of the spirit: for the letter killeth, but the spirit giveth life"* (2 Corinthians 3:6).

I love to study and promote higher education at every opportunity. For several years I have tried to read at least three to five books a week plus dozens of other spiritual magazines and my Bible. But when bookworm intellectuals, who would rather read than pray, replace the prophets of God who can say, "I heard from God today," our denominations die. The inherent danger of the ministry as Roscoe Russell has pointed out is that "ministers begin to traffic in unfelt truth." If a truth from God's Word doesn't grip your soul with reality, it will deaden you, or as Paul says, "It will kill you," so that after weeks and years your heart and feelings become stone.

Christian, beware lest the things of God become commonplace. If you are unmoved and calloused to what you read and hear, you are causing others to fall by the wayside, because when the unbeliever looks to you he only sees a lukewarm saint instead of a red-hot soul winner.

Recently I received a letter from a lady who said, "My tears are for those people who refuse any effort to evangelize or to get your evangelistic team to our town. They are so snuggled in their individual churches—they don't want to reach out. The churches have built fences rather than bridges. They are too comfortable to work for Jesus. Please pray for my church. We need a spiritual leader. We are like sheep without a shepherd."

Lukewarm or Hot?

In Revelation 2 and 3 you can read the letters Jesus wrote to the seven churches of Asia Minor. Notice how He was trying to correct their course even then.

* Jesus told the Ephesian Christians to repent because they had left their first love
   (Revelation 2:4).
* Jesus told the Pergamos Christians to repent because they allowed teachers to say
   that compromising with idolatry and living
   immorally was okay (Revelation 2:14,15).
* Jesus told the Thyatira Christians to repent

because they also allowed false teachers to compromise the congregation in the area of morals and separation from the world (Revelation 2:20).

* Jesus told the Christians at Sardis to repent because they had His name, but they didn't have His flame burning in their hearts (Revelation 3:1).

* Jesus wrote to the Laodicean Christians commanding them to repent because they were lukewarm (Revelation 3:16).

Because these are the last days of the Laodicean era, it would be good to read everything that Jesus says to us, *"I know thy works, that thou art neither cold nor hot: I would thou wert cold or hot.*

"So then because thou art lukewarm, and neither cold nor hot, I will spue [spit] *thee out of my mouth.*

"Because thou sayest, I am rich, and increased with goods, and have need of nothing; and knowest not that thou are wretched, and miserable, and poor, and blind, and naked" (Revelation 3:15-17).

Jesus reveals His revulsion of Christians who are not aflame for God, Christians who are rich with goods, nice houses, good jobs, comfortable churches and who basically feel they don't need a thing. Jesus said, *"Repent of your lukewarmness"* because you are wretched, miserable, poor, and blind and naked (Revelation 3:17).

I know these are stern words, but Jesus gave

them to you and me to save us from condemnation. The question, however, that keeps coming back to me is, "If you have a difficult time keeping your heart hot for God, how will you ever survive a cold, dead church?"

The message of Revelation 17 is that God will judge the Apostate Church. You want to be sure you are *not* part of it when it happens.

9

The Rise and Fall of Russia!

Today the free world is on a collision course with communism. Everyone realizes that sooner or later these forces will collide. A recent poll reveals that 68 percent, that is nearly seven out of ten Americans, believe there will be a nuclear war between the United States and Russia.

We dare not diminish the communist threat. Recently the President of the United States said, "I do have to point out that everything that has been said and everything in their manuals indicate that unlike us, the Soviet Union believes that a nuclear war is possible, and they believe it is winnable."

Alexander Solzhenitsyn, a Soviet writer who fled to the West after suffering in Soviet prison camps for many years, has given many startling predictions about the future. He says, "All warnings to the West about the pitilessness and the insatiable nature of the communist regimes have proven to be in vain because the acceptance of such a view would be too terrifying. For decades, it has been the standard practice to deny reality—the reality of the Russian aggression, by citing peaceful coexistence, détente, and the Kremlin leadership's pursuit of peace. Meanwhile, communism envelops country after country and achieves new missile capabilities."

Former President Jimmy Carter thought he understood the Russians, and he even believed their peace-talk until they invaded Afghanistan and killed thousands. Then Mr. Carter said his eyes were opened to the communist menace. We should never forget what Joseph Stalin, one of the fathers of communism, said, "As long as capitalism and socialism exist, we cannot live in peace. In the end one or the other will triumph. A funeral dirge will be sung either over the Soviet republic or over world capitalism." Stalin also said, "The theory of communism may be summed up in one sentence: ABOLISH ALL PRIVATE PROPERTY."

So the free world should not deceive itself that it can make peace with the communist anti-God system. If peace is offered by the communists, it is only to consolidate their gains. Henry Kissinger, former Secretary of

State for the United States, has said, "We [the U.S.] are sliding toward a world out of control with our relative military power declining, with our economical lifeline increasingly vulnerable to blackmail [the Arabs can cut 50 percent of the U.S. oil supply whenever they want to], with hostile radical forces growing in every continent, and with the number of countries willing to stake their future on our friendship dwindling."

Alexander Solzhenitsyn also has said, "You, the Western world [U.S. and Canada], have the impression that democracy can last, but democracies are islands lost in an immense river of history. The water is always rising. You have forgotten the meaning of liberty. When you acquired liberty, it was as a sacred notion, but you have forgotten. *Liberty without obligation and responsibility cannot survive because today, throughout the free world, nobody is ready to die for it."*

Beginning with Korea, the Western World embarked upon the foolish philosophy of "limited wars." In other words, do not damage the enemy too badly. Former President Harry Truman fired Douglas MacArthur because he wanted to bomb the sanctuaries that the North Koreans were using in China. Once MacArthur received an okay to bomb one of the bridges the Koreans were using as long as he bombed the right end. How ridiculous! Therefore, thousands of American men died in Korea for nearly nothing.

Again, the philosophy of limited war was used in Viet Nam. Another 55,000 American lives were given. How tragic! Today MacArthur's words ring louder than ever. He said, "Timidity breeds conflict, and courage often prevents it. Never enter a conflict unless you are committed to victory."

I believe history confirms MacArthur's statement to be true. Whenever a nation allows itself to become weak, it invites the aggressor to attack. This is why a strong America will not start a war; it will keep a war from happening. And the United States and Canada, along with the rest of the Western Nations, should serve notice that we will not provide "sanctuary" for the enemy in the event of a conflict. To do so only prompts the enemy to move against us.

When Solzhenitsyn received an honorary doctorate from Harvard he said, "The fight for our planet, physical and spiritual, a fight of cosmic proportions, is not a vague matter of the future; it has already started. The forces of evil have begun their decisive offensive. You can feel their pressure, and yet your [television and film] screens and publications are full of prescribed smiles and raised glasses. What is the joy about?"

If it were not for the Bible prophecies that

foretell the coming fall of Soviet Russia, I would not be able to laugh at all. In fact, I would be trembling in fear this very moment.

War Predictions

The chairman of Communist China recently said, "A third world war is inevitable." When Pope Paul II appeared before the United Nations he said, "Continual preparation for war demonstrated by evermore sophisticated weapons shows the desire for war. Sometime...somewhere...somehow...someone can set into motion the terrible mechanism of general destruction."

Today the nations of the world are spending over one billion dollars a day, over one million dollars a minute, preparing for World War III that, according to Bible prophecy, will break out in the Mideast.

The CBS television network presented a prime-time special revealing what would happen if the Russians exploded a 15-megaton nuclear warhead over Omaha, Nebraska. Within weeks over two million would die from the blast and from radiation poisoning.

After Hiroshima and Nagasaki, when the United States used the A-bomb for the first time, General MacArthur said, "A new era is upon us. The utter destruction of the war potential, through progressive advances in scientific discovery, has in fact now reached a point which revises the traditional concept of war. Men, since the beginning of time, have sought peace, military alliances, balances of power. Leagues of nations, all in turn, have failed, leaving the only path to be by the way of the crucible of war. *We have had our last chance. If we do not now devise some greater and more equitable system, Armageddon will be at our door."*

MacArthur was right. Armageddon IS at our door. For the first time in history mankind has the power to destroy everything on earth! Keep in mind that the Russians have 1,400 missiles aimed at the heartland of the United States. It would only take 18 minutes for them to reach us. And the United States probably has a similar number aimed at the U.S.S.R.

I recently read that the United States and Russia have a combined force of 50,000 to 60,000 nuclear devices. It has been this "balance of terror" that has kept the leaders of the world from "pushing the button." But the world is counting down to a zero when many of these weapons will be used.

The Federal Emergency Management Agency estimates that if a large-scale nuclear attack were to be launched by the Russians against the United States, 140 million Americans would die. In the event of such an attack, the President and all 16 of his successors would board a windowless specially-shielded $250 million version of the Boeing 747 jet that sits on permanent alert at the Andrews Air Force Base near Washington. If the President did not take to the air, a small one-megaton bomb dropped on the White House would instantly vaporize every structure within two miles. Residents five miles away would suffer second or third degree burns and bellowing clouds of radiation would stretch for 100 miles.

Our government even has emergency plans to protect the national archives in case of a nuclear attack. A 50-ton vault has been built beneath the display case that holds the Declaration of Independence, the Constitution and the Bill of Rights. As soon as a guard presses a switch, it starts to lower the case into this vault designed to protect the documents from fire, shock, heat, water and atomic explosion. Harry Truman dedicated the vault in 1952 and said, "It is as safe from destruction as anything that the wit of modern man can devise. So I confidently predict that what we are doing today is placing before the eyes of many generations to come the symbols of a living faith."

Russia Will Fail

Of Russia, history will record that communism was a colossal failure. The only right it knows is might. William Buckley recorded the purges and persecutions set forth by the communists against their own Russian people and said, *"For the 32-year period between 43 million and 52 million Russians [were] killed."* Can you imagine the persecution by a system of government that butchers millions of its own people? As I have pointed out in another section of this book, the Russians and the communist nations are the only countries that must protect themselves from their own people. Their border guards are faced inward to keep their people from escaping to freedom.

Today there are many anti-Nuke demonstrators marching in rallies of western countries, crying out for our leaders to disarm in the face of the Russians. Where are the Russian people who protest their government policies? In Siberian concentration camps.

The world witnessed what happened when the people of Poland tried to organize and influence their government—they were imprisoned when the army took over. This same thing happened in Czechoslovakia and in Hungary. Why do the Russians want to escape? Why did Joseph Stalin's own daughter Svetlana flee Russia and come to the United States? Because she wanted the spiritual and emotional liberty that is not available in her homeland.

Communism has also failed to meet the needs of its own people. Most Russians do not own cars and if they did they would have to pay around $2 a gallon for gasoline. Did you know the average Russian earns only $229 a month? With this small income, most Russians are forced to stand in lines to get the most basic foods that they need.

Ezekiel's Vision of Israel

The question is, When will the Russians and the West go to war? Seven out of ten Americans believe it will happen soon. What do the scriptures have to say about this nation? Thankfully the Bible mentions Russia by name. The Prophet Ezekiel was given a vision of the last days in chapters 37, 38 and 39. The first part of his prophecies refer to Israel.

"Thus saith the Lord God; Behold, I will take the children of Israel from among the heathen, whither they be gone, and will gather them on every side, and bring them into their own land: And I will make them one nation in the land upon the mountains of Israel" (Ezekiel 37:21,22).

This scripture, along with others, reveals that God will gather Israel into her homeland exactly as He has done. Since 1947 we have been living in what the scriptures refer to as "the last days."

Ezekiel 37:25 says, *"And they shall dwell in the land I have given unto Jacob my servant...for ever."* From this scripture we know that Israel will never be destroyed or driven into the Mediterranean Sea as the Arabs have predicted. I also predict that Israel will never give up Jerusalem. Prime Minister Menachem Begin said Jerusalem is "the eternal capital of our country, our people, our faith, our civilization."

Chief Rabbi Shlomo Goren says, "Jerusalem is our brain, our head, our soul." The Bible says that Israel will never be dislodged from their promised land again.

But now you can see how the confrontation between the Russians and the West will build up. Israel is the land-bridge between three continents—Europe, Asia and Africa. Today, Israel is the only nation that keeps the Russians from taking over the Mideast. With the United States receiving 50 percent of its oil from the Mideast, Europe receiving 70 percent and Japan receiving 90 percent, the Russians could win control of the world by simply taking possession of the Mideast oil fields.

Ezekiel's Vision of Russia

Here is what the Bible says is going to happen. According to the prophecies of Ezekiel 38, Russia and her allies will launch an invasion against Israel very soon.

"And the word of the Lord came unto me, saying, Son of man, set thy face against Gog, the land of Magog, the chief prince of Meshech and Tubal, and prophesy against him, And say, Thus saith the Lord

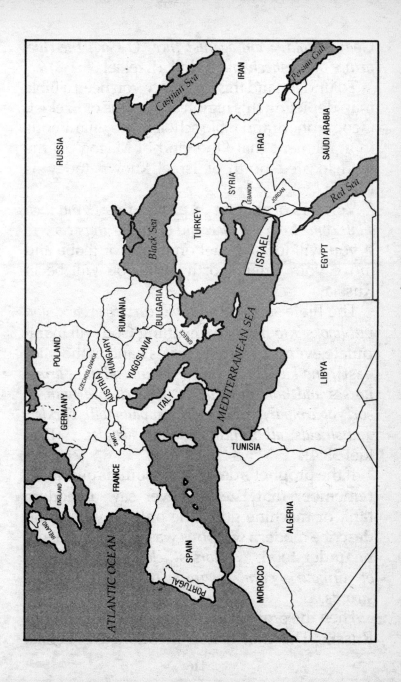

God; Behold, I am against thee, O Gog, the chief prince of Meshech and Tubal" (Ezekiel 38:1-3).

To understand this prophecy you need a Bible map depicting this region at the time of Ezekiel. Geographers and Bible scholars are unanimous in agreement that "the land of Magog" is the land located north of Israel known today as Russia.

Verse 15 of chapter 38 proves this: *"And thou shalt come from thy place out of the north parts...."* If you will locate Israel on a map or globe and move your finger northward, you will be in Russia.

The Bible says, *"And I will turn thee back, and put hooks into thy jaws* [meaning God will manipulate events to force Russia's hand in the Mideast], *and I will bring thee forth, and all thine army, horses and horsemen, all of them clothed with all sorts of armour, even a great company with bucklers and shields, all of them handling swords..."* (Ezekiel 38:4).

If the prophet's description sounds outdated, remember that Ezekiel never saw a modern tank or machine gun. The only way he could describe modern weapons was with the imagery he understood. *"...Horses...clothed with all sorts of armour, even a great company...handling swords...."*

Then the prophet lists the nations that will join Russia. The first nation mentioned is Persia.

This is the old name for Iran. For 18 years, prior to the overthrow of the Shah, I preached that Iran would ally with the Russians. This appeared foolish because the Shah was one of the West's great allies. But the Shah is gone and Iran drifts closer and closer into the Russian orbit.

The next ally mentioned in this prophecy is Ethiopia. It wasn't very long ago that Haile Selassie was in power and allied with the West. Now he is gone and his nation is in the hands of communists.

Libya is the third ally of the Russians in this invasion of Israel. Libya was once pro-West, but the radical Khadaffy overthrew the government in a coup and is now anti-American and sponsoring terrorism around the world.

"Gomer" is used to describe Russia's fourth ally. Gomer refers to Eastern Germany and the balkan states of Romania—Yugoslavia, Bulgaria Czechoslovakia and Poland. Old maps show that Gomer covered these areas. Most of these nations will join Russia in her assault against Israel.

The last nation mentioned in this prophecy is Turkey. It is referred to in scripture as "Togarmah." Today Turkey is a member of NATO (the North Atlantic Treaty Organization). However, the Bible says that there will be a change in the government's policy and that Turkey will join the Russians against Israel.

Remember that this nation is inhabited mostly by Muslims and a Khomeini-type religious revolt could topple the present military junta just like the Muslims overthrew the Shah of Iran. When this happens or when the government becomes pro-Russian, watch carefully because soon afterward the Russians will invade Israel.

The Bible says of Russia, *"In the latter years* [or the last day] *thou shalt come into the land that is brought back from the sword, and is gathered out of many people, against the mountains of Israel..."* (Ezekiel 38:8).

Israel Will Be Safe

The Bible says that God will protect the Israelis from the Russian armies. Ezekiel 38:8 ends with, *"And they* [Israel] *shall dwell safely all of them."*

The Bible graphically describes the Russian air attack saying, *"Thou shalt ascend and come like a storm"* (Ezekiel 38:9).

When the nations of the West see what Russia and her allies are up to, they will rush to Israel's defense. Even Saudi Arabia will ally with Israel against the Russians. The Bible says, *"Sheba and Dedan* [the old names for the region that is now called Saudi Arabia] *and the merchants of Tarshish, with all the young lions...shall say, 'Art thou come to take a spoil?'"* (verse 13).

The phrase, "merchants of Tarshish" is the

only uncertain part of this prophecy. Tarshish was a sea-faring nation that most prophecy teachers believe is Great Britain. "And the young lions thereof" refers to the United States, Canada, Australia and the other nations that Great Britain colonized and which have since become independent.

I believe this is the correct interpretation, for it is obvious that if the Russians tried to take over the oil supply of the world, the rest of the West would rally together against them.

One thing is certain: Many nations will come to Israel's defense (not because they are pro-Israeli, but because they are pro-oil). But I doubt that these nations will do much fighting. The reason God has allowed events to bring them to this land is to witness the miraculous delivery of Israel out of Russia's hands.

The Intervention of God

The Bible says, *"Surely in that day there shall be a great shaking in the land of Israel; So that the fishes of the sea, and the fowls of the heaven, and the beasts of the field, and all creeping things that creep upon the earth, and all the men that are upon the face of the earth shall shake at my presence, and the mountains shall be thrown down, and the steep places shall fall, and every wall shall fall to the ground.*

"And I will call for a sword against him throughout all my mountains, saith the Lord God: every man's

sword shall be against his brother" (Ezekiel 38:19-21).

When this great horde of Russian communists and their allies invade Israel, God is going to intervene and confuse their hosts by sending a great earthquake to the region. This earthquake will be felt around the world. In the confusion, the armies will destroy themselves.

There may be a nuclear exchange at this time, or else God will send fire from heaven as He did upon Sodom. *"And I will plead against him with pestilence and with blood; and I will rain upon him, and upon his bands, and upon the many people that are with him, an overflowing rain, and great hailstones, fire, and brimstone"* (Ezekiel 38:22).

This supernatural intervention by God will shock the nations of the world. The prophecy continues, *"Thus will I magnify myself, and sanctify myself; and I will be known in the eyes of many nations, and they shall know that I am the Lord"* (Ezekiel 38:23).

According to chapter 39, five-sixths of the Russian army will be destroyed and the Israelis will spend seven months burying the dead and seven years burning the war materials.

I believe it is possible and very probable that there will be a thermo-nuclear exchange between Russia and the western nations at this time. This will cause the world to cry out "Never again!" And the peoples of the world will look for a superman to bring peace at any price. This will prepare the way for the coming antichrist.

The Bible says, *"Why do the heathen rage, and the people imagine a vain thing?*

"The kings of the earth set themselves, and the rulers take counsel together, against the Lord, and against his anointed, saying, 'Let us break their bands asunder, and cast away their cords from us.'

"He that sitteth in the heavens shall laugh: the Lord shall have them in derision [He scoffs at them]. *Then shall he speak unto them in his wrath, and vex them in his sore displeasure.*

"Yet have I set my king upon my holy hill of Zion" (Psalm 2:1-6).

Regardless of what the godless systems and governments try to do, God is going to set up Jesus Christ as the ruler of the world. It reminds me of what happened when Billy Graham visited Winston Churchill during a London Crusade. Churchill asked, "Is there hope for this world?" Billy replied, "Yes! I have read the last chapter of the Bible and it says 'we win!'"

A New World Is Coming

Yes, there is a new world coming! God is building His new kingdom even now. This is what the great German composer, George Frederick Handel, must have seen when he wrote the famous words and music to "The Messiah." This great piece of music has been sung and heard by hundreds of millions of people since it was first presented in 1742.

In Handel's biography, Newman Flower describes Handel's experience this way: "It was the achievement of a giant inspired. The work of one, who by some extraordinary mental feat had drawn himself completely out of this world. What happened was that Handel passed through a superb dream. He was unconscious of its press and call. Handel's whole mind was in a trance. He did not leave his house. His servant brought him food, and as often as not, returned in an hour to the room to find the food untouched and his master staring into vacancy.

"When he had completed part two with the Hallelujah Chorus, his servant found him at the table, tears streaming from his eyes. Handel said, 'I did think I did see all of heaven before me, and the great God Himself.'"

Of a certainty, Handel saw a kingdom greater than this world.

When the Queen of England heard the performance of "The Messiah" and the choir sang, "the Lord God omnipotent reigneth," the Queen arose from her throne, took off her crown and knelt in prayer. Through Handel's "Messiah" the Queen had seen a kingdom greater than her own. It was the kingdom of the everlasting God, and she had the sense to humble herself before the Lord.

So, no matter what the communists or capitalists try to do, don't let your heart be troubled. Jesus said, *"Ye believe in God, believe also in me"* (John 14:1).

"Wherefore God also hath highly exalted him, and given him a name which is above every name:

"That at the name of Jesus every knee should bow, of things in heaven, and things in earth, and things under the earth;

"And that every tongue should confess that Jesus Christ is Lord, to the glory of God the Father" (Philippians 2:9-11).

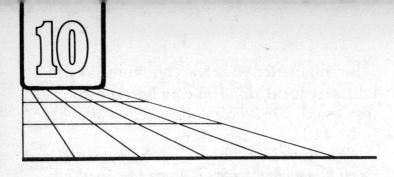

The Coming Antichrist

The Club of Rome is an elite group of world leaders who periodically meet to review the world situation. Recently they released a report entitled "Mankind at the Crossroads." The document stated, "Suddenly, virtually overnight, when measured on an historical scale, mankind finds itself confronted by a multitude of unprecedented crises: First, the population crisis; second, the environmental crisis; third, the world food crisis; fourth, the energy crisis; and fifth, the raw materials crisis— to name just a few." The report concludes, "The only alternatives *without a global plan* are division and conflict, hate and destruction."

The United Nations Secretary General has declared, "I do not wish to seem overdramatic, but I can only conclude from the information that is available to me as secretary general that the members of the United Nations have perhaps 10 years left in which to subordinate their ancient quarrels and launch a global partnership to curb the arms race, to improve the human environment, to de-fuse the population explosion, and to supply the required momentum to world development efforts." The alternative is a situation *"beyond our capacity to control."* The perilous position of our planet has leaders of the world talking about a new world government that will guarantee peace at any price.

A Princeton professor published a comprehensive work on the arms race entitled "Thinking About the Unthinkable." He said, "THE ONLY WAY TO SOLVE THE PROBLEM IS MAYBE SOME FORM OF WORLD GOVERNMENT."

The threat of nuclear war is so great that five nuclear arms experts at Harvard University and the Massachusetts Institute of Technology recently warned, "A VERY NASTY KIND OF WORLD GOVERNMENT MAY BE THE ONLY WAY TO KEEP THE WORLD FROM BLOWING ITSELF UP IN A NUCLEAR WAR."

In 1860, the French scientist, Pierre Berchelt, stated that "inside of one hundred years of physical and chemical science, man will know what the atom is. It is my belief that when science reaches this stage, God will come down to earth with His big ring of keys and will say to humanity, 'Gentlemen, it's closing time.'''

I wish I didn't have to write this chapter, but there are dark days ahead and you need to be prepared. We are nearing the time when a satanic-superman is going to appear. THIS ANTI-AGE is going to produce an antichrist.

The Apostle John describes this sinister character in these words: *"Little children, it is the last time: and as ye have heard that antichrist shall come, even now there are many antichrists; whereby we know that it is the last time"* (1 John 2:18).

The early Christians were aware that an antichrist would arise in the last days.

Paul Foresaw an Evil One

Paul the apostle wrote a special letter to the Thessalonian Christians about the satanic superman to come. The Thessalonians were afraid they were going through the Great Tribulation because of the persecution they were suffering. Paul told them that the Great Tribulation period in the last days would be introduced by the antichrist—a man of lawlessness. Then he goes into detail: *"Concerning the coming of our Lord Jesus Christ and our being gathered to him, we ask you, brothers, not to become easily unsettled or alarmed by some prophecy, report or letter supposed to have come from us, saying that the day of the Lord* [the tribulation] *has already come.*

"Don't let anyone deceive you in any way, for that day will not come until the rebellion occurs and the man of lawlessness is revealed, the man doomed to destruction. He opposes and exalts himself over everything that is called God or is worshiped, and even sets himself up in God's temple, proclaiming himself to be God.

"Don't you remember that when I was with you I used to tell you these things? And now you know what is holding him back, so that he may be revealed at the proper time. For the secret power of lawlessness is already at work; but the one who now holds it back will continue to do so till he is taken out of the way. And then the lawless one will be revealed, whom the Lord Jesus will overthrow with the breath of his mouth and destroy by the splendor of his coming.

"The coming of the lawless one will be in accordance with the work of Satan displayed in all kinds of counterfeit miracles, signs and wonders, and in every sort of evil that deceives those who are perishing. They perish because they refused to love the truth and so be saved. For this reason God sends them a powerful delusion so that they will believe the lie and so that all will be condemned who have not believed the truth but have delighted in wickedness" (2 Thessalonians 2:1-12, NIV).

From what Paul says, this man is one of the most important figures in prophecy. In fact, next to Jesus Christ, the antichrist is the most powerful man described in the Bible.

Daniel Predicts an Evil Power

The Prophet Daniel has a lot of amazing things to say about this coming evil one. *"In the latter part of their reign, when rebels have become completely wicked, a stern-faced king, a master of intrigue, will arise. He will become very strong, but not by his own power. He will cause astounding devastation and will succeed in whatever he does. He will destroy the mighty men and the holy people.*

"He will cause deceit to prosper, and he will consider himself superior. When they feel secure, he will destroy many and take his stand against the Prince of princes. Yet he will be destroyed, but not by human power" (Daniel 8:23-25, NIV).

Daniel continues, *"The king will do as he pleases. He will exalt and magnify himself above every god and will say unheard-of things against the God of gods"* (Daniel 11:36, NIV).

READ THIS NEXT PASSAGE CAREFULLY, BECAUSE JESUS SAYS THIS PROPHECY DANIEL GIVES US IS A GREAT KEY TO UNDERSTANDING END – TIME EVENTS.

"Yea, he magnified himself even to the prince of the host, and by him the daily sacrifice was taken away, and the place of the sanctuary was cast down. And an host was given him against the daily sacrifice by reason of transgression, and it cast down the truth to the ground; and it practised, and prospered" (Daniel 8:11,12).

God revealed to Daniel that the antichrist will take away the daily Jewish sacrifices (which will soon be reestablished) and will set himself up in the Jewish temple showing himself as God almighty.

The Gospels Confirm Daniel's Prophecy

This prophecy will help you understand the words of Jesus Christ in two of the Gospels. They run parallel according to the pattern we have followed throughout this book.

"When ye therefore shall see the abomination of desolation, spoken of by Daniel the prophet, stand in the holy place, (whoso readeth, let him understand:) Then let them which be in Judaea flee into the mountains: Let him which is on the housetop not come down to take any thing out of his house: Neither let him which is in the field return back to take his clothes. And woe unto them that are with child, and to them that give such in those days! But pray ye that your flight be not in the winter neither on the sabbath day" (Matthew 24:15-20).

"But when ye shall see the abomination of desolation, spoken of by Daniel the prophet, standing where it ought not, (let him that readeth understand,) then let them that be in Judaea flee to the mountains: and let him that is on the housetop not go down into the house, neither enter therein, to take any thing out of his house: And let him that is in the field not turn back again for to take up his garment. But woe to

them that are with child, and to them that give suck in those days! And pray ye that your flight be not in the winter" (Mark 13:14-18).

The "abomination of desolation" that Jesus mentions is when the antichrist sets himself up as God in the Jewish temple. This act will signal the most terrible time ever to come upon this world—especially upon Israel. Jesus warns the Jewish believers to flee Jerusalem the instant they see the antichrist in the temple.

It's easy to see how such a satanic superman could rise to power today. People everywhere are crying for a strong man to lead the world out of economic turmoil and to protect us from World War III. There is a growing "Peace Movement" in Europe and the United States.

Historian Arnold Toynbee could see where the world was headed when he said, "By forcing on mankind more and more lethal weapons, and at the same time making the world more and more interdependent economically, technology has brought mankind to such a degree of distress that we are ripe for the deifying of any new Caesar who might succeed in giving the world unity and peace."

Sydney J. Harris, writing for the *Chicago Daily News*, made this comment in an article titled, "WE WANT A MESSIAH, NOT A LEADER":

"People keep saying, we need a leader...but that is not what they really mean. What most are looking for is not a leader, because a true leader does not tell us what we *want* to hear, but what we *ought* to hear. What we are looking for is neither a true leader nor a true Messiah, but a false messiah—a man who will give us oversimplified answers, who will justify our ways....In short, we are invoking magic, we are praying for the coming of a WIZARD....What we are looking for is a leader who will show us how to be the same old man, only more successfully—and his ancient name is Satan."*

Characteristics of the Antichrist

There are several unusual characteristics about the antichrist. In the vision God gave Daniel (see Daniel 7), the great kingdoms of history are revealed. The first was Babylon (verse 4) which was in existence in Daniel's day: next, Medo-Persia (verse 5), Greece (verse 6), and Rome (verse 7), and then it mentions the antichrist (verse 8). *"In this horn were eyes like the eyes of man, and a mouth speaking great things."* That this is the antichrist is confirmed by the fact that he is the last ruler just before the Ancient of Days sets up His kingdom.

Another thing that stands out is the striking appearance of this evil man. The prophet men-

---

* Reprinted by permission of
Sydney J. Harris and *Field
Newspaper Syndicate*

tions his eyes several times. *"...that horn [the antichrist] that had eyes, and a mouth that spake very great things, whose look was more stout than his fellows"* (Daniel 7:20).

"In the latter time...a king of fierce countenance, and UNDERSTANDING DARK SENTENCES, shall stand up" (Daniel 8:23). This means the antichrist will have occult connections with Satan and the demonic underworld.

Daniel 11:21 says he will have such a striking personality that he will overcome his opposition with flatteries.

Daniel tells us the antichrist will most likely arise out of the area that comprised the old Roman Empire, the present Europe and Middle East. My reasons for believing this are two-fold:

First, in Daniel 7:7,8 we see that *"the little horn"* antichrist is an offshoot of the old Roman Empire. (Rome was the fourth great empire.)

Second, Daniel 8:9 says, *"And out of one of them came forth a little horn, which waxed exceeding great, toward the south, and toward the east, and toward the pleasant land [Israel]."*

The antichrist will begin as the head of a small country. He is repeatedly called "the little horn," but he grows rapidly. *"And after the league made with him he shall work deceitfully: for he shall come up, and shall become strong with a small people"* (Daniel 11:23).

The Seventy Weeks

The antichrist shall make a seven-year covenant with the Jews, but will break his contract with them after three and one half years. From what I have studied, the antichrist will come up with a Mideast peace plan that will win the favor of the Jews. They rejected the true Christ when He walked among them, but in an effort to establish peace they will be deceived by a false Christ. *"And he shall confirm the covenant with many for one week: and in the midst of the week* [seven year period of time] *he shall cause the sacrifice and the oblation to cease..."* (Daniel 9:27).

Don't let the week, which represents seven days (or seven years) of judgment puzzle you. The literal translation is "seventy sevens" or seventy "seven lengths" of time. Since the only English word denoting time as a group of seven is "week," it was translated at "seventy weeks." Because Israel had sinned against God, they were to be punished for seventy seven-lengths of time, or 490 years, (see Daniel 9:24-27). According to this prophecy, 69 of these weeks of years have already taken place, which leaves one week to go to complete the prophecy. This last week of time will begin the moment the Jews make a covenant with the false Christ.

John's Revelation

The Apostle John was given a revelation of this satanic superman in Revelation 13:1, *"And I stood upon the sand of the sea [humanity], and saw a beast* [the antichrist] *rise up out of the sea* [of humanity] *having seven heads and ten horns* [ten nations allied with him], *and upon his horns ten crowns and upon his heads the name of blasphemy."*

John says the antichrist will experience a satanic resurrection. Just as God raised Jesus from the dead, Satan will raise the antichrist back to life. *"And I saw one of his heads as it were wounded to death; and his deadly wound was healed: and all the world wondered after the beast"* (Revelation 13:3).

When Satan brings the antichrist back to life, it will shock the world. Imagine how the world would have wondered if former President John F. Kennedy had risen from the dead after the assassin's bullet had blown away much of his head.

Supernatural Power Displayed

The antichrist will have supernatural power. *"And they worshipped the dragon* [Satan] *which gave power unto the beast* [the antichrist]: *and they worshipped the beast, saying, Who is like unto the beast? who is able to make war with him?"* (Revelation 13:4).

Although the antichrist will not control the whole world (see Daniel 11:30,44), he will have phenomenal power to make war. In fact, the nations will fear him and will only fight in self-defense.

With nations arming themselves with intercontinental ballistic missiles today, with the U.S. and Russia in possession of H-bombs, cruise missiles, nuclear submarines, etc., it seems amazing that the nations will say, "Who is able to make war with him?" The only answer is that the antichrist will be armed with some kind of super secret weapon—stronger than H-bombs and missiles.

The antichrist will persecute the tribulation saints. *"And it was given unto him to make war with the saints, and to overcome them: and power was given him over all kindreds, and tongues, and nations"* (Revelation 13:7).

The False Prophet

The antichrist will be aided by another demonically-controlled man described as the false prophet. *"And I beheld another beast coming up out of the earth; and he had two horns like a lamb, and he spake as a dragon* [the devil]. *And he exerciseth all the power of the first beast before him* [the antichrist], *and causeth the earth and them which dwell therein to worship the first beast* [the antichrist], *whose deadly wound was healed.*

135

"And he doeth great wonders, so that he maketh fire come down from heaven on the earth in the sight of men, And deceiveth them that dwell on the earth by means of those miracles which he had power to do in the sight of the beast; saying to them that dwell on the earth, that they should make an image [idol] to the beast, which had the wound by a sword, and did live.

"And he had power to give life unto the image of the beast, that the image of the beast should both speak, and cause that as many as would not worship the image of the beast should be killed" (Revelation 13:11-16).

Can you imagine the impact it will make on the masses of people when the idol of the antichrist is erected and begins to speak as a man? Just as the magicians of Egypt were able to do many miraculous things when Moses appeared before them, so Satan will work wonders through the false prophet to turn people to the antichrist (see Exodus 7:10-13.)

The Mark of the Beast

The false prophet will require that all people have a mark on their hand or forehead. *"And he causeth all, both small and great, rich and poor, free and bond, to receive a mark in their right hand, or in their foreheads: And that no man might buy or sell, save he that had the mark, or the name of the beast, or the number of his name.*

136

"Here is wisdom. Let him that hath understanding count the number of the beast: for it is the number of a man; and his number is Six hundred three score and six [666]" (Revelation 13:16-18).

Now, more bizarre speculations have been made about "the mark of the beast" than any other last day event. I am constantly receiving tracts and booklets on the subject. It makes for speculative reading and with computers, Master Charge and Visa, social security numbers and the new check-out system in our stores, it is easy to see how the antichrist could get hold of everyone in a material sense.

Empire of the Antichrist

However, we must remember the antichrist will not, I repeat, will *not* control the whole world politically. From what I can see in prophecy, he will only control a revived Europe and at the most—the Mideast. (See map.)

Note what Daniel says, *"For the ships of Chittim shall come against him* [the antichrist]: *therefore he shall be grieved, and return"* (Daniel 11:30).

Whatever countries "the ships of Chittim" represent, they will stop the antichrist from invading other countries. This proves that the antichrist does *not* rule the whole world. For instance, the United Nations and the Catholic Church are worldwide entities and have enormous influence, but they do not totally control

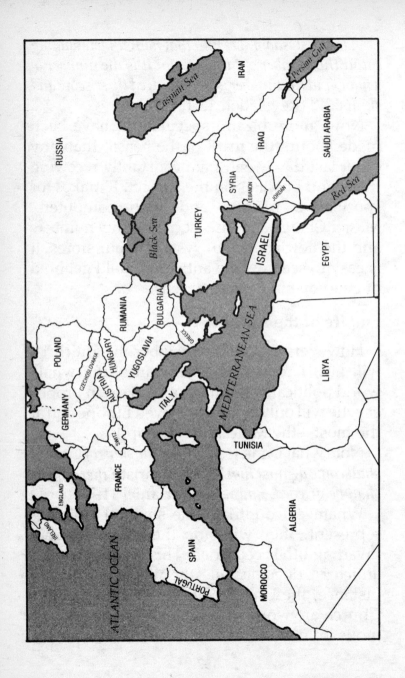

countries politically.

"He shall enter also into the glorious land...But tidings out of the east and out of the north shall trouble him" (Daniel 11:41,44).

This means that the nation north of Israel (Russia) and an eastern nation (possibly Red China) will cause the antichrist to ponder what is going to happen.

People living in the sphere of the antichrist's influence will be required to have a mark on their forehead or in their hand so they will be able to buy or sell. But this doesn't mean that all people will take the mark or that those who do will be totally under his control. The question is simple: If the antichrist cannot keep nations from attacking him or stopping his invasions, how could he require their people to obey him completely? The answer is, "He cannot!" Remember, just because the Bible says, *"He causeth all, to receive a mark"* (Revelation 13:16), does not mean the whole world will receive it. The Bible also says that Caesar sent out a decree that all the world should be taxed (Luke 2:1), but the whole world was not taxed, only the territory he had jurisdiction over.

I'm not trying to downplay the danger of the antichrist's rule. I'm simply saying that many people have made more of this mark than they should have. They have made it universal when the antichrist's control is in varying degrees in various places.

Who Wins in the End?

How will everything end? God's Word assures us of the final outcome. The antichrist *will* fail! Daniel said, *"I beheld, and the same horn made war with the saints, and prevailed against them; Until the Ancient of days [Jesus Christ] came, and judgment was given to the saints of the Most High; and the time came that the saints possessed the kingdom"* (Daniel 7:21,22).

The Apostle John says, *"And the beast [the antichrist] was taken, and with him the false prophet that wrought miracles before him, with which he deceived them that had received the mark of the beast, and them that worshipped his image. These both were cast alive into a lake of fire burning with brimstone"* (Revelation 19:20).

Praise God, the antichrist and his followers are going to lose. The saints of the Most High are going to win. But this will not happen until there is a great struggle that I'll tell you about in the next chapter.

11

The Great Tribulation

If you have a feeling that the world is headed for disaster—you're right. The coming holocaust will be worse than anything that the world has ever known.

Jesus said, *"Unless God shortens the days—there will be no survivors"* (see Matthew 24:22). This coming calamity is known as the great tribulation.

"For then shall be Great Tribulation, such as was not since the beginning of the world to this time, no, nor ever shall be. And except those days should be shortened, there should no flesh be saved: but for the elect's sake those days shall be shortened. Then if any man shall say unto you, Lo, here is Christ, or there; believe it not. For there shall arise false Christs, and false prophets, and shall shew great signs and

141

wonders; insomuch that, if it were possible, they shall deceive the very elect. Behold, I have told you before. Wherefore if they shall say unto you, Behold, he is in the desert; go not forth: behold, he is in the secret chambers; believe it not. For as the lightning cometh out of the east, and shineth even unto the west; so shall also the coming of the Son of man be. For wheresoever the carcass is, there will the eagles be gathered together" (Matthew 24:21-28).

"For in those days shall be affliction, such as was not from the beginning of the creation which God created unto this time, neither shall be. And except that the Lord had shortened those days, no flesh should be saved: but for the elect's sake, whom he hath chosen, he hath shortened the days. And then if any man shall say to you, Lo, here is Christ; or, lo, he is there; believe him not: For false Christs and false prophets shall rise, and shall shew signs and wonders, to seduce, if it were possible, even the elect. But take ye heed: behold, I have foretold you all things" (Mark 13:19-23).

"For these be the days of vengeance, that all things which are written may be fulfilled. But woe unto them that are with child, and to them that give suck, in those days! for there shall be great distress in the land, and wrath upon this people. And they shall fall by the edge of the sword, and shall be led away captive into all nations: and Jerusalem shall be trodden down of the Gentiles, until the times of the Gentiles be fulfilled" (Luke 21:22-24).

God's purpose in this time of terror will be to bring men and women to repentance. Just as a father punishes his boy to save him from a rebellion that ends in ruin, God is going to punish this planet to save all He can from eternal destruction.

You can read much more about these end-time tribulation events in the book of Revelation where God gave John a vision of the last days.

If you are studying the book of Revelation, I am offering you a simple outline to follow. You can write these guidelines at the beginning of each chapter. If you are not interested in these details, skip to the end of the shaded area.

OUTLINE OF REVELATION

CHAPTER

1 An introduction to Jesus Christ—who He is and where He stands.

2,3 Letters from Jesus Christ to the seven churches of Asia Minor. These churches are typical of churches today.

4 John gets a vision of Jesus Christ in heaven.

5 Jesus prepares to open the books of last-day prophecy.

6 A quick review of events taking place from the resurrection of Jesus

Christ to the last days.
7 A close, in-depth view of what will happen during the Tribulation.
8-11 Events of the Great Tribulation (the seven trumpets).
12 The final conflict in heaven.
13 The antichrist described in greater detail.
14,15 View of heaven.
16 The final plagues poured out upon the earth.
17 Apostate Christian religion described and punished.
18 The godless commerce system of this world described and punished.
19 Jesus prepares to return. Beginning with verse 11 heaven opens and He comes with all His saints.
20 Satan is bound for 1,000 years, then loosed for a season and cast into a lake of fire. Beginning with verse 11, the great white throne judgment where all the wicked dead will be judged.
21 The earth renewed, the holy city described.
22 The future foretold and final comments made.

Most teachers of Bible prophecy place Revelation 6 with the six seals at the beginning of the tribulation period. I believe this interpretation is wrong for three reasons.

1. It does not correspond with the words of Jesus in Matthew, Mark and Luke which are the key to both Revelation and the book of Daniel.

2. The events of Revelation 6 will require many years to take place, more time than can be allotted in the seven-year tribulation period. I'll never forget when the Lord first showed me this in Bible college. After the teacher tried to get all of Chapter 6 and the following events of Revelation into a seven-year period, I asked, "How can you reasonably say all this will happen in such a short period?" He looked up and the realization of my comment struck home in his heart. Doubt swept over his face and he said, "Lowell, you might be right."

3. Almost every prophecy teacher says the antichrist comes on the world scene during a time of peace and prosperity. (They are correct.) How then could there be peace and prosperity with the four horsemen racing across the earth and the six seals breaking loose during the first three-and-a-half years of the tribulation period? (Read almost any prophecy book

and you will catch the writer in this terrible inconsistency.)

I say again, I believe Revelation 6 was a panoramic vision shown to John of all the major events from the resurrection of Jesus Christ up to His return to the Mount of Olives. It was a quick review of this entire period.

I believe the proper interpretation of Revelation 6 is as follows:

The white horse, the first seal, is Jesus Christ and the gospel going forth conquering and to conquer.

As the gospel goes forth, false teachers arise. This corresponds with Matthew 24:5 where Jesus said, *"Many shall come in my name, saying, I am Christ; and shall deceive many."* (See also Mark 13:6 and Luke 21:8.)

The red horse, the second seal, is War.

This corresponds with Jesus' words in Matthew 24:6, *"Ye shall hear of wars and rumors of wars."* (See also Mark 13:7 and Luke 21:9.)

The black horse, the third seal, is Famine.

This corresponds with Jesus' words in Matthew 24:7, *"There shall be famines."* (See also Mark 13:8 and Luke 21:8.)

The pale horse, the fourth seal, is Pestilence.

I have read that the Black Plague that swept the world from 1347 to 1351 destroyed one-third of the inhabitants of the earth.

This corresponds with Jesus' words in Matthew 24:7, *"There shall be...pestilences."* (See also Mark 13:8, *"There shall be troubles,"* and Luke 21:11.)

The fifth seal is the saints from all the ages in heaven finally becoming impatient over the wicked who rule the earth and crying out for vengeance.

This corresponds with Jesus' words in Matthew 24:9, *"Then shall they deliver you up to be afflicted, and shall kill you: and ye shall be hated of all nations for my name's sake."* (Also Mark 13:12,13 and Luke 21:12.)

The sixth seal is the Final Judgment at the end of the Tribulation when the stars fall from heaven.

This corresponds with a passage we have not come to yet in our chronological study of the end-time events from Matthew, Mark and Luke. Jesus says, *"Immediately after the tribulation of those days shall the sun be darkened, and the moon shall not give her light, and the stars shall fall from heaven, and the powers of the heaven shall be shaken"* (Matthew 24:29). Also see Mark 13:24,25 and Luke 21:25,26.

Tribulation Events

Here are some of the events that will take place during the Tribulation.

* 144,000 Jews will repent of their sins, believe in Jesus Christ and be sealed by God, protected against the antichrist's persecution (Revelation 7:1-8).
* One-third of all the trees and grass will be burned up (Revelation 8:7).
* One-third of the sea will turn to blood (Revelation 8:8).
* One-third of marine life and sailors and their ships will be destroyed (Revelation 8:9).
* One-third of all the waters of the earth will be turned bitter (Revelation 8:10,11).
* One-third of the sun, moon and stars will be smitten so they will dim, causing the earth to turn cold and eerie (Revelation 8:12,13).

This is just the beginning of God's judgments. In your mind, review what has already happened. One-third of all the trees and grass have been burned up, the waters of the oceans have turned red, and one-third of the sailors and their ships have been lost. The waters of many wells inland have turned bitter while the sun, moon and stars have dimmed by 33 percent. What happens next makes my blood run cold. Into this cold, eerie world God looses demonic locusts.

The Bottomless Pit Opened

"And he opened the bottomless pit; and there arose a smoke out of the pit, as the smoke of a great furnace; and the sun and the air were darkened by reason of the smoke of the pit. [A hellish "atomic-like" cloud will rise when God opens the belly of the earth.]

"And there came out of the smoke locusts [giant grasshopper-like creatures] *upon the earth: and unto them was given power, as the scorpions* [poisonous spiders] *of the earth have power.*

"And it was commanded them that they should not hurt the grass of the earth [their common food], *neither any green thing, neither any tree; but only those men which have not the seal of God in their foreheads.*

"And to them it was given that they should not kill them, but that they should be tormented five months: and their torment was the torment of a scorpion, when he striketh a man.

"And in those days shall men seek death, and shall not find it; and shall desire to die, and death shall flee from them" (Revelation 9:2-6).

I have read in history that Roman soldiers were so disciplined against pain that often they would not cry out when one of their arms were cut off. Yet during the Roman army's conquest of Egypt, many soldiers were bit by scorpions and even though they were hardened, the pain was so bad they screamed out loud. Just imagine the terror that will seize men when these giant demonic locusts are loosed upon the earth!

No wonder the Bible says, *"During those days men will seek death, but will not find it; they will long to die, but death will elude them"* (Revelation 9:6, NIV).

Giant Locusts Will Terrify People

The scriptures even describe these hellish locusts in greater detail. *"The locusts looked like horses prepared for battle. On their heads they wore something like crowns of gold, and their faces resembled human faces. Their hair was like women's hair, and their teeth were like lions' teeth. They had breastplates like breastplates of iron, and the sound of their wings was like the thundering of many horses and chariots rushing into battle. They had tails and stings like scorpions, and in their tails they had power to torment people for five months. They had as king over them the angel of the Abyss, whose name in Hebrew is Abaddon, and in the Greek, Apollyon"* (Revelation 9:7-11, NIV).

As these giant demonic locusts hunt men and women in the gray twilight, the terrifying screams of the victims will be heard everywhere. People will pray for death, but it will not come.

Yet something worse is ahead.

One-third of the People Destroyed

"The sixth angel blew his trumpet, and I heard a voice coming from the horns of the golden altar that is before God. It said to the sixth angel who had the trumpet, 'Release the four angels who are bound at

the great river Euphrates.' And the four angels who had been kept ready for this very hour and day and month and year were released to kill a third of mankind. The number of the mounted troops was two hundred million....

"The horses and riders I saw in my vision looked like this: Their breastplates were fiery red, dark blue, and yellow as sulfur. The heads of the horses resembled the heads of lions, and out of their mouths came fire, smoke and sulfur.

"A third of mankind [today that would be over one billion five hundred million], *was killed by the three plagues of fire, smoke and sulfur that came out of their mouths. The power of the horses was in their mouths and in their tails; for their tails were like snakes, having heads with which they inflict injury"* (Revelation 9:13-19, NIV).

Ever since Mao Tse-tung said he could raise an army of 200 million, a popular interpretation of this army of 200 million is to say it belongs to Red China. But I believe these are special demonic creatures that God has prepared for the last days.

The purpose of these frightening creatures is to bring the world to repentance. God is not a madman playing games of torture like a cat playing with a mouse. God, our Father in heaven, is using every possible means to soften men's rebellious hearts.

The Bible describes what happens after these 200 million demonic assassins have finished. *"The rest of mankind that were not killed by these plagues still did not repent of the work of their hands; they did not stop worshiping demons, and idols of gold, silver, bronze, stone and wood—idols that cannot see or hear or walk. Nor did they repent of their murders, their magic arts, their sexual immorality or their thefts"* (Revelation 9:20,21, NIV).

Beware, Watch and Pray

Now, if you are a committed Christian, you don't have to worry about this terrible time that is coming upon the earth. Although I will deal with this subject in greater detail later in this book, I will say now that Jesus Christ is going to come for His church and take us to heaven before these frightening events take place.

Jesus said, *"And take heed to yourselves, lest at any time your hearts be overcharged with surfeiting, and drunkenness, and cares of this life, and so that day come upon you unawares. For as a snare shall it* [the Tribulation] *come on all them that dwell on the face of the whole earth. Watch ye therefore, and pray always, that ye may be accounted worthy to escape all these things that shall come to pass, and to stand before the Son of man"* (Luke 21:34-36).

Many other dreadful events will take place during the Great Tribulation that I will continue to describe in the next chapter, but it is really easy to see why Jesus said, *"Except those days should be shortened, there should no flesh be saved"* (Matthew 24:22).

The Great Tribulation - Part 2

A great question arises regarding the tribulation period: if the church of true believers is taken to heaven and the antichrist is in power persecuting everyone who believes in Jesus Christ, who will preach to the inhabitants of earth during the days of God's judgment? How will people on earth know and understand what is taking place?

Two Witnesses Revealed

The Bible in Revelation 11 tells us what's coming next: God will send two prophets to Jerusalem where they will preach with great power. If the antichrist tries to stop them with soldiers, fire will come forth out of their mouths and devour them.

"They [the Gentiles] *will trample on the holy city for 42 months* [three-and-a-half years]" (Revelation 11:2, NIV).

This means that even though Israel has possession of the Holy City today, the antichrist will break his treaty with the Jews and will possess the city with his armies.

Here's where the two prophets of God are described: *"And I will give power to my two witnesses, and they will prophesy for 1,260 days* [approximately three-and-a-half years], *clothed in sackcloth. If anyone tries to harm them, fire comes from their mouths and devours their enemies. This is how anyone who wants to harm them will die. These men have power to shut up the sky so that it will not rain during the time they are prophesying; and they have power to turn the waters into blood and to strike the earth with every kind of plague as often as they want"* (Revelation 11:3,5,6, NIV).

Remember, this chapter is an insert into the tribulation picture. As stated in the last chapter, the trees and grass will be burned up and the oceans and seas will turn to blood. Chances are these two prophets have called these judgments down upon the earth.

There has been a lot of speculation as to who these men are. Some say they are Elijah and Moses, but I would favor Elijah and John the apostle. The reason is that the angel said to John at the end of Revelation 10, *"Thou must prophesy again before many peoples, and nations, and tongues, and kings"* (Revelation 10:11).

155

God will not be without His witnesses in this world. Just imagine how it will frustrate the antichrist and the sinful masses when these faithful men pronounce judgments and call the world to repentance. Surely the world, like wicked King Ahab of ancient Israel, will think these prophets are causing the problems, but it will be their sins that have brought God's judgments. (See 1 Kings 18:17.)

God Protects His Children

The unbeliever has a difficult time understanding why God punishes the wicked. He resents God because God punishes sin, because God created hell, because God separates the wicked from the righteous. The sinner in his darkened mind thinks God is a monster rather than a loving Father.

Let me ask, "Would a loving father expose his children to a deadly disease?" Never! He'll protect them with his life. So it is with God. He loves His children and wants to protect them from the disease of sin present in evil people. If God separates the sinners from the just, it is because He is doing so out of love.

The Witnesses Resurrected and Seen Worldwide

When the two prophets have finished their prophesying, something happens that causes the world to rejoice.

"Now when they have finished their testimony, the beast that comes up from the Abyss will attack them and overpower and kill them. [Remember, this beast and his hordes have been hunting down people all over the world.] *Their bodies will lie in the street of the great city, which is figuratively called Sodom and Egypt, where also their Lord was crucified* [Jerusalem]. *For three-and-a-half days men from every people, tribe, language and nation will gaze on their bodies and refuse them burial. The inhabitants of the earth will gloat over them and will celebrate by sending each other gifts, because these two prophets had tormented those who live on the earth.*

"But after the three-and-a-half days a breath of life from God entered them, and they stood on their feet [they are resurrected!], *and terror struck those who saw them. Then they heard a loud voice from heaven saying to them, 'Come up here.' And they went up to heaven in a cloud, while their enemies looked on.*

"At that very hour there was a severe earthquake and a tenth of the city collapsed. Seven thousand people were killed in the earthquake, and the survivors were terrified and gave glory to the God of heaven" (Revelation 11:7-13, NIV).

In the past, this remarkable passage of scripture was often refuted by skeptics of the Bible who said, "How could all the inhabitants of the world see these two dead prophets in the streets of Jerusalem? It's impossible! The Bible must be wrong."

But now, via television and communication satellites, the world has become a global village. It will be very easy for the world to see the two witnesses lying dead in Jerusalem's streets. A local Israeli station will focus its cameras on the victims and then, through an up-link beam, transmit the photos and commentaries to satellite stations throughout the world. Millions of people will see the two prophets of God dead and then raised to life right on their home TV sets!

Revelation 12 and 13 Summarized

After the prophets are caught up into heaven, the Apostle John (in Revelation 12) is shown how the Jews, who have accepted Jesus Christ as their Messiah (and this could include some of the Gentile believers who come to Jesus Christ during the tribulation), will escape the persecution of the antichrist.

Chapter 13 of Revelation describes the antichrist in greater detail than we have in Chapter 12.

God's Judgments Continue

Then the judgments of God proceed again. John says, *"And I saw another angel fly in the midst of heaven, having the everlasting gospel to preach unto them that dwell on the earth, and to every nation, and kindred, and tongue, and people.*

"Saying with a loud voice, Fear God, and give glory to him; for the hour of his judgment is come: and worship him that made heaven, and earth, and the sea, and the fountains of waters" (Revelation 14:6,7).

Imagine it! The angel of God flying through the heavens preaching to the inhabitants of the world, commanding them to repent of their sins.

"And the third angel followed them, saying with a loud voice, If any man worship the beast and his image, and receive his mark in his forehead, or in his hand, The same shall drink of the wine of the wrath of God" (Revelation 14:9,10).

Before God unleashes His final fury, He is going to warn the peoples of the world what is coming to pass. He gives them another chance to change their ways.

God's Final Wrath Outpoured

Finally, *"I heard a loud voice from the temple saying to the seven angels, 'Go, pour out the seven bowls of God's wrath upon the earth.'*

"The first angel went and poured out his bowl on the land, and ugly and painful sores broke out on the people who had the mark of the beast and worshiped his image.

159

"The second angel poured out his bowl upon the sea, and it turned into blood like that of a dead man, and every living thing in the sea died." [Notice: In the first judgments of God only one-third perished; now everyone dies!]

"The third angel poured out his bowl on the rivers and springs of water, and they became blood. Then I heard the angel in charge of the waters say:

"'You are just in these judgments, you who are and who were, the Holy One, because you have so judged; for they have shed the blood of your saints and prophets, and you have given them blood to drink as they deserve.'

"And I heard the altar respond [the martyred saints]: 'Yes, Lord God Almighty, true and just are your judgments.'

"The fourth angel poured out his bowl on the sun, and the sun was given power to scorch people with fire." (Notice: In the first judgments the sun is dimmed and the earth becomes a dreary, errie place. Now the curtain of darkness is pulled back and the sun is allowed to scorch people with its terrible heat.]

"They were seared by the intense heat and they cursed the name of God, who had control over these plagues, but they refused to repent and glorify him" (Revelation 16:1-9, NIV).

It is awesome to see how sin has such a great hold on people. After all their punishments, the

160

greater number of people on earth will only curse God instead of crying out for His mercy.

Then, *"The fifth angel poured out his bowl [of punishments] on the throne of the beast [the antichrist], and his kingdom was plunged into darkness. Men gnawed their tongues in agony and cursed the God of heaven because of their pains and their sores, but they refused to repent of what they had done"* (Revelation 16:10,11, NIV).

Preparing for Armageddon

Now the climax of history is nearing as Christ and Satan battle for planet earth. *"Then I saw three evil spirits that looked like frogs; they came out of the mouth of the dragon [Satan], out of the mouth of the beast [the antichrist], and out of the mouth of the false prophet. They are spirits of demons performing miraculous signs, and they go out to the kings of the whole world, to gather them for the battle on the great day of God Almighty"* (Revelation 16:13,14, NIV).

The antichrist has called the nations of the world together for the showdown battle for planet earth. Armageddon is in the making.

The Prophet Zechariah foresaw this moment and said, *"The day of the Lord cometh....For I will gather all nations against Jerusalem to battle"* (Zechariah 14:1,2).

As these great armies of the world head toward Jerusalem for battle, other horrors will take place.

Terrors From the Sky

"The seventh angel poured out his bowl [of judgments] *into the air, and out of the temple came a loud voice from the throne, saying 'It is done!' Then there came flashes of lightning, rumblings, peals of thunder and a severe earthquake. No earthquake like it has ever occurred since man has been on earth, so tremendous was the quake. The great city* [Jerusalem] *split into three parts, and the cities of the nations collapsed... Every island fled away and the mountains could not be found. From the sky huge hailstones of about a hundred pounds each fell upon men. And they cursed God on account of the plague of hail, because the plague was so terrible"* (Revelation 16:17-21, NIV).

This is the time Jesus speaks of in all three gospels. In Matthew He says, *"Immediately after the tribulation of those days shall the sun be darkened, and the moon shall not give her light, and the stars shall fall from heaven, and the powers of the heaven shall be shaken"* (Matthew 24:29).

Mark records Jesus' words this way: *"After that tribulation, the sun shall be darkened, and the moon shall not give her light, And the stars of heaven shall fall, and the powers that are in heaven shall be shaken"* (Mark 13:24,25).

Luke remembered Jesus' words and wrote them saying, "*And there shall be signs in the sun, and in the moon, and in the stars; and upon the earth distress of nations, with perplexity; the sea and the waves roaring* [because of the immense earthquakes]; *Men's hearts failing them for fear, and for looking after those things which are coming on the earth: for the powers of heaven shall be shaken*" (Luke 21:25,26).

Can you imagine the terror that will seize men when the stars begin to fall from heaven? When giant meteors plunge toward earth? The heavens will be ablaze with objects plummeting downward.

The Apostle John saw this day and said, "*And the sun became black as sackcloth of hair, and the moon became as blood: And the stars of heaven fell unto the earth, even as a fig tree casteth her untimely figs, when she is shaken of a mighty wind.*

"*And the heaven departed as a scroll when it is rolled together; and every mountain and island were moved out of their places.*

"*And the kings of the earth, and the great men, and the rich men, and the chief captains, and the mighty men, and every bondman* [slave], *and every free man, hid themselves in the dens and in the rocks of the mountains;*

"*And said to the mountains and rocks, Fall on us, and hide us from the face of him that sitteth on the throne, and from the wrath of the Lamb: For the great day of his wrath is come; and who shall be able to stand?''* (Revelation 6:12-17).

Accept God's Salvation Now

Events are moving swiftly now and we are nearing the day when God's wrath will be poured out upon the wicked.

All I can say is, pray now and make your peace with God while you can, because in the dark days ahead you'll wish you had been ready when Jesus came, so you could have escaped the Tribulation.

"Dear friends, this is now my second letter to you. I have written both of them as reminders to stimulate you to wholesome thinking. I want you to recall the words spoken in the past by the holy prophets and the command given by our Lord and Savior through your apostles.

"First of all, you must understand that in the last days scoffers will come, scoffing and following their own evil desires. They will say, 'Where is this coming he promised? Ever since our fathers died, everything goes on as it has since the beginning of creation.' But they deliberately forgot that long ago by God's word the heavens existed and the earth was formed out of water and with water. By water also the world of that time was deluged and destroyed. By the same word the present heavens and earth are reserved for fire, being kept for the day of judgment and destruction of ungodly men.

"But do not forget this one thing, dear friends: With the Lord a day is like a thousand years, and a thousand years are like a day. The Lord is not slow in keeping his promise, as some understand slowness. He is patient with you, not wanting anyone to perish, but everyone to come to repentance.

"But the day of the Lord will come like a thief. The heavens will disappear with a roar; the elements will be destroyed by fire, and the earth and everything in it will be laid bare.

"Since everything will be destroyed in this way, what kind of people ought you to be? You ought to live holy and godly lives as you look forward to the day of God and speed its coming. That day will bring about the destruction of the heavens by fire, and the elements will melt in the heat. But in keeping with his promise we are looking forward to a new heaven and a new earth, the home of righteousness.

"So then, dear friends, since you are looking forward to this, make every effort to be found spotless, blameless and at peace with him" (2 Peter 3:1-14, NIV).

"For God hath not appointed us to wrath, but to obtain salvation by our Lord Jesus Christ" (1 Thessalonians 5:9).

Jesus also wrote to the faithful church at Philadelphia, and to all the faithful living in these last days, *"Because thou hast kept the word... I also will keep thee from the hour of temptation, which shall come upon all the world, to try them that*

dwell upon the earth.
   "Behold, I come quickly" (Revelation 3:10,11).

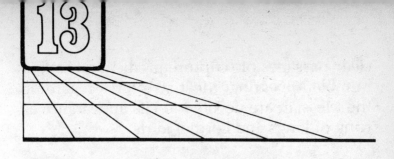

The Great Escape

Have you ever wondered why the Jewish people rejected Jesus Christ as their Messiah? I believe there are three reasons. First, I believe that they did not truly believe in God as they should have. Jesus told them, *"If God were your Father, ye would love me"* (John 8:42).

Second, I believe their sins blinded them to the "Light of the world." The Bible says, *"The god of this world hath blinded the minds of them which believe not, lest the light of the glorious gospel of Christ, who is the image of God, should shine unto them"* (2 Corinthians 4:4).

Third, I believe that they were not aware that Jesus was to come as the Lamb of God to die for the sins of the world. When I read the Old Testament, I can understand how they might have missed this suffering Messiah. With the exception of Isaiah 53, there really are not many clear passages of scripture predicting His first humble appearing. Most scriptures regarding the Messiah are devoted to His appearance as King of kings and Lord of lords.

A Sudden Disappearance

Unless you and I are careful, it will be as easy for us to miss the second coming of Jesus Christ as it was for the Jews to miss His first. This is why you should be prepared for an event that is going to take the world by surprise. I will tell you now that literally millions of committed Christians are going to disappear when Jesus Christ returns in secret to take His church out of the world prior to the Great Tribulation.

Christians call this event "the rapture." Even though this word does not appear in the Bible, a description of the event does. The term "rapture" comes from the Latin word *rapio*, which means to seize, to transport and to snatch so as to remove something or someone from one place to another. The equivalent Greek word is found in the passage of 1 Thessalonians 4:16,17 where Paul the apostle says, *"For the Lord himself shall descend from heaven with a shout, with the voice of the archangel, and with the trump of God: and the dead in Christ shall rise first: Then we which are alive and remain shall be caught up* [rapio, raptured] *together with them in the clouds,* to meet the Lord in the air: and so shall we ever be with the Lord."

I must tell you here that there are many committed Christians who do not believe in the rapture. They believe that the church is going to go through the Great Tribulation when God pours out His wrath upon the unbelieving world. But there are several reasons why I believe we will be caught away before that time.

Why I Believe in the Rapture

First, the scriptures clearly declare we will escape. Jesus said, *"And take heed to yourselves, lest at any time your hearts be overcharged with surfeiting* [eating too much], *and drunkenness, and cares of this life, AND SO THAT DAY COME UPON YOU UNAWARES.*

"For as a snare shall it [the Tribulation] *come on all them that dwell on the face of the whole earth.*

"Watch ye therefore, and pray always, THAT YE MAY BE ACCOUNTED WORTHY TO ESCAPE ALL THESE THINGS THAT SHALL COME TO PASS, AND TO STAND BEFORE THE SON OF MAN" (Luke 21:34-36).

My questions are: Why would Jesus warn us to be prepared to escape the Tribulation if we were going to go through it? Why would Jesus tell us to pray always, so we could stand before Him, unless we were to be caught up before the Tribulation shakes this earth?

In Revelation 3:10 Jesus speaks to the faithful Philadelphia church (a type of truly committed Christians present at the end of the age), *"Because thou hast kept the word of my patience, I also will keep thee from the hour of temptation, which shall come upon the world, to try them that dwell upon the earth."*

In this passage Jesus clearly teaches that if you and I are faithful, He will keep us from the great tribulation trials.

If the church is going through the Tribulation, "Why isn't it mentioned in any detail after Revelation 3? The absence of the church prompts one to ask, "Where has it gone?" I believe the church is in heaven. Paul wrote to the Christians in Thessalonica saying, *"For God hath not appointed us to wrath, but to obtain salvation by our Lord Jesus Christ"* (1 Thessalonians 5:9).

Consider These Points

I also believe that typology teaches the rapture. Typology is the study of how one event illustrates an even greater event. (For example, the ark of Noah is a type of Jesus Christ. All who enter are saved from destruction.)

Jesus said His coming would be similar to the days of Noah and the days of Sodom and Gomorrah (see Matthew 24:37 and Luke 17:29). In both of these instances God rescued His faithful followers BEFORE He poured out His wrath upon the wicked. The very fact that Jesus speaks of Noah and Lot in reference to His return emphasizes that they are types of the rapture.

History has shown that nations usually recall their ambassador before they declare war. I believe God will recall His ambassadors (the true Christians) before He pours His wrath out upon the earth.

There is another wonderful scriptural type. The Church is called the Bride of Christ and Jesus is the Bridegroom. The Bible refers to our coming together as *"the wedding"* (See Revelation 19:7-9). Have you ever noticed that it is usually not a custom of the groom to beat up the bride before the wedding?

To say the church is going through the Tribulation defies the laws of logic.

If you study Matthew 24, Mark 13 and Luke 21 (the master outline for Bible prophecy I have set forth in this book), Jesus outlines many of the tribulation events such as the antichrist in the temple (Matthew 24:15); the moon being darkened, the stars falling from heaven, and the powers of the heavens being shaken (Matthew 24:29). And then He says, *"Watch therefore: for ye know not what hour your Lord doth come"* (Matthew 24:42). He also likens His return to that of a thief (see Matthew 24:43-51).

My question is, "Do you think any Christian

would *not be aware of the hour* if he has seen the antichrist rise to power, the mark of the beast given (Revelation 13:15-17), and the moon darkened and the stars falling? By this time even the wicked will be crying out for the rocks and mountains to fall upon them; *"For the great day of his wrath has come; and who shall be able to stand?"* (Revelation 6:17).

Even the most unobservant Christians will be alerted to the return of Jesus Christ after these calamities have taken place. Consequently, the return of Christ would no longer be the unexpected event that Jesus declares it will be. There is only one answer—the true saints have been "caught away" during a relatively peaceful hour prior to the Great Tribulation.

Parables Tell of Christ's Return

Also, the parables of Jesus show that the hour of His return is peaceful. In Matthew 25 you can read about the foolish virgins—a type of lazy unprepared Christians who are sleeping. Ask yourself these questions: If the Christians are going through the Tribulation, when "all hell" is breaking loose on earth, with stars falling from heaven, do you think anyone will be sleeping? Do you think there is any possibility someone could sleep?

Remember, the return of Jesus Christ for His

church is an unexpected event. This is why Jesus says in Mark 13:32-37, *"But of that day and that hour knoweth no man, no, not the angels which are in heaven, neither the Son, but the Father.*

"Take ye heed, watch and pray: for ye know not when the time is.

"For the Son of man is as a man taking a far journey, who left his house, and gave authority to his servants, and to every man his work, and commanded the porter to watch.

"Watch ye therefore: for ye know not when the master of the house cometh, at even, or at midnight, or at the cockcrowing, or in the morning:

"Lest coming suddenly he find you sleeping.

"And what I say unto you I say unto all, Watch."

CHRISTIAN, WHY WOULD JESUS SAY, "WATCH!" IF YOU WOULD NOT ESCAPE THE TRIBULATION?

If you think we are going through the Great Tribulation, another passage of scripture to consider is Matthew 24:30 where it says, *"Then shall appear the sign of the Son of man in heaven: and then shall all the tribes of the earth mourn, and they shall see the Son of man coming in the clouds of heaven with power and great glory."*

In this appearing, which I believe is at the end of the Great Tribulation, the nations have time to gather themselves for battle, the Jews have time to mourn. THIS COMING IS NOT THE SUD-

DEN SECRET EVENT AS THE RAPTURE IS DESCRIBED.

And another thing, if the true Christians do not rise up to join Christ until the end of the Great Tribulation, we would only be going up to do a great big U-turn in the sky. Why go up to come right back down? I believe the Lord will take us up to heaven, judge us and give us our rewards and positions in His new kingdom so we will be ready to rule with Him when He returns to reign!

His Return Is Secret

The day Jesus ascended into heaven the two angels standing by said, *"Ye men of Galilee, why stand ye gazing up into heaven? this same Jesus, which is taken up from you into heaven, shall so come in like manner as ye have seen him go into heaven"* (Acts 1:11).

When Jesus departed, it was a *secret departure*. Only His chosen disciples were present. This means when Jesus returns only His chosen disciples will rise to greet Him.

When Jesus departed, it was *sudden*. *"While they beheld, he was taken up"* (Acts 1:9). This means the return of Christ for His church will be sudden—much different from the way He appears at the end of the tribulation. When Jesus departed, the clouds received Him out of their sight (Acts 1:9). So it will be when Jesus returns.

We Should Be Excited

If you are wondering why Christians are looking forward to this event, I'll tell you.

First, when Jesus returns we will see Him face to face. The Bible says, *"For the Lord himself shall descend from heaven"* (1 Thessalonians 4:16). I have never seen Jesus face to face, but it will be a wonderful moment when we see Him in all of His glory. When Peter, James and John saw Him transfigured (made radiant by the power of God) on the mountain, they were so inspired they wanted to build shrines to commemorate Moses, Elijah and Jesus. The Bible says they said these things because they were afraid.

However, if you are a Christian, it will be a wonderful moment when you see our Lord and Savior in person. John the apostle saw Jesus in the Revelation and wrote, "[He was clothed] *with a golden girdle. His head and his hairs were white like wool, as white as snow; and his eyes were as a flame of fire; And his feet like unto fine brass, as if they burned in a furnace* [this means the power of God so infused the body of Jesus that the energy caused His feet to appear to be changing colors, like brass heated hot in the flames]; *and his voice as the sound of many waters"* (Revelation 1:13-15).

The greatest moment in your life and mine will be when we see Jesus face to face.

Our Bodies Will Change

When Jesus returns, we will be changed. Paul the apostle writes, *"Behold, I shew you a mystery; We shall not all sleep, but we shall all be changed,*

"In a moment, in the twinkling of an eye, at the last trump: for the trumpet shall sound, and the dead shall be raised incorruptible, and we shall be changed" (1 Corinthians 15:51,52).

John the apostle writes, *"Beloved, now are we the sons of God, and it doth not yet appear what we shall be: but we know that; when he shall appear, we shall be like him; for we shall see him as he is"* (1 John 3:2).

A great transformation is going to take place when Jesus appears. You will receive a new incorruptible body. You will never get sick again. You will never get old. You will never die.

Won't it be great to have a new body? Think of those who suffer on beds of affliction with arthritis, heart trouble, muscular dystrophy, multiple sclerosis. They will never suffer again.

I have seen the crippled in their wheelchairs and my heart has gone out to them. I always tell them, "When Jesus comes, I'm going to have a footrace with you in heaven."

One of the most tragic sights I have ever seen was a baby born without eyes. As I held that helpless child, my heart ached. Praise God she is going to see very soon. For when Jesus Christ returns, He is going to give His children glorified bodies. We will never hurt again!

Heaven Reunites Us With Loved Ones

When Jesus returns, we will join our loved ones and be together forever.

"For the Lord himself shall descend from heaven… and the dead in Christ shall rise first: Then we which are alive and remain shall be caught up together with them in the clouds, to meet the Lord in the air: and so shall we ever be with the Lord.

"Wherefore comfort one another with these words" (1 Thessalonians 4:16-18).

If you have ever lost a loved one, you know how much this promise means. Death is cruel. I'll never forget the death of my baby brother, LaVerne. He was the happiest little guy. He would jump up and down in his crib when I'd play my guitar.

Now he is buried at the cemetery near our home, along with my godly grandmother. Like you, I realize I'll have to make many trips to the cemetery should the Lord tarry. And each time I lay one of my loved ones to rest, part of me will die.

But as a Christian, you and I have a wonderful hope. It is the promise of our Lord's return and our reunion with our loved ones in heaven.

Won't it be wonderful to hug your mother and dad again? Just imagine the joy of seeing your mate in glory. Thanks to Jesus, you will see your child again. You're going to laugh with your brothers and sisters and reminisce about "old times" back on earth. I cannot express the ecstatic happiness you will experience when Jesus comes and we are caught up together.

Our Works Rewarded

When Jesus comes, you and I will be rewarded for our labors.

Jesus clearly said, *"Behold, I come quickly; and my reward is with me, to give every man according as his work shall be"* (Revelation 22:12). If you have served the Lord for any length of time, you know the pain and shame you have suffered. Jesus said your labors will not go unrewarded. Even a cup of water given in His name will be remembered.

Before I came to Jesus Christ, I had the dream of becoming a top country entertainer on the "Grand Ole Opry." I turned my back on the world to follow Jesus because I saw that the reward of serving Him was so much greater than serving myself. The Bible says that Moses had this same realization. *"By faith Moses, when he was come to years, refused to be called the son of Pharaoh's daughter; Choosing rather to suffer affliction with the people of God, than to enjoy the pleasures of sin for a season;*

"Esteeming the reproach of Christ greater riches than the treasures in Egypt: for he had respect unto the…reward" (Hebrews 11:24-26).

Moses knew that the glory of God was greater than the glory of Egypt. This is why he refused to be called an Egyptian.

Are You Ready for the Rapture?

Friend, don't lose sight of the goal. Don't forget eternity is forever. You may live to be 80 or 90 years old, but eternity is forever!

Many of the prophetic signs of our Savior's return have been fulfilled. He will return very soon. If you are not ready for the rapture, repent of anything in your life that is not pleasing to God.

John the apostle said, *"Every man that hath this hope in him purifieth himself"* (1 John 3:3).

You can tell if you're ready for the rapture by examining your heart and life. Are you free from the habits of sin? Are you looking for His appearing? The Bible says, *"…Unto them that look for him shall he appear the second time without sin unto salvation"* (Hebrews 9:28).

Time is short. Whatever you are going to do for Jesus Christ you must do today. In a moment, in a twinkling of an eye, Jesus is going to appear. If you're not ready, pray and dedicate your life to Jesus Christ.

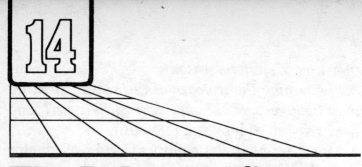

The Judgment Seat of Christ

The first event that will take place in heaven after the rapture will be the judgment seat of Christ. This is the time when Jesus Christ awards His saints for their service. This is when you are given your position in the kingdom of God. Remember always that you are saved by grace but rewarded by works.

The Bible says, *"For we must all appear before the judgment seat of Christ; that every one may receive the things done in his body, according to that he hath done, whether it be good or bad.*

"Knowing therefore the terror of the Lord, we persuade men…" (2 Corinthians 5:10,11).

Do not confuse the judgment seat of Christ with the Great White Throne Judgment in Revelation (Revelation 19:12-15) or the Judgment of the Nations in Matthew 25. The judgment seat of Christ is the believer's judgment, whereas the other two judgments are for the nonchristians.

The three judgments appear in this order:

1. When Jesus returns for His true Church, and we are raptured (caught up) to heaven with our loved ones, we will immediately be brought before Him to be judged for our service.

2. When Jesus returns with His saints to rule at the end of the great tribulation period, *"Before him shall be gathered all nations; and he shall separate them one from another, as a shepherd divideth his sheep from the goats"* (Matthew 25:32).

3. At the end of the 1,000-year reign of Jesus Christ, called the millenium (I will deal with this in a coming chapter), the wicked dead of all the ages will appear before God to be judged and cast into hell (see Revelation 20:11-15).

Our Works Judged by Fire

For many Christians, the judgment seat of Christ is going to be a surprise. Today there is a feeling among many that everyone in heaven will receive the same reward. Nothing could be farther from the truth.

"For other foundation can no man lay than that is laid, which is Jesus Christ.

"Now if any man build upon this foundation gold, silver, precious stones, wood, hay, stubble; [Notice the types of material; three are perishable and three are lasting.]

"Every man's work shall be made manifest: for the day shall declare it, because it shall be revealed by fire; and the fire shall try every man's work of what sort it is" (1 Corinthians 3:11-13).

I believe the fire that will try our works at the judgment seat of Christ will be the eyes of Jesus. The Bible says, *"His eyes were as a flame of fire"* (Revelation 1:14).

If your motives in working for the Lord were wrong or your deeds were not lasting, your works will be burned up when Jesus beholds them. His flaming eyes will burn up everything that is not genuine.

"If any man's work abide which he hath built thereupon, he shall receive a reward.

"If any man's work shall be burned, he shall suffer loss: but he himself shall be saved; yet so as by fire" (1 Corinthians 3:14,15).

What an awesome statement! The Bible says that many will be scarcely saved, by the "skin of their teeth."

These passages of scripture should settle the question about degrees of reward. Some are going to rule on thrones (see Luke 21:28-30) and others will barely make it to heaven.

A Place Better Than Heaven

This is why one old-time minister used to preach a sermon titled, "A Better Place Than Heaven." The scriptures I just mentioned were his text. He also pointed out the scripture, *"It is appointed unto men once to die, after this the judgment"* (Hebrews 9:27).

Once you face Jesus Christ in judgment, you will never be able to change your standing in eternity. Just imagine the careless Chistian who lived "the easy life" without committing himself fully. When he stands before the Lord and receives nearly nothing, while others are given positions of authority, ruling on thrones with Christ, he will cry out and say, "Lord, please give me another chance. Allow me to return to earth and live my life again."

Because of his awareness then, he will want to come back to earth, but it will be too late. In that sense, there is a better place than heaven; it is right here on earth serving Jesus Christ with all your heart.

There is another way in which you can truthfully say that earth is better than heaven. If God wanted you in heaven, He could promote you there in less than a second. Obviously, God doesn't want you there yet, so your service to Jesus Christ now is winning others to the Savior—it is God's perfect will.

This is why Paul the apostle said, *"For to me, living means opportunities for Christ, and dying— well, that's better yet! But if living will give me more opportunities to win people to Christ, then I really don't know which is better, to live or die! Sometimes I want to live and at other times I don't, for I long to go and be with Christ. How much happier for me than being here! But the fact is that I can be of more help to you by staying.*

"Yes, I am still needed down here and so I feel certain I will be staying on earth a little longer, to help you grow and become happy in your faith" (Philippians 1:21-25, *The Living Bible*).

The judgment seat of Christ will change your priorities. If the manner in which you are living today will not be rewarded then, you should change your life-style now.

Your Monetary Giving Is Important

Jesus taught His disciples saying, *"There was a certain rich man, which had a steward* [manager or accountant]; *and the same was accused unto him that he had wasted his goods.*

"And he called him, and said unto him, How is it that I hear this of thee? give an account of thy stewardship; for thou mayest be no longer steward. [In other words, the manager got his two-week notice.]

"Then the steward said within himself, What shall I do? for my lord taketh away from me the steward-

ship: I cannot dig; to beg I am ashamed.

"I am resolved what to do, that, when I am put out of the stewardship, they may receive me into their houses. [In simple language, he said, I am going to obligate my lord's debtors to me.]

"So he called every one of his lord's debtors unto him, and said unto the first, How much owest thou unto my lord?

"And he said, An hundred measures of oil. And he said unto him, Take thy bill, and sit down quickly, and write fifty.

"And said he to another, And how much owest thou? And he said, An hundred measures of wheat. And he said unto him, Take thy bill, and write [80].

"And the lord commended the unjust steward, because he had done wisely: for the children of this world are in their generation wiser than the children of light" (Luke 16:1-8).

This is an amazing statement by Jesus. He says that nonchristians are wiser at handling their money in this world than Christians are.

He continues, *"And I say unto you, Make to yourselves friends of the mammon of unrighteousness* [money]; *that, when ye fail, they may receive you into everlasting habitations"* (Luke 16:9).

I have chosen to use the classic King James Version of the Bible in this passage because I believe it offers the truth as no other translation does. What Jesus is saying to you and me is, "Make to yourselves friends, or converts, with your money, so that when you fail (or die), then the converts you have won with your money will receive you into heaven."

The results of your giving will appear at the judgment seat of Christ. This is when you want to have hundreds and even thousands gathered around the throne of God as a result of your giving to ministries.

I am afraid that many Christians haven't even thought of this aspect of their giving. This is why Jesus said,

"Lay not up for yourselves treasures upon earth, where moth and rust doth corrupt, and where thieves break through and steal:

"But lay up for yourselves treasures in heaven, where neither moth nor rust doth corrupt, and where thieves do not break through nor steal:

"For where your treasure is, there will your heart be also" (Matthew 6:19-21).

Jesus says, "If you have anything the moths are going to eat, clothing in your closets, attics, basement or garage, if you have anything that will rust such as an old car, sewing machine, motorboat or snowmobile, if you have anything the thieves will steal in your safe deposit box such as gold, silver, diamonds, stocks, bonds, or paid-up insurance that you do not need, sell or give away the items to support God's work, and transfer your treasures to heaven." Jesus is not telling you to give away your treasures—

only to transfer them from earth to heaven.

Just think how much could be done for the kingdom of God with the money from the proceeds of garage sales. Imagine how many souls could be won through possessions that are rusting. Only God knows how many millions could be converted with the gold, silver, stocks, bonds, jewels and cash that Christians have locked up in bank vaults.

You Cannot Serve Two Masters

Jesus says, *"He that is faithful in that which is least is faithful also in much: and he that is unjust in the least is unjust also in much.*

"If therefore ye have not been faithful in the unrighteous mammon [or money], *who will commit to your trust the true riches?*

"And if ye have not been faithful in that which is another man's, who shall give you that which is your own?

"No servant can serve two masters: for either he will hate the one, and love the other; or else he will hold to the one, and despise the other. Ye cannot serve God and mammon [money]*"* (Luke 16:10-13).

Jesus said you cannot live for this world and the next one at the same time. He said if you are convinced of the rewards at the judgment seat of Christ, you will not amass material possessions.

The early church lived with this philosophy.

The Bible says, *"And with great power gave the apostles witness of the resurrection of the Lord Jesus: and great grace was upon them all.*

"Neither was there any among them that lacked: for as many as were possessors of lands or houses sold them, and brought the prices of the things that were sold.

"And laid them down at the apostles' feet: and distribution was made unto every man according as he had need.

"And...Barnabas...having land, sold it, and brought the money, and laid it at the apostles' feet" (Acts 4:33-37).

Just to show you how far we have drifted from the concepts of the early church, when is the last time people of your congregation have sold lands and houses to support God's work? There are times when someone dies and leaves his possessions to the church, but the early Christians gave their treasures while they lived.

I believe it is much more honorable to give your treasures to God while you are alive. If you only give money in your will, it means God has to promote you to heaven to get it.

Kindness Brings Reward

There is a true story told of a weary traveler and his wife who came to a modest hotel in search of a room. The clerk informed him that

all the rooms were occupied, but the businessman said, "I have tried every hotel in the area
and there is nothing available."

The young clerk was touched at the man's
plight and said, "Sir, I will give you my room.
Please give me a few moments to clean it."

The businessman protested, but the young
clerk prevailed. The couple spent the night in the
clerk's apartment while he slept on the sofa in
the lobby.

The next morning the businessman said,
"Young man, I will reward you for your act of
kindness. How would you like to manage your
own hotel?"

The clerk smiled and expressed his apprecia-
tion for the man's intentions. The clerk did not
see the man for many years. One day the clerk
was surprised to receive a call from the businessman, who asked him to come to New York.
When he arrived, he was taken by limousine to
the center of town. The businessman walked
with him down the street, and when they came
around the corner an incredibly beautiful hotel
towered up before them, sparkling in the
morning light.

The man turned to the young clerk and said,
"It's yours! You can manage it for me."

The gentleman was John Jacob Astor, one of
the legendary greats of New York. He rewarded
the clerk's kindness beyond anything anyone

could have imagined.

The same will be true of Jesus Christ. Jesus said, *"I come quickly; and my reward is with me"* (Revelation 22:12).

Trust Not in Riches

Are you living for the judgment seat of Christ? Paul did. He said, *"I have fought a good fight, I have finished my course, I have kept the faith:*

"Henceforth there is laid up for me a crown of righteousness, which the Lord, the righteous judge, shall give me at that day: and not to me only, but unto all them also that love his appearing" (2 Timothy 4:7,8).

If God has blessed you with possessions and the means to make money, keep the judgment seat of Christ in mind. You may be tempted to hoard your wealth instead of investing it. This is why Paul the apostle said, *"Charge them that are rich in this world, that they be not highminded, nor trust in uncertain riches, but in the living God, who giveth us richly all things to enjoy;*

"That they do good, that they be rich in good works, ready to distribute, willing to communicate [to give];

"Laying up in store for themselves a good foundation against the time to come, that they may lay hold on eternal life" (1 Timothy 6:17-19).

While the world is going through the Great Tribulation, you and I will appear at the judgment seat of Christ. If you hope to have a great reward on that day, begin by giving your best to God's work today.

The Great Celebration

There is also another event that will take place immediately after judgment. It is called the "Marriage Supper of the Lamb."

The Bible says, *"Let us be glad and rejoice, and give honour to him: for the marriage of the Lamb is come, and his wife hath made herself ready.*

"And to her was granted that she should be arrayed in fine linen, clean and white: for the fine linen is the righteousness of saints.

"And he saith unto me, Write, Blessed are they which are called unto the marriage supper of the Lamb" (Revelation 19:7-9).

This celebration will be the greatest in the history of the Church, this will be the fulfillment of our love affair with our Savior, Jesus Christ. Jesus looked forward to this moment before He died. He told His disciples at the last supper before the crucifixion, *"For I say unto you, I will not any more eat thereof, until it be fulfilled in the kingdom of God.*

"And he took the cup, and gave thanks, and said, Take this, and divide it among yourselves:

"For I say unto you, I will not drink of the fruit of the vine, until the kingdom of God shall come" (Luke 22:16-18).

Just imagine having holy communion with Jesus Christ in person! This will be a moment of fellowship and unity far greater than anything you and I have ever experienced.

Stewardship Involves Responsibility Now

Are you ready for the Marriage Supper of the Lamb? Are you prepared to give account of your stewardship? How many are saved and in heaven today because of your investment of time, energy, prayers and gifts?

If you want to be ready then, prepare now— for the trumpet is about ready to sound. Remember, you cannot wait to work for the Lord until you are ready to die. If you want to rule on a throne, if you want a reward for a lifetime of service, you need to serve God today.

15

When Christ Returns to Reign!

If you have ever prayed The Lord's Prayer, this chapter will be exciting. When Jesus Christ returns to reign, it will be the literal fulfillment of the words:

"THY KINGDOM COME. Thy will be done in earth, as it is in heaven" (Matthew 6:9,10).

When Jesus gave His discourse on the last days, He emphatically declared that one day He would return to rule this planet.

He said, *"And then shall appear the sign of the Son of man in heaven: and then shall all the tribes of the earth mourn, and they shall see the Son of man coming in the clouds of heaven with power and great glory. And he shall send his angels with a great sound of a trumpet, and they shall gather together his elect from the four winds, from one end of heaven to the other"* (Matthew 24:30,31).

"And then shall they see the Son of man coming in the clouds with great power and glory. And then shall he send his angels, and shall gather together his elect from the four winds, from the uttermost part of the earth to the uttermost part of heaven" (Mark 13:26,27).

"And they asked him, saying, Master, but when shall these things be? and what sign will there be when these things shall come to pass?" (Luke 21:7).

After the world has been shaken to the point of despair by the Tribulation judgments, "the sign of the Son of man" will appear in the heavens. This means the world will be able to see Jesus coming with His saints. Enoch saw this day centuries ago when he said, *"Behold, the Lord cometh with ten thousands of his saints, To execute judgment upon all..."* (Jude 14,15).

Armageddon: The Last Battle

However, the most amazing thing will happen then. When Christ returns to reign the antichrist will rally the kings of the earth and their armies together and will declare war on the Son of God. They will angrily defend themselves against what appears to be an invasion from outer space.

Jerusalem Besieged by Nations

Remember, prior to our Savior's return with His saints, the antichrist is ruling from the desecrated Jewish temple in Jerusalem. During

194

this period, the nations of the world are going to gather for the last great battle. The nations will think they are gathering to make war against the antichrist, but at the last moment they will be persuaded by the antichrist to make war against the Lamb of God! The Prophet Zechariah saw it in a vision and said,

"Behold, I will make Jerusalem a cup of trembling unto all the people roundabout, when they shall be in the siege both against Judah and against Jerusalem.

"And in that day will I make Jerusalem a burdensome stone for all people: all that burden themselves with it shall be cut in pieces, THOUGH ALL THE PEOPLE OF THE EARTH BE GATHERED TOGETHER AGAINST IT" (Zechariah 12:2,3).

The vision of Zechariah continues:

"Behold, the day of the Lord cometh....For I will gather all nations against Jerusalem to battle; and the city shall be taken, and the houses rifled [possessions taken], *and the women ravished* [raped]; *and half of the city shall go forth into captivity, and the* [remainder] *of the people shall not be cut off from the city"* (Zechariah 14:1,2).

When the city is surrounded by the armies of the antichrist and the nations of the world, THEN the Jewish people will cry out to God and repent of their sins and receive Jesus Christ as their Messiah. This is what Jesus meant when He said, *"Then shall appear the sign of the*

195

Son of man in heaven: and then shall all the tribes of the earth mourn, and they shall see the Son of man coming in the clouds of heaven with power and great glory" (Matthew 24:30).

Just imagine the grief the Jewish people will experience when they see Jesus coming and realize that this Savior they have rejected for so many centuries is really their Messiah.

When the nation of Israel cries out to God, the Bible says, *"Then shall the Lord go forth, and fight against those nations, as when he fought in the day of battle.*

When the Antichrist Fights the King of Kings

The Apostle John was given a vision of this last battle and describes it saying, *"And I saw heaven opened, and behold a white horse; and he that sat upon him was called Faithful and True, and in righteousness he doth judge and make war. His eyes were as a flame of fire, and on his head were many crowns; and he had a name written, that no man knew, but he himself. And he was clothed with a vesture dipped in blood: and his name is called The Word of God. And the armies which were in heaven followed him upon white horses, clothed in fine linen, white and clean.*

"And out of his mouth goeth a sharp sword, that with it he should smite the nations: and he shall rule them with a rod of iron: and he treadeth the winepress of the fierceness and wrath of Almighty God. And he

*hath on his vesture and on his thigh a name written,
KING OF KINGS, AND LORD OF LORDS.*

*"And I saw an angel standing in the sun; and he
cried with a loud voice, saying to all the fowls that fly
in the midst of heaven, Come and gather yourselves
together unto the supper of the great God; That ye
may eat the flesh of kings, and the flesh of captains,
and the flesh of mighty men, and the flesh of horses,
and of them that sit on them, and the flesh of all men,
both free and bond, both small and great"* (Revelation
19:11-18).

Imagine it! God is going to summon the
buzzards and vultures of the Mideast together
for this great conflict. They will serve as a divine
clean-up committee!

Notice what happens when the antichrist
and the leaders of the world see Jesus Christ
and His armies approaching.

"AND I SAW THE BEAST [the antichrist],
*AND THE KINGS OF THE EARTH, AND THEIR
ARMIES, GATHERED TOGETHER TO MAKE
WAR AGAINST HIM THAT SAT ON THE
HORSE, AND AGAINST HIS ARMY.*

"And the beast [the antichrist] *was taken, and
with him the false prophet that wrought miracles
before him, with which he deceived them that had
received the mark of the beast, and them that worshiped his image. These both were cast alive into a
lake of fire burning with brimstone.*

"And the remnant were slain with the sword of

him that sat upon the horse, which sword proceeded out of his mouth: and all the fowls were filled with their flesh" (Revelation 19:19-21).

Jesus Christ Becomes Supreme Ruler

"AND THE LORD SHALL BE KING OVER ALL THE EARTH" (Zechariah 14:9).

The first time Jesus came to earth as the Lamb of God to die for the sins of the world. But the second time He will return as the Lion of the tribe of Judah (see Revelation 5:5).

This will be the beginning of a new era in world leadership. Isaiah saw it and said, *"For unto us a child is born, unto us a son is given: and the government shall be upon his shoulder: and his name shall be called Wonderful, Counsellor, The mighty God, The everlasting Father, The Prince of Peace. Of the increase of his government and peace there shall be no end"* (Isaiah 9:6,7).

This is the hour that the world has waited for since the beginning of time: Christ the Lord, will rule and reign from Jerusalem—the center of the world!

Daniel the prophet said, *"I saw in the night visions, and, behold, one like the Son of man came with the clouds of heaven, and came to the Ancient of days....*

"And there was given him dominion, and glory, and a kingdom, that all people, nations and languages,

198

should serve him: his dominion is an everlasting dominion, which shall not pass away, and his kingdom...shall not be destroyed" (Daniel 7:13,14).

We Will Reign With Christ

The return of Jesus Christ is great news for every believer, because you and I as Christians are going to share in the leadership of this new kingdom with our Lord.

Daniel says, *"...the Ancient of days came, and judgment was given to the saints of the Most High; AND THE TIME CAME THAT THE SAINTS POSSESSED THE KINGDOM"* (Daniel 7:22).

"And the kingdom and dominion, and the greatness of the kingdom under the whole heaven, SHALL BE GIVEN TO THE PEOPLE OF THE SAINTS OF THE MOST HIGH, whose kingdom is an everlasting kingdom, and all dominions shall serve and obey him" (Daniel 7:27).

This is why Jesus said, *"He that overcometh, and keepeth my works unto the end, TO HIM WILL I GIVE POWER OVER THE NATIONS"* (Revelation 2:26).

Just imagine, ruling and reigning with Jesus Christ! Many men and women have longed for power and position in this world, but Jesus will give it to the humble. He said, *"Blessed are the meek: for they shall inherit the earth"* (Matthew 5:5).

If you can see what God has planned for you, it will help you through your trials and discouragements. Paul the apostle was awaiting execution by the headsman's axe in Rome when he wrote to Timothy, *"If we suffer, we shall also reign with him"* (2 Timothy 2:12). Toward the last of his final letter Paul writes, *"For I am now ready to be offered, and the time of my departure is at hand.*

"I have fought a good fight, I have finished my course, I have kept the faith:

"Henceforth there is laid up for me a crown of righteousness, which the Lord, the righteous judge, shall give me at that day [the day of His return to reign]: *and not to me only, but unto all them also that love his appearing"* (2 Timothy 4:6-8).

Looking For That Day

Believer, don't let anything discourage you. The Lord is coming and this is our greatest hope. He will take vengeance upon your enemies and those who have used and abused you.

What a grand and glorious future awaits us. I wrote a song several years ago that says,

"I'll tell you this world needs someone
Someone to show it the Way;
It needs the One who is the Lord
To reign forevermore.
I've been a-lookin' for that day!

Someday the blind man's gonna see
And the poor man's gonna be
As rich as a millionaire.
The lame are gonna walk again
And suffering shall end
And every man will be free.

I'm lookin' for that day
When every man will say,
'I love you, brother, here's my hand.'
The Lord's gonna come again
And suffering will end.
I'm a-lookin' for the day
When He will be the Lord of the land.
I'm a-lookin' for the day
He will be the Lord of the land."

I'm A-lookin' for the Day

Lundstrom/Lundstrom Music/SESAC © 1972

16

The Coming 1,000 Years of Peace and Prosperity

This world is going to experience a marvelous transformation when Jesus Christ returns to rule this earth with His saints. It is so exciting I can hardly wait to tell you about it.

One of the most memorable pieces of English literature is John Milton's *Paradise Lost*. This twelve-part epic poem depicts the fall of man as the most awesome event in history. *Paradise Lost* covers the time from the fall of Lucifer to the sacrifice of Jesus Christ on the cross.

However, Milton knew this was not the end of the story. He knew that Jesus Christ was going to return to rule this world. This prompted him to write another shorter epic titled *Paradise Regained*. This work covers the time from the temptation of Jesus by Satan in the wilderness to eternal bliss.

As my friend, Kenneth Schmidt, has pointed

out, "Although it complemented *Paradise Lost* as far as literature was concerned, it was never widely accepted. The simple reason is that man can feel the terrible loss of Eden, but it takes faith to look forward to a new paradise."

Paul the apostle wrote, *"I consider that our present sufferings are not worth comparing with the glory that will be revealed in us. THE CREATION WAITS IN EAGER EXPECTATION FOR THE SONS OF GOD TO BE REVEALED"* (Romans 8:18,19, NIV).

Every type of human government has failed, Roman imperialism, fascism, nazism, socialism, communism and even capitalism.

Why the World is Becoming Desperate for a Strong Leader

Henri Spaak, early planner of the European Common Market and Secretary General of NATO said in one of his speeches: "We do not want another committee—we have too many already. What we want is a man of sufficient stature to hold allegiance of all people, and to lift us out of the economic morass into which we are sinking. *Send us such a man, and be he God or Devil, we will receive him."*

A prime minister of Belgium has said, "The truth is that the method of international committees [the League of Nations and the United Nations] has failed. *What we need is a PERSON,* someone of the highest order, of great experience and great authority, of wide influence and of great energy. Let him come, and let him come quickly. Either a civilian or a military man—no matter what his personality—one who will cut all the red tape, shove out of the way the committees, wake up the people and galvanize all governments into action. The man we need and for whom we wait will take charge...once more I say it is not too late, but high time."

You and I as Christians know the world is going to choose a "superman" who will turn out to be the antichrist. But after the antichrist leads the world to destruction and is punished, Jesus Christ will take charge and transform this planet. Nearly everyone realizes we need the Lord to take charge now.

Our World is Deteriorating

Time-Life book editors recently published an awesome series of articles on the deterioration of our present civilization. They said, "Man's confidence in his power to control his world is suddenly at a low ebb. The scientists themselves are now depressed to realize that their universe is far more complex than they recently thought and that they have fewer solutions than hoped."

Sometimes it appears as if the world has gone mad.

Recently I counselled with an angry, broken-hearted father whose four-year-old daughter was raped by a 13-year-old boy. The child is still in shock and cries continously. She doesn't want her father to touch her or hold her anymore.

The man cannot press charges because the rapist is a minor—even the authorities cannot do a thing. The rapist's parents just want to forget what happened and refuse to correct him. As the father talked, his hands trembled and his eyes filled with tears. His anguish and rage over the injustice of his dilemma was tearing him apart.

After conversing with this father, I walked back to my room and turned on the television. Great Britian and Argentina were preparing to go to war over the Falkland Islands, and the question of U.S. involvement, the possibility of a nuclear exhange between the United States and Russia was being discussed.

On the same telecast CBS News reported the tragic story of three men in New York City who tried to rescue a woman who was being abducted by a stranger. He was trying to push her into his van. When the three men tried to help, they were shot dead—executed in gangland style.

Then, yesterday, outside of my motel three men jumped two others. They kicked and stomped their victims. One grabbed a triangular steel post and began swinging it like a wild man. He then beat his victim on the back and finally struck him in the head, giving him a 4-inch gash. When the police were called, the attackers fled.

I did not see it happen, but as soon as I heard what happened, I ran to the side of the fallen man. He was nearly unconscious and could barely see or hear me talk as I prayed with him.

As I heard the wailing of the approaching police and ambulance sirens, as I saw this innocent man's blood oozing from his head onto the ground, I cried inside and said, "When, oh when, will this brutal violence end?"

A Period of Peace

I am thankful the Bible tells us of a coming kingdom when Jesus Christ will rule and reign for 1,000 years in peace and prosperity. Bible scholars call this 1,000 years "The Millennium." It comes from the Latin words *mille* which means "thousand" and *annus* which means "year." Although the word "millennium" does not appear in the Bible, this thousand-year reign of peace is mentioned six times in Revelation 20.

This period of unparalleled peace has been foretold by the prophets. The Prophet Zechariah says, *"And the Lord shall be king over all the earth:*

in that day shall there be one Lord, and his name one" (Zechariah 14:9).

The Prophet Isaiah said, *"For unto us a child is born, unto us a son is given: and the government shall be upon his shoulder: and his name shall be called Wonderful, Counsellor, The mighty God, The everlasting Father, THE PRINCE OF PEACE. Of the increase of his government and peace there shall be no end, upon the throne of David, and upon his kingdom, to order it, and to establish it with judgment and with justice from henceforth even for ever"* (Isaiah 9:6,7).

I realize that today's news is frightening. The world is headed for judgment and an antichrist will soon rise to power and deceive the nations of the world. Yet I am optimistic because of what is going to follow.

The Image Revealed

Many centuries ago King Nebuchadnezzar, the king of Babylon, had an unusual dream: He saw an image with a head of gold, breast and arms of silver, belly and thighs of brass, legs of iron, and feet of iron and clay. God gave him this dream to show him the makeup of the kingdoms to come. The sketch on the following page depicts what history shows the image to be.

NEBUCHADNEZZAR'S DREAM
(Daniel 2)

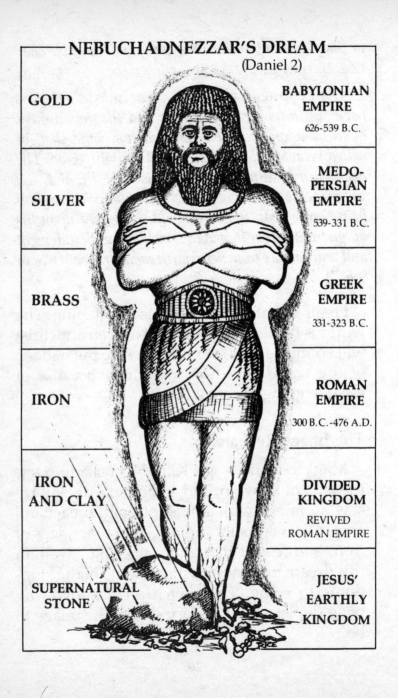

GOLD

BABYLONIAN
EMPIRE

626-539 B.C.

SILVER

MEDO-
PERSIAN
EMPIRE

539-331 B.C.

BRASS

GREEK
EMPIRE

331-323 B.C.

IRON

ROMAN
EMPIRE

300 B.C.-476 A.D.

IRON
AND CLAY

DIVIDED
KINGDOM

REVIVED
ROMAN EMPIRE

SUPERNATURAL
STONE

JESUS'
EARTHLY
KINGDOM

Interpretation of the Image

When King Nebuchadnezzar could not remember his dream or interpret it, he asked his magicians and astrologers for its explanation. They could not tell him. This made the king angry and he commanded that all the wise men in Babylon be put to death.

Daniel was among this number, and when he heard the decree he asked the king for time to interpret the dream.

Daniel and his three Hebrew friends prayed for God's mercy and wisdom so they would be spared. Then God revealed the mystery to Daniel through a vision in the night. Daniel praised God and said, *"Blessed be the name of God for ever and ever: for wisdom and might are his: And he changeth the times and the seasons: he removeth kings, and setteth up kings: he giveth wisdom unto the wise, and knowledge to them that know understanding:*

"He revealeth the deep and secret things: he knoweth what is in the darkness, and the light dwelleth with him.

"I thank thee, and praise thee, O thou God of my fathers, who hast given me wisdom and might, and hast made known unto me now what we desired of thee: for thou hast now made known unto us the king's matter" (Daniel 2:20-23).

Daniel revealed the dream to the king,

explaining the kingdoms that would come upon the earth. He said, *"You, O king, are* [a] *king of kings. The God of heaven has given you dominion and power and might and glory...he has made you ruler over...all. You are that head of gold.*

"After you, another kingdom will rise, inferior to yours. Next, a third kingdom, one of bronze, will rule over the whole earth. Finally, there will be a fourth kingdom, strong as iron...and as iron breaks things to pieces, so it will crush and break all the others.

"Just as you saw that the feet and toes were partly of baked clay and partly of iron, so this will be a divided kingdom; yet it will have some of the strength of iron in it, even as you saw iron mixed with clay. And just as you saw the iron mixed with baked clay, so the people will be a mixture and will not remain united, any more than iron mixes with clay" (Daniel 2:37-41,43, NIV).

Then Daniel told the king the meaning of the stone cut without hands that crushed the image. He said, *"And in the days of these kings* [world leaders during the last days, represented by the feet of the image] *shall the God of heaven set up a kingdom, which shall never be destroyed: and the kingdom shall not be left to other people, but it shall break in pieces and consume all these kingdoms, AND IT SHALL STAND FOR EVER"* (Daniel 2:44).

The scriptures give us a glorious glimpse into the future. Even though governments are wobbly and broken down (remember it is impossible to mix clay and iron as shown in the feet of the image), we are looking for the day when the stone, Jesus Christ, will smash the power of sinful empires and set up His own glorious government.

When the angel appeared unto the Virgin Mary and announced that she would give birth to the Messiah, he said, *"Behold, thou shalt conceive in thy womb, and bring forth a son, and shalt call his name Jesus. He shall be great, and shall be called the Son of the Highest: and the Lord God shall give unto him the throne of his father David: AND HE SHALL REIGN OVER THE HOUSE OF JACOB FOR EVER; AND OF HIS KINGDOM THERE SHALL BE NO END"* (Luke 1:31-33).

Why Doesn't God Intervene Now?

For centuries millions have wondered why God doesn't do something to stop wars as well as crime and violence. There is a reason for God's delay. Just as a wise doctor allows a festering boil to come to a head before he lances it, God in His infinite wisdom and patience is allowing evil to run its course.

If God moved in and destroyed every evil person and stopped every unrighteous act, there would be no one left to convert. God is building a kingdom that requires millions of tried-and-tested saint administrators. It is for this reason God has waited so many years to complete the Church. When the Church has been completed, this age will come to an end.

A New World Order

After the nuclear wars and ravages of the antichrist, the world will be ready to follow the PRINCE OF PEACE. Jesus Christ is coming to establish a new world order.

The first step Jesus Christ will take when He sets up His millennial kingdom on earth is that He will have Satan bound.

For centuries Satan has accelerated the process of evil by deceiving men and women into rebelling against God. He has stirred up strife and prompted people into committing terrible sins. When Jesus returns with His saints to reign, the first thing He will do is confine Satan to the abyss.

The Bible says, *"And I saw an angel come down from heaven, having the key of the bottomless pit and a great chain in his hand. And he laid hold on the dragon, that old serpent, which is the Devil, and Satan, and bound him a thousand years, And cast him into the bottomless pit, and shut him up, and set a seal upon him, that he should deceive the nations no more, till the thousand years should be fulfilled: and after that he must be loosed a little season"* (Revelation 20:1-3).

Down through the ages men and women have cried, "What's wrong with the world?" The answer is simple:

1. *The devil is in the wrong place.* He has been running to and fro throughout the earth—when he should be in hell. During the millennium Jesus Christ will cast him into the bottomless pit.

2. *Jesus Christ has been in the wrong place.* He is in heaven now—when He needs to be on earth. It is not that He has failed, because He is working through His saints by the Holy Spirit, preparing them for a leadership role in the new world. However, it will be wonderful when He is revealed as King of kings and Lord of lords and rules in person from Jerusalem with His saints.

3. *The saints have been in the wrong place.* We have been put down and persecuted, while the wicked have been in power. During the millennium the roles will be reversed. As I have mentioned in the last couple of chapters, Jesus says, *"He that overcometh, and keepeth my works unto the end, to him will I give power over the nations"* (Revelation 2:26).

If you are wondering how we can live a life of peace and victory in spite of everyone being in the wrong place—this story may help.

One evening a man was watching the evening news on TV. He was very depressed by the events of the day. As he contemplated what was happening in the world, his little girl kept interrupting him with small talk. Finally, to keep her occupied, he took the evening newspaper, with a map of the world showing all the points of conflict, and tore it up. Then he told her to go into the other room and put the puzzle together.

In just a few moments she reappeared with the map put back together with Scotch tape. The father was amazed, because he knew she didn't know much about geography and the different nations of the world.

He said, "Honey, how did you do it so quickly?"

The little girl replied, "Daddy, there was a picture of a man on the other side of the puzzle. When I put the man together, the world turned out right."

The same is true of you and me. If we will allow God to put us together, the world will turn out right no matter how mixed up it may appear.

When Jesus returns to rule and reign during the coming Millennium, He is going to set everything in order. This will result in great peace and prosperity. Sometime ago I wrote a song with these words, "My Day Is Gonna Come."

"I've been tempted by the devil
    since the first day I was saved;
I've been tortured by the demons
    who would drive me to the grave.
I've been 'put down' by the mockers,
   'made a fool of' by the dumb,
But I will not be discouraged
    'Cause I say one day my day
       is gonna come.

"Well, my day is gonna come—
    I say my day is gonna come
When Jesus comes in glory
    To reward us for what we've done,
He'll rule the world with an iron hand;
    No man of sin will ever stand.
We'll rejoice because we've won
    Yes, I say one day my day
       is gonna come!"*

In the next chapter, I am going to share some exciting changes Jesus is going to make when He rules the world with His saints.

---

* Lundstrom, Lundstrom Music © 1980

The Millennium —
Part 2

A great day is coming! It will be so wonderful that it is almost impossible to describe. Jesus Christ is going to rule the world for 1,000 years in peace and the changes He will make will be phenomenal!

The Bible says, *"And he will dwell with them... And God shall wipe away all tears from their eyes; and there shall be no more death, neither sorrow, nor crying, neither shall there be any more pain: for the former things are passed away.*

"And he that sat upon the throne said, Behold, I make all things new" (Revelation 21:3-5). Can you imagine all the new things God is going to make in the coming kingdom of the Lamb?

Arthur Bloomfield, in his excellent book *All Things New*, published by Bethany Fellowship, shares a tremendous outline of truth. When man sinned he lost three things:

1. *MAN LOST HIS SOUL. "For in the day that thou eatest thereof thou shalt surely die"* (Genesis 2:17). *"The soul that sinneth, it shall die"* (Ezekiel 18:4).
2. *MAN LOST HIS BODY.* He could no longer eat of the tree of life, and he began to get old. *"For dust thou art, and unto dust shalt thou return"* (Genesis 3:19).
3. *MAN LOST THE EARTH.* He lost dominion over the earth. It produced a living for him only by hard labor. It developed weeds and pests, disease and plagues. It passed into the control of Satan (Genesis 3:17-18).*

However, when Jesus Christ returns, He will deliver us from the curse and penalty of sin. He will redeem us completely. The three main events in redemption are:

1. *CONVERSION:* When Christ saves the soul.
2. *RESURRECTION:* When Christ redeems the body.
3. *THE SECOND COMING OF CHRIST:* When Christ redeems the earth.

It will be a glorious day when redemption is completed.

---

* Reprinted by permission from
All Things New
by Arthur E. Bloomfield
Published and copyrighted 1959
Bethany House Publishers
Minneapolis, MN 55438

Jesus Will Establish Perfect Justice

One visit to a penitentiary will reveal that there is very little true justice here on earth. This is what makes the rehabilitation of criminals so difficult. While they are suffering for their crimes, many greater offenders go free. It makes prisoners cynical and rebellious to know the judicial system is corrupt. Statistics show that the system favors the rich while it punishes the poor.

During the Millennium this inequality will be set straight. Jesus is going to set up His kingdom in righteousness and will establish true justice. The Prophet Jeremiah wrote, *"Behold, the days come, saith the Lord, that I will raise unto David a righteous Branch, and a King shall reign and prosper, AND SHALL EXECUTE JUDGMENT AND JUSTICE IN THE EARTH"* (Jeremiah 23:5).

No longer will the courts be jammed and prisons overcrowded while attorneys argue their cases before weary juries. No longer will the wealthy be allowed to "buy" their freedom by employing crafty lawyers who twist the truth. Jesus Christ is going to rule the world with His saints, and perfect justice will be established, because we will have access to the knowledge of God.

The Bible says, *"Do ye not know that the saints shall judge the world?"* (1 Corinthians 6:2). When the saints are supplied with God's knowledge of events, when they are seated as judges, it is going to revolutionize the judicial system of the world.

Do you realize that God is trying to prepare you for a position as a judge in this new world? Jesus promised leadership positions to his 12 apostles. He said, *"Ye are they which have continued with me in my temptations. And I appoint unto you a kingdom, as my Father hath appointed unto me; That ye may eat and drink at my table in my kingdom, AND SIT ON THRONES JUDGING THE TWELVE TRIBES OF ISRAEL"* (Luke 22:28-30).

Again let me quote the Apostle Paul, *"If we suffer, we shall also reign with him"* (2 Timothy 2:12). John the apostle says, *"And I saw thrones, and they sat upon them, and judgment was given unto them...and they lived and reigned with Christ a thousand years"* (Revelation 20:4).

Jesus Will Provide Complete Safety

Think of the millions of city dwellers who live behind bolted doors, afraid to go into the streets at night for fear of getting mugged, raped or killed. The majority of people living in major cities of the world do not dare venture out into the night without placing their lives in jeopardy.

Jesus will change all this. The Prophet Micah wrote, *"But they shall sit every man under his vine and under his fig tree; AND NONE SHALL MAKE*

219

THEM AFRAID: for the mouth of the Lord of hosts hath spoken it" (Micah 4:4).

If you go into the wilderness, you won't have to worry about the wild animals. The Prophet Ezekiel said, *"And I will make with them a covenant of peace, and will cause the evil beasts to cease out of the land: AND THEY SHALL DWELL SAFELY IN THE WILDERNESS, AND SLEEP IN THE WOODS"* (Ezekiel 34:25).

The Prophet Isaiah adds, *"The wolf and the lamb shall feed together, and the lion shall eat straw like the bullock: and dust shall be the serpent's meat. They shall not hurt nor destroy in all my holy mountain, saith the Lord"* (Isaiah 65:25).

Think how wonderful it will be to roam at will in forests, the wilderness or in cities at night, knowing you are perfectly safe.

Jesus Will Improve Everyone's Health

We are not given many details, but you can be certain the Lord's medical program will be beyond anything Medicare, Medicaide, Blue Cross, Blue Shield or any medical organization has ever dreamed of. The Bible says, *"And the inhabitant shall not say, I AM SICK: the people that dwell therein shall be forgiven their iniquity"* (Isaiah 33:24).

Divine health will be the rule of the day in the new kingdom. The Prophet Isaiah continues, *"Never again will there be in it an infant that lives*

220

but a few days, or an old man who does not live out his years; HE WHO DIES AT A HUNDRED WILL BE THOUGHT A MERE YOUTH; he who fails to reach a hundred will be considered accursed.

"They will build houses and dwell in them; they will plant vineyards and eat their fruit. No longer will they build houses and others live in them, or plant and others eat.

"For as the days of a tree, so will be the days of my people; my chosen ones will long enjoy the works of their hands.

"They will not toil in vain or bear children doomed to misfortune; for they will be a people blessed by the Lord" (Isaiah 65:20-23, NIV).

The blind and deaf will receive their sight and hearing during the Millennium. The Bible says, *"In that day the deaf will hear the words of the scroll, and out of gloom and darkness the eyes of the blind will see"* (Isaiah 29:18, NIV).

People of the Kingdom

Remember, during the Millennium there will be people living on earth other than the saints and the chosen ones of Israel. In fact, these are the three groups of people in the Millennium who will participate in Christ's kingdom:

1. The unsaved Gentiles (called the servants of the bride of Christ), who will multiply and rebuild the nations. These did *not* partake in the first resurrection.

221

2. Saved Jews, who will rebuild Israel and enjoy favored nation status as they inherit the promises made to Abraham. These are the 144,000 which are saved out of the tribulation.
3. The believers of ALL AGES who return with Jesus as His "bride." They will reign with Christ over the Jews and Gentiles (Revelation 5:10;20:6). They *did* partake in the *first* resurrection (the rapture).

Jesus Will Restore Universal Joy and Happiness

The Prophet Jeremiah gives us a glimpse of this gladness. He says, *"'Then maidens will dance and be glad, young men and old as well. I will turn their mourning into gladness; I will give them comfort and joy instead of sorrow. I will satisfy the priests with abundance, and my people will be filled with my bounty,' declares the Lord"* (Jeremiah 31:13,14, NIV).

The scriptures are alive with the promises of joy and happiness. Read what Zephaniah says, *"Sing, O Daughter of Zion; shout aloud, O Israel! Be glad and rejoice with all your heart, O Daughter of Jerusalem! The Lord has taken away your punishment, he has turned back your enemy. The Lord, the King of Israel, is with you; never again will you fear any harm.*

"On that day they will say to Jerusalem, 'Do not fear, O Zion; do not let your hands hang limp. The Lord your God is with you, he is mighty to save. He will take great delight in you, he will quiet you with his love, HE WILL REJOICE OVER YOU WITH SINGING" (Zephaniah 3:14-17, NIV).

Can you imagine what it will be like to hear a song sung by Jesus Christ? If you love music, this will be the greatest song ever!

The Prophet Isaiah continues, *"The ransomed of the Lord will return. They will enter Zion with singing; everlasting joy will crown their heads. Gladness and joy will overtake them, and sorrow and sighing will flee away"* (Isaiah 51:11, NIV).

"I will rejoice over Jerusalem and take delight in my people; the sound of weeping and of crying will be heard in it no more" (Isaiah 65:19, NIV).

Jesus Will Make Jerusalem the Capital of the World

When Jesus Christ conquers the nations at the end of the Tribulation, He will declare Jerusalem as the capital of His new kingdom.

The Bible says, *"Then the survivors from all the nations that have attacked Jerusalem will go up year after year to worship the King, the Lord Almighty, and to celebrate the Feast of Tabernacles. If any of the peoples of the earth do not go up to Jerusalem to worship the King, the Lord Almighty, they will have no rain. If the Egyptian people do not go up and take part, they will have no rain. The Lord will bring on them the plague he inflicts on the nations that do not go up...*" (Zechariah 14:16-18, NIV).

"*And many peoples and powerful nations will come to Jerusalem to seek the Lord Almighty and to entreat him*" (Zechariah 8:22, NIV).

And then there is the amazing prophecy of which part is inscribed on the plaque of the United Nations, "*For out of Zion shall go forth the law, and the word of the Lord from Jerusalem.*

"*And he shall judge among the nations, and shall rebuke many people: AND THEY SHALL BEAT THEIR SWORDS INTO PLOW SHARES* [the steel cutting edge on plows used to prepare the soil for seeding], *AND THEIR SPEARS INTO PRUNING HOOKS: NATION SHALL NOT LIFT UP SWORD AGAINST NATION, NEITHER SHALL THEY LEARN WAR ANY MORE*" (Isaiah 2:3,4).

Won't it be wonderful when nations no longer squander their wealth on weapons of destruction? Today nations are spending a million dollars a minute preparing for a nuclear holocaust that could turn this world into an inferno. But when Jesus comes to reign, He will put an end to this madness. The wealth of this world will not be spent on destruction but on production that will feed the hungry and provide for the needy.

The Prophet Micah said, "*But in the last days it shall come to pass, that the mountain of the house of the Lord shall be established…and people shall flow unto it. And many nations shall come, and say, Come, and let us go up to the mountain of the Lord, and to the house of the God of Jacob; and HE WILL TEACH US HIS WAYS, and we will walk in his paths: for the law shall go forth of Zion, and the word of the Lord from Jerusalem"* (Micah 4:1,2).

Jerusalem is the center of much controversy in the world today. But in the new world, it will become the very center of the kingdom government, education and worship.

Jesus Will Establish a Universal Language

If you have travelled the world at all, you know that language barriers divide people almost more than personal prejudices. There are literally hundreds of languages and dialects. No wonder the American Bible Society has had to translate the Bible into 1,647 languages.

However, when Jesus Christ returns, He will establish a universal language. The Prophet Zephaniah declares, *"For then will I turn to the people a pure language, that they may all call upon the name of the Lord, to serve him with one consent"* (Zephaniah 3:9).

Jesus Will Lift the Curse From the Earth

When our parents, Adam and Eve, sinned in the garden of Eden, they brought a curse upon the earth. The world has suffered because of it ever since. When Jesus comes to rule and reign, He will lift the curse and this will turn the earth into a paradise. Here is a quick review:

"And I will multiply the fruit of the tree, and the increase of the field" (Ezekiel 36:30).

"The Lord shall make bright clouds, and give them showers of rain, to every one grass in the field" (Zechariah 10:1).

"And the desolate land shall be tilled...[and] become like the Garden of Eden" (Ezekiel 36:34,35).

"In that day shall the branch of the Lord be beautiful and glorious, and the fruit of the earth shall be excellent" (Isaiah 4:2).

"For the seed shall be prosperous; the vine shall give her fruit, and the ground shall give her increase, and the heavens shall give their dew..." (Zechariah 8:12).

One of the greatest quotes regarding the abundance to come, as a result of Jesus lifting the curse from the earth, is found in the words of the Prophet Amos.

"Behold, the days come, saith the Lord, that THE PLOWMAN SHALL OVERTAKE THE REAPER, and the treader of grapes him that soweth seed; and the mountains shall drop sweet wine" (Amos 9:13).

The lifting of the curse will forever solve the problems of famine throughout the world. The earth will reach its fullest potential during the millennial reign of Jesus Christ.

Jesus Will Solve the Arab-Israeli Conflict

Since the 1900s the Arab-Israeli conflict has kept the world at the brink of war. Do you realize the Arab-Israeli problem is the result of an act of unbelief? Years ago God promised Abraham a son. When it appeared that his wife Sarah would die childless, Abraham went in to Sarah's handmaid, Hagar, and she bore a son named Ishmael. Soon after, Sarah bore a son by Abraham named Isaac.

There was instant conflict. Hagar and Ishmael were thrown out of the house, and Isaac and Sarah continued to live with Abraham. These two sons of Abraham became two nations. Isaac became the father of the Jews. Ishmael became the father of the Arabs.

There has been fighting between these two nations ever since. Actually, the Mideast conflict is a theological one. The Arabs say they are heirs to the promised land by Ishmael, and the Jews say they are heirs to the promised land by Isaac. This explains why politicians do not have the answer; it is a spiritual problem, not a political one.

When Jesus returns to reign, He will solve the Arab-Israeli conflict. First, He will change the hearts of the Jewish people who have often been so hard on others, including God. The Bible says, *"I will put a new spirit within you; and*

227

I will take the stony heart out of their flesh, and will give them an heart of flesh:

"That they may walk in my statutes, and keep my ordinances, and do them: and they shall be my people, and I will be their God" (Ezekiel 11:19,20).

"But this shall be the covenant that I will make with the house of Israel; After those days, saith the Lord, I will put my law in their inward parts, and write it in their hearts; and will be their God, and they shall be my people.

"And they shall teach no more every man his neighbour, and every man his brother, saying, Know the Lord: for they shall all know me, from the least of them unto the greatest of them, saith the Lord: for I will forgive their iniquity, and I will remember their sin no more" (Jeremiah 31:33,34).

The Jews will be truly converted. This will give them a new attitude toward the Arabs and the rest of the Gentile world. I've noticed how true conversion changes homes. When a husband and wife both have new "spiritual hearts" it enables them to get along so much better. They are quick to forgive and forget their differences. Love wins!

Here is what will happen during the Millennium. The Bible says, *"In that day shall five cities in the land of Egypt speak the language of Canaan [Jewish]....*

"In that day shall there be an altar to the Lord in the midst of the land of Egypt.

"In that day shall there be a highway out of Egypt to Assyria, and the Assyrian shall come into Egypt, and the Egyptian into Assyria, and the Egyptians shall serve with the Assyrians.

"In that day shall Israel be the third with Egypt and with Assyria, even a blessing in the midst of the land:

"Whom the Lord of hosts shall bless, saying, Blessed be Egypt my people, and Assyria the work of my hands, and Israel mine inheritance" (Isaiah 19:18,19,23-25).

The three antagonists of the Mideast—the Jews, Arabs and Syrians—will be united when Jesus Christ returns. The Lord will work a change in everyone's hearts which will solve one of the greatest feuds in history, a feud that has claimed literally tens of thousands of lives.

Jesus Will Oversee the Evangelization of the World

During the Millennium you and I will witness the fullness of the prophecy, *"And it shall come to pass...that I will pour out my spirit upon all flesh...and whosoever shall call upon the name of the Lord will be delivered"* (Joel 2:28,32).

Satan has bound many by superstitions, demons, religious lies and misunderstandings. In the new world, knowledge shall increase and the Lord will pour out His Spirit upon all flesh. There will be a worldwide awakening and

229

turning to God. What a difference this will make in everything! Can you imagine how kindly people will act when the Spirit of God is in their hearts?

Jesus Will Rule With Supreme Power

The problem with rulers has been that if they were good, they were too weak and died too soon; if they were bad, they were too strong and lived too long. When Jesus rules from Jerusalem, He will not only be good, but He will have the power it takes to govern well.

The Bible says, *"And he shall rule them with a rod of iron"* (Revelation 2:27). *"And she* [Israel] *brought forth a man child, who was to rule all nations with a rod of iron"* (Revelation 12:5). One thing about the rod of iron is that it is an inflexible standard. Man cannot "bend" it so that he can measure up. The "ROD" of Jesus Christ will truly bring justice without respect or prejudice.

"And out of his mouth goeth a sharp sword [the Word of God] *that with it he should smite the nations.* [Remember when Judas and his band of soldiers came to take Jesus by force? Jesus spoke three words, "I AM HE," and the soldiers fell to the ground. His words are so powerful that when he speaks in truth, they can destroy all who oppose Him.] *And he shall rule them with a rod of iron"* (Revelation 19:15).

230

Thank God, there is no chance that Jesus will fail. He will command and demand that this world become the paradise God intended it to be!

When the earth has been transformed, when all weapons of war have been abolished, when the curse upon nature has been lifted, when perfect peace and health are present, when joy and laughter are heard everywhere, when holiness and purity are exalted, then Jesus will do something wonderful: He will give this perfect world back to God who created it.

The Bible says, *"THEN THE END WILL COME, WHEN HE HANDS OVER THE KING- DOM TO GOD THE FATHER AFTER HE HAS DESTROYED ALL DOMINION, AUTHORITY AND POWER. FOR HE MUST REIGN UNTIL GOD HAS PUT ALL HIS ENEMIES UNDER HIS FEET*

"WHEN HE HAS DONE THIS, THEN THE SON HIMSELF WILL BE MADE SUBJECT TO HIM WHO PUT EVERYTHING UNDER HIM, SO THAT GOD MAY BE ALL IN ALL" (1 Corinthians 15:24,25; 28, NIV).

This will be the ultimate moment in history, when Jesus turns a perfect creation back to God. When all the inhabitants of the world fall down upon their knees and glorify God. At that moment even Jesus Himself will kneel down, lift up His hands to God and pray, "O Father,

231

glorify Yourself with the creation You have given Me!"

Praise God forever! What a glorious day this will be!

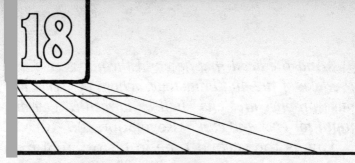

The Final Cleansing of the Earth

After enjoying 1,000 years of unparalleled peace and prosperity during the reign of Jesus Christ, you would imagine that all mankind would be grateful to God for His blessings. But the madness of man is shown in this next unbelievable event.

The Bible says, *"And when the thousand years are expired, Satan shall be loosed out of his prison, And shall go out to deceive the nations which are in the four quarters of the earth, Gog and Magog, to gather them together to battle: the number of whom is as the sand of the sea.*

"And they went up on the breadth of the earth, and compassed the camp of the saints about, and the beloved city [Jerusalem]: and fire came down from God out of heaven and devoured them.

"And the devil that deceived them was cast into the lake of fire and brimstone, where the beast and false prophet are, and shall be tormented day and night for ever and ever" (Revelation 20:7-10).

This is the second time in history that man has gone haywire in paradise. The first time was when Adam and Eve sinned in the Garden of Eden by eating the fruit of the forbidden tree (see Genesis 3).

Now again, at the end of the age, men and women will rebel against God, even while they are enjoying the fruits of a world that Jesus has turned into paradise. The sinister character behind this rebellion is Satan. His revolt against God began long before man was created. If you research Satan's rebellion, you will learn a lot about the devastating power of evil.

Who is Satan?

Satan was once one of God's most exalted angels. He was probably in the class of Michael or Gabriel. But pride entered into his heart, and the Bible records his downfall in Ezekiel 28. In this passage of scripture the king of Tyre is mentioned, but Satan is the one whom the prophet is really describing. This is one of the two-fold teachings that refer both to a man and the motivator behind him, which in this case is Satan.

"You were in Eden,
   the garden of God;
every precious stone adorned you:
   ruby, topaz and emerald,
   chrysolite, onyx and jasper,
   sapphire, turquoise and beryl.
Your settings and mountings were
   made of gold;
on the day you were created
   they were prepared.
You were anointed as a guardian
   cherub,
   for so I ordained you.
You were on the holy mount of God;
   you walked among the fiery stones.
You were blameless in your ways
   from the day you were created
   till wickedness was found in you.
Through your widespread trade,
   you were filled with violence,
      and you sinned.
So I drove you in disgrace from the
   mount of God,
and I expelled you, O guardian
   cherub,
   from among the fiery stones.
Your heart became proud
   on account of your beauty,
and you corrupted your wisdom
   because of your splendor.

235

So I threw you to the earth"
                    (Ezekiel 28:13-17, NIV).

Another passage of scripture that describes Satan's fall is found in Isaiah 14. The king of Babylon is mentioned, but as it was with Ezekiel's description of the king of Tyre, it is Satan whom the prophet Isaiah is describing.

"How are thou fallen from heaven, O Lucifer, son of the morning! how art thou cut down to the ground, which didst weaken the nations! For thou hast said in thine heart, I will ascend into heaven, I will exalt my throne above the stars of God: I will sit also upon the mount of the congregation, in the sides of the north:
"I will ascend above the heights of the clouds; I will be like the Most High. Yet thou shalt be brought down to hell [Sheol and Hades, the grave of departed spirits], *to the sides of the pit"* (Isaiah 14:12-15).

These two portions of scripture describe in great detail the fall of Satan. First we see that Lucifer was a beautiful creature. God speaks of him as having splendor (Ezekiel 28:17). Beauty is dangerous because it corrupts the judgment of both the possessor and the beholder. When Satan saw how majestic he was, he should have given glory to God his Creator. But Satan forgot, or decided to exalt himself even further.

Second, we see that Lucifer misused his self-will. He says,

I will—ascend into heaven.

I will—exalt my throne above the stars of God.

I will—sit upon the mount of the congregation in the sides of the north.

I will—ascend above the heights of the clouds.

I will—be like the Most High.

"I" is the middle letter of PRIDE. "I" is the middle letter of SIN. "I" is the middle letter of LUCIFER.

The misuse of this vertical pronoun was Satan's downfall. It turned him from a beautiful angelic creature into a monster of evil.

Evil is the Absence of God

Down through the ages many Christians and nonchristians have wondered where evil comes from. The answer is, "Evil doesn't come from anywhere. Evil is simply the absence of righteousness." It is like asking the question, "Where does darkness come from?" It doesn't come from anywhere. Darkness is simply the absence of light. If you turn out the light, darkness rushes in. Spiritually speaking, if you turn out the light and energy of righteousness, evil rushes in like the darkness. *"He that believeth on him is not condemned: but he that believeth not is condemned already, because he hath not believed in the name of the only begotten Son of God. And this is the condemnation, that light is come into the world,*

237

and men loved darkness rather than light, because their deeds were evil. For every one that doeth evil hateth the light, neither cometh to the light, lest his deeds should be reproved. But he that doeth truth cometh to the light, that his deeds may be made manifest, that they are wrought in God" (John 3:18-21).

So remember, evil is simply the absence of God.

Why Are We Tempted?

Other questions people ask are, "If God is good, why does He allow Satan to exist? Why does He allow me to be tempted?"

To answer this question you must understand God's purpose in creating you. God did not want you to be a mechanical robot, programmed to walk about praising Him. God created you as a sovereign, an emperor with authority over your own life. God has given you a "free will" to choose good or evil. One of the main reasons God has placed you on earth is to develop the proper use of your self-will. God gives you approximately 70 years to practice resisting evil before He allows you to rule and reign in eternity.

It is true that God did not ask you if you wanted to be created, but being God—the option should be His. Wouldn't you rather be created, even with the temptations and hassle, than to never have existed at all?

So here you are. You must make life-changing decisions, and there are serious consequences. What will you do? Your choice determines your destiny. All that Satan does is to accelerate the process of evil. If you have it in your heart to love and serve God, there are not enough demons in hell or enough temptations to defeat you. The Bible says,

"There hath no temptation taken you but such as is common to man [in other words, we all face similar trials]: *BUT GOD IS FAITHFUL, WHO WILL NOT* [allow] *YOU TO BE TEMPTED ABOVE* [what you are able to bear]; *BUT WILL WITH THE TEMPTATION ALSO MAKE A WAY TO ESCAPE, THAT YE MAY BE ABLE TO BEAR IT"* (1 Corinthians 10:13).

So the devil doesn't have the advantage over you. The odds are more than even. *If you want to win, you will; if you don't, you won't.* Or as the old story goes, "God voted for me, the devil voted against me, and I broke the tie!"

But the stakes are high. You cannot fail or you will pay an eternal penalty. God will not destroy you just because you chose to rebel against Him. You are an eternal creation of God. You will *never* die in the truest sense of the word. You will spend eternity in heaven or hell depending on the choices you make.

Hell is Real

Jesus said, *"And these* [the wicked] *shall go away into everlasting punishment: but the righteous into life eternal"* (Matthew 25:46).

The same Greek word translated "everlasting" in this phrase "everlasting punishment" is also used in the phrase "life eternal." There is no way you will burn up in hell and cease to exist. Jesus spent a lot of time in Luke 16:19-31 telling how a rich man died and was constantly tormented for his sins.

The critic cries, "But an everlasting hell doesn't sound reasonable." But does an everlasting heaven for repentant sinners sound reasonable? Heaven is as unreasonable (humanly speaking) as hell, but people choose to believe in heaven because it sounds better than hell.

Jesus said, *"If your hand causes you to sin, cut it off. It is better for you to enter life maimed than with two hands to go into hell, where the fire never goes out. And if your foot causes you to sin, cut it off. It is better for you to enter life crippled than to have two feet and be thrown into hell. And if your eye causes you to sin, pluck it out. It is better for you to enter the kingdom of God with one eye, than to have two eyes and be thrown into hell, where their worm does not die and the fire is not put out.*

"Everyone will be salted with fire" (Mark 9:43-49, NIV).

If you cannot accept eternal hell as a reality, you had better bend your brain into believing it because it is true. And don't forget—rejecting God's plan of salvation is an eternal crime that demands an eternal punishment.

Today some religions have even created a place where the evil is burned out of you. People who believe in such an in-between place pay to have prayers prayed for their departed loved ones. This doesn't make sense, because if there were such a place, the rich would escape and the poor would be doomed to suffer. What does a man do if he doesn't have any wealthy relatives? Such a place does not exist. It is only the reasoning of men trying to work out a way to save the lost who refuse to repent. There is no "second chance." *"It is appointed unto men once to die and then the judgment"* (Hebrews 9:27).

Satan's Release

If you think that being punished brings about a change of heart, take a look at Satan. He will spend 1,000 years in the bottomless pit (see Revelation 20:2). Can you imagine anything more terrible than falling endlessly in darkness for 1,000 years? Will this frightening experience change his mind about sin? Not at all. When he is set free from his prison, he will immediately prompt men to rebel against God again.

The awesome fact is that once evil enters your heart, the only cure is Jesus Christ. This is why Jesus said, *"Ye must be born again!"* (John 3:3). Unless you experience the Holy Spirit quickening your heart, unless you experience your sins being washed away by the sacrificial blood of Jesus Christ, you will be hopelessly evil forever.

Weary of Righteousness

The question rises, why will the people of the world try to overthrow the kingdom of God that has blessed them with 1,000 years of peace and prosperity? The answer is, it is possible to get weary of righteousness. C. S. Lovett brings out this important truth in his helpful book, *Latest Words on the Last Days*.

"You can get tired of doing good.

"You can get weary of righteousness.

"You can get bored with holy things.

"You can get fed up with praying and reading your Bible—unless you are really hungry for righteousness."

The most famous story Jesus ever told was that of the prodigal son (see Luke 15:12-32). The young man was bored with the righteousness of his father. He yearned to get away from home so he could experience the thrills of evil.

This will happen during the Millennium. People will begin to tell stories about "the good old days" when they were free to gamble, drink, fight and commit immorality. Millions will feel restricted by the police and the uncompromising law and order. Sin is subtle: It seduces you into wondering what it is like to do wrong. When you and I are tempted we are usually viewing the temptation from the "saved" side. In our position of safety we are not experiencing the pain of guilt, the remorse of regret, the tragic consequences of actions, etc. All we see is the pleasure of the *act*—not the pain of the consequences.

When the lords of the Philistines wanted to destroy Samson, the powerful man who could singlehandedly slay 1,000 men, they hired a prostitute named Delilah to *"entice him"* (Judges 16:5). The New International Version says, *"See if you can lure him into showing you the secret of his great strength."*

So remember, sin is a satanic trap. The devil has baited it well to entice you, to lure you into its hold. The moment you partake of sin's pleasures, the trap will snap shut and you'll cry, "God, why?"

I'll never forget counselling a tear-stained teenager who was only 14 and pregnant. She kept repeating, "Oh, if there just weren't consequences. Oh, if there just weren't consequences."

You Need a Spiritual Appetite

Christian friend, the way to keep from becoming weary of righteousness is to sincerely seek God daily by reading your Bible and praying earnestly. This is why Jesus said, *"Blessed are they which do hunger and thirst after righteousness: for they shall be filled"* (Matthew 5:6).

You can read the Bible mechanically and pray empty words that are hardly worth repeating, but you can also seek God with a hungry heart. If you are not hungry for God, search your heart to see what has destroyed your appetite. I remember the time I felt impressed to buy a bum a hamburger steak dinner. The poor fellow ate the salad and bread but apologized for not eating the meat. He said, "Mr. Lundstrom, please don't be offended. I only get 38 cents a day from the city to eat. The only place I can survive on 38 cents a day is eating at a 'slop joint' down the street that grinds up old bones into a watered-down soup. I've eaten that slop so long I cannot eat this meat. It's too rich for me."

If you do not have a spiritual appetite, it is because you have allowed "worldly slop" to replace the meat of God's Word. Chances are that trashy TV shows, smutty books, secular conversation, impure jokes, and worldly thoughts have ruined your appetite for the Bread of life.

Paul the apostle writes, *"And I, brethren, could not speak unto you as unto spiritual, but as unto carnal, even as unto babes in Christ"* (1 Corinthians 3:1).

A carnal Christian is a "half-breed." His soul is saved, but he is controlled by the appetites and lusts of his body.

Carnal Christians are really miserable people. They are like the generation of Israelites that lacked the faith to cross over into the Promised Land of milk and honey. Yet they knew too much to go back to Egypt! Thus their lust for flesh pots, leeks and garlics condemned them to wandering in the wilderness for 40 years.

Let's look at the same passage in The New International Version, *"Brothers, I could not address you as spiritual but as worldly—mere infants in Christ. I gave you milk, not solid food, for you were not ready for it. Indeed, you are still not ready. You are still worldly. For since there is jealousy and quarreling among you, are you not acting like mere men?"* (1 Corinthians 3:1-3).

The writer to the Hebrews says, *"We have much to say...but it is hard to explain because you are slow to learn. In fact, though by this time you ought to be teachers, you need someone to teach you the elementary truths of God's Word all over again. You need milk, not solid food! Anyone who lives on milk, being still an infant, is not acquainted with the teaching about righteousness. But solid food is for the mature, who by constant use have trained themselves to distinguish good from evil"* (Hebrews 5:11-14, NIV).

If you do not have the spiritual hunger you need, cut out the things in your life that are destroying your spiritual appetite. When you are growing weary of righteousness, your hunger for God's Word and prayer is the first to go.

Search the Scriptures

It also helps to read the Bible with a searching soul. Seek to discover a fresh glimpse into the marvelous character of God. For instance, after David sinned with Bathsheba and killed her husband, God was so hurt that He sent His prophet Nathan to David and said in essence, "I've blessed you beyond measure. I made you king of Israel and delivered you out of the hand of Saul. I gave you many wives and gave you Israel and Judah to rule." And then God adds, *"If this was too little, I would have given you more"* (see 2 Samuel 12:7,8).

It has always touched my heart to think of what God said to David, *"I would have given you more."* It gives me a glimpse into the heart and character of God. It helps me to love Him better and encourages me to pray. We have not because we ask not.

So study the Bible with a hungry heart, and search out the obscure scriptures that reveal God in such a wonderful way. It will help you to love Him more. It will keep you fresh in your soul.

Satan Cast into Fire

So, after 1,000 of the best years men have ever enjoyed, people will become careless with their souls and weary of righteousness. When Satan suggests they destroy God's kingdom, like madmen they will march toward Jerusalem.

Their evil plot will end when God sends fire down from heaven and destroys them. Then Satan will be cast alive into the lake of fire to burn forever with the beast (antichrist) and the false prophet.

The lesson of all this is to learn how completely evil corrupts and why it is necessary to keep a fresh touch of the Holy Spirit on your life. David the psalmist declares, *"He restoreth my soul"* (Psalm 23:3). If your soul needs restoration, stop a moment at the end of this chapter and pray. Ask God to do something special in your life. Remember what God told David, "If you had only asked, I would have done more for you." Jesus says, *"Ask—that your joy be full!"* (John 16:24).

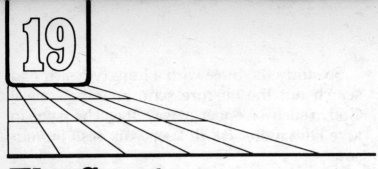

The Great White Throne Judgment

The most awesome day in the history of eternity for nonchristians will be the Great White Throne Judgment. Can you imagine the terror lost men and women will experience when they meet their Creator face to face?

Judgment day is not only a fact of Bible prophecy, it is rooted in the conscience of man. The Prophet Daniel declares, *"And many...that sleep in the dust of the earth shall awake, some to everlasting life, and some to shame and everlasting contempt"* (Daniel 12:2).

The Apostle John saw a vision of this Great White Throne Judgment and said, *"And I saw the dead, small and great, stand before God; and the books were opened: and another book was opened, which is the book of life: and the dead were judged out of those things which were written in the books, according to their works.*

"And the sea gave up the dead which were in it; and death and hell delivered up the dead which were in them: and they were judged every man according to their works. And death and hell were cast into the lake of fire. This is the second death. AND WHO-SOEVER WAS NOT FOUND WRITTEN IN THE BOOK OF LIFE WAS CAST INTO THE LAKE OF FIRE" (Revelation 20:12-15).

In an earlier chapter I pointed out how Christians will be judged and rewarded for their works at the judgment seat of Christ. However, this judgment (The Great White Throne) is not for Christians but for *all* the unbelievers who have ever lived. You can see from this passage of scripture that it is clear that some will be saved and others damned. The important truth is "What standard determines whether a man will be saved or lost?"

All Will Stand Before God

Let's examine this event verse by verse. John says, *AND I SAW THE DEAD, SMALL AND GREAT, STAND BEFORE GOD"* (Revelation 20:12).

The greats from history will appear on this day: caesars, emperors, czars, kings, queens, pharaohs and dictators. Hitler, Stalin, Genghis Kahn, Khrushchev, Alexander the Great and Mao Tse-tung will be present. There will also be billions of unknowns present on that day:

Farmers, ranchers, clerks, waitresses, lawyers, carpenters, bricklayers, assembly line workers, peasants, serfs, slaves, etc.

This great multitude, as far as eye can see, will stand before God. I believe the saints of God will be there too—not as defendants, but as witnesses to this awesome judgment. This is the only time in history that all living souls will assemble at once. It will never happen again.

Our Lives Exposed

"AND THE BOOKS WERE OPENED." God has kept a complete record of every person who has ever lived—from their first breath to their last. Years ago this sounded like an impossible task, but modern day computers are able to store the history of millions of consumers on a few tiny silicone chips.

However, God has not only kept a detailed account of our deeds, but also of our thoughts, wishes and secret plans. Think how foolish it is for people to try to live a secret life. Jesus said, *"That which is done in secret shall be shown openly and that which was whispered shall be shouted from the housetops"* (see Luke 12:2,3).

There will be no secrets. At the Great White Throne Judgment, God will give an instant readout of every soul who stands before Him. No wonder Jesus said there will be weeping and wailing and gnashing of teeth.

The Lamb's Book of Life Opened

"AND ANOTHER BOOK WAS OPENED, WHICH IS THE BOOK OF LIFE" (Revelation 20:12).

Millions are unaware of this book. Many believe they will have to give an account of themselves on Judgment Day, but they have never stopped to consider there will be TWO books, not just one, that will determine their destiny. The second book is called The Lamb's Book of Life. This is the book in which God writes the names of all who repent of their sins and receive Jesus Christ as their personal Savior. The moment you turn your life over to Jesus Christ, God writes your name in the Lamb's Book of Life. This is why Jesus said, *"He that overcometh, the same shall be clothed in white raiment; and I WILL NOT BLOT OUT HIS NAME OUT OF THE BOOK OF LIFE, but I will confess his name before my Father, and before his angels"* (Revelation 3:5).

Judgment of the Heathen

John the apostle continues, *"AND THE DEAD WERE JUDGED OUT OF THOSE THINGS WHICH WERE WRITTEN IN THE BOOKS, ACCORDING TO THEIR WORKS"* (Revelation 20:12).

The questions arise, "What is God going to do about the heathen who have never heard about Jesus Christ? Will they go to hell?"

This passage of scripture answers these questions. Because they have never heard the gospel, they will be judged according to their works.

Jesus said, *"That servant who knows his master's will and does not get ready or does not do what his master wants will be beaten with many blows. BUT THE ONE WHO DOES NOT KNOW AND DOES THINGS DESERVING PUNISHMENT WILL BE BEATEN WITH FEW BLOWS. From everyone who has been given much, much will be demanded; and from the one who has been entrusted with much, much more will be asked"* (Luke 12:47,48, NIV).

When Abraham was interceding for his nephew Lot who dwelt in Sodom, he said to the Lord, *"Shall not the Judge of all the earth do right?"* (Genesis 18:25). I believe God will judge the heathen fairly. Jesus said the ignorant will be beaten with fewer stripes. He did not dare say they would be saved, or Christians would not sacrifice their lives to evangelize the lost. But God will be fair. However, if you have ever heard the gospel once, you cannot claim the mercies that will be extended to the heathen. You are obligated before God to serve Jesus Christ today.

No One Escapes the Judgment

"AND THE SEA GAVE UP THE DEAD WHICH WERE IN IT; AND DEATH AND HELL DELIV-

ERED UP THE DEAD THAT WERE IN THEM"
(Revelation 12:13).

No one will escape. Unbelievers who had their bodies cremated and ashes thrown into the sea will find themselves standing before God. New scientific discoveries show that your entire body can be reconstructed from just one cell. Each person has a DNA factor, a numbering system, that is unique. Even though a body is decomposed at sea and the remains lost, God will be able to call forth a "number" and suddenly the man who tried to escape by cremation will appear out of nowhere.

"AND THEY WERE JUDGED EVERY MAN ACCORDING TO THEIR WORKS" (Revelation 20:13).

Again and again and again, John is gripped by the systematic, unrelenting, methodical and meticulous judgment of the wicked dead.

Can a Man Die Twice?

"AND DEATH AND HELL WERE CAST INTO THE LAKE OF FIRE. THIS IS THE SECOND DEATH" (Revelation 20:14).

John saw that a man can die twice. He dies once, and his body is buried in the ground. But he dies the second time when his soul is cast into the lake of fire.

Here is a mystery: If you are only born once,

you will die twice, but if you are born twice, you will only die once. The interpretation is: If you have never been "born again" as the scriptures teach, you have only been born once (physically). This means you will die twice—once in the flesh and the second time spiritually. But if you are born twice, once in the flesh and again in the Spirit, you will only die once.

Not Good Enough

John's final statement is very significant, *"AND WHOSOEVER WAS NOT FOUND WRITTEN IN THE BOOK OF LIFE WAS CAST INTO THE LAKE OF FIRE"* (Revelation 20:15).

The great question is: Has your name been written in the Lamb's Book of Life? It is recorded that you have repented of your sins and received Jesus Christ, by faith, as your personal Savior?

It is tragic that so many people do not understand or see the necessity of repenting and turning to Jesus Christ. Sometime ago, I took a flight to Pittsburgh and the gentleman sitting next to me was a vice-president of one of America's largest corporations. When I began to tell him about Jesus Christ, he was insulted and said, "Well, Mr. Lundstrom, I want you to know that I am a good man."

What could I say? I could tell from visiting with him that he was a great guy. But just then the Holy Spirit gave me the answer, I said, "Sir, it is obvious that you are a good man, but your problem is that YOU ARE NOT GOOD ENOUGH!"

The Bible says, *"For all have sinned and come short of the glory of God"* (Romans 3:23).

The truth of this scripture was made real to me several years ago by a minister I met at one of our crusade rallies. The man had tears in his eyes when he said, "Lowell, this is the saddest day in my life."

When I asked why, he said, "My boy always dreamed of attending West Point. He wanted to become an officer in the United States Army. He was a terrific athlete and scholar in school. His grades were so good our congressman recommended him to West Point.

"When he went for his interview, he passed the mental and physical tests with flying colors. But the academy turned him down. They refused to admit my son."

By now I could see the anguish of this father's soul. When I asked why his son was refused, he said, "Because he was one inch too short." He wasn't tall enough to meet the minimum height requirements for a military cadet.

This is why the Bible says, *"All have sinned and come short of the glory of God"* (Romans 3:23). Without Jesus as our Savior, you and I just cannot measure up. Jesus Christ was the only perfect man who ever lived, and without His atoning sacrifice, without His blood covering for our sins, we will never stand a chance on Judgment Day.

Take This Test

Many times you'll get the feeling from people that they are "good." This is so deceiving. To show you why, honestly compare your life to Exodus 20:3-17, the Ten Commandments.

1. *"THOU SHALT HAVE NO OTHER GODS BEFORE ME."*

    Have you ever put anything ahead of God? Have you ever decided to do your own will rather than His? Please mark one.

    ☐ guilty   ☐ innocent

2. *"THOU SHALT NOT MAKE UNTO THEE ANY GRAVEN IMAGE."*

    Have you ever worshiped any object or materialistic thing more than God? (Whether it be a person or a house, car, boat, etc.)

    ☐ guilty   ☐ innocent

3. *"THOU SHALT NOT TAKE THE NAME OF THE LORD THY GOD IN VAIN."*

    Have you ever cursed or used God's name in a vain or disrespectful manner?

    ☐ guilty   ☐ innocent

4. *THOU SHALT "REMEMBER THE SAB-BATH DAY TO KEEP IT HOLY."*

Have you ever dishonored the Lord on His holy day? Have you ever used God's sacred day for your own selfish pleasure or for work that could have waited?

☐ guilty   ☐ innocent

5. *"HONOR THY FATHER AND MOTHER."*

Have you ever rebelled against your parents' wishes or failed to show them the respect they deserve?

☐ guilty   ☐ innocent

6. *"THOU SHALT NOT KILL."*

Have you ever resented or hated someone so much you wished they were dead? Jesus taught that to hate a man without a cause is committing murder, endangering your soul (see Matthew 5:22-24 and 1 John 3:15).

☐ guilty   ☐ innocent

7. *"THOU SHALT NOT COMMIT ADUL-TERY."*

Jesus said, *"You have heard that it was said by them of old time, Thou shalt not commit adultery: But I say unto you, That whosoever looketh on a woman to lust after her hath committed adultery with her already in his heart.*

"And if thy right eye offend thee, pluck it out, and cast it from thee: for it is profitable for thee that one of thy members should perish, and not that thy whole body should be cast into

hell" (Matthew 5:27-29).

Have you ever looked with lust in your eye at someone who was not yours?

☐ guilty   ☐ innocent

8. *"THOU SHALT NOT STEAL."*

Have you ever stolen anything?

☐ guilty   ☐ innocent

9. *"THOU SHALT NOT LIE."*

Have you ever deceived anyone, cheated on a test in school, or failed to tell the whole truth?

☐ guilty   ☐ innocent

10. *"THOU SHALT NOT COVET."*

Have you ever wished that you owned something that belonged to another, with the feeling that you deserved it as much or more than he?

☐ guilty   ☐ innocent

How did you fare on this righteousness test? As I review my life in the light of these paragraphs, I can see that I have broken every one of them in thought, word or deed. I've never killed a man, but I've hated several. I've never committed adultery but I've lusted in my heart. So this is why the Bible says, *"All have sinned and come short of the glory of God"* (Romans 3:23). We have all failed to measure up to God's standard of righteousness. This is why we all must repent of our sins and receive Jesus Christ by faith as our personal Savior. Jesus died for our sins, and His blood justifies us before God.

Possessing Jesus is the Key

There is a life-changing story told of an old Methodist minister who dreamed he died and went to heaven.

When he arrived at heaven's gate, the angels told him he could not enter. The minister was shocked and said, "There must be some mistake. I am Reverend So-and-So. Go in and tell God I'm out here."

The angels went in and reappeared a few moments later with the same message: He was not admitted. God would not allow him to enter heaven.

Then the minister, sensing the seriousness of the moment, began to tell his life story. He told the angels how he began to preach the gospel when he was a teenager, how he had been a "circuit-riding" preacher for many years, traveling from one small church to the next on horseback. He told of the many sacrifices he had made, riding through the rain, snow and cold, giving himself in service to the Lord.

The angels were so moved by his story they went back into heaven. A few moments later they returned and said, "God has granted you permission to plead your own cause before His throne."

Just then the gates of heaven swung open

and the minister was ushered into the presence of God. Everything was so holy and pure that, as he approached the steps leading to the throne of God, he felt so unworthy he dared not even look up to behold God on His throne.

Just then God spoke and said, "Mortal man, why do you stand here before Me?" When the minister heard God speak, he was so over-whelmed with God's majesty and power, he began to weep. He realized then that he would never be good enough to enter heaven. He would never be able to give enough money, pray enough prayers or be able to sacrifice his life in a way to merit spending eternity with God.

As he stood there weeping with the realization of his own sinfulness, he felt the presence of Jesus Christ. Then Jesus walked over, stood by his side, slipped His arm around his waist and said, "Father, this is one of mine."

Just then the minister awakened from his dream. But he was never the same again because he knew from that moment he wasn't going to get to heaven because he was good or because he prayed, gave money or sacrificed for the church. *He knew the only reason he would ever make heaven was because he belonged to Jesus!*

You Can Escape Damnation

My question is, Do you belong to Jesus? Does

He possess your heart, soul, mind and body? If you don't have the Lord in your heart, if your name is not written in the Lamb's Book of Life, you are in great jeopardy. If your heart stops beating before you finish this chapter, you will spend eternity in hell.

Remember the Bible says, *"And whosoever was not found written in the book of life WAS CAST INTO THE LAKE OF FIRE"* (Revelation 20:15).

If you have never asked Jesus Christ into your heart, sincerely pray this prayer right now:

"My Father in heaven, please have mercy on me and forgive my sins. I believe that Jesus Christ, Your Son, died in my place on the cross, and that You raised Him from the dead.

"I repent of my sins and receive Jesus Christ into my heart as my personal Savior. I will serve Him with all my heart and keep His commandments. In Jesus' name, Amen."

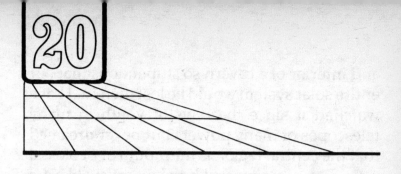

Superlife!

One of the most thrilling discoveries by astronomers in recent times has been the great empty space in the nebula of the Orion constellation: A heavenly cavern so gigantic that the mind of man cannot comprehend it and so beautiful that words cannot adequately describe it.

Powerful telescopes, utilizing long-exposure photographic plates, can peer into the depths of interstellar space and glimpse its vastness. The opening within the Orion constellation is perhaps more than 16,740,000,000,000 miles in diameter. The diameter of the earth's orbit is 186 million miles, but the Orion opening is 90 thousand times as wide! Thirty thousand solar systems like ours could be stretched side by side across the entrance of the Orion opening, and there would be room to spare.

Professor Learkin of Mount Lowe Observatory gives us the following description of the Orion nebula: "These photographs reveal the opening and interior of a cavern so stupendous that our entire solar system would be lost therein. I have watched it since the days of youth in many telescopes of many powers but never dreamed that the central region is the mouth of a colossal cave. Pen of writer and brush of artist alike are lifeless and inert in any attempt to describe this interior."

Surpassing the immensity of its size is its exquisite beauty. The luminous colors are unlike any upon earth: "For the depths of the Orion nebula appear like torn and twisted objects and river masses of shining glass, irregular pillars, columns of stalactites in glittering splendor and stalagmites from the mighty floor. The appearance is like that of light shining and glowing behind the clear walls of ivory and pearls, studded with millions of diamond shining stars."*

Now, there must be a reason for this spectacular constellation in space. Could this be heaven itself? Chances are it is just one of the many wonders of God's universe. But if He can create a constellation so beautiful that a trained astronomer has been fascinated with it for a lifetime, can you imagine how amazing the Holy City will be?

---

* Reprinted by permission from
  Editor John Denmark
  Evangelistic Outreach
  Apache Junction, AZ

A River of Life

Our new home in heaven will be more than minerals and jewels. The Bible says that a beautiful river will flow through it. *"And he shewed me a pure river of water of life, clear as crystal, proceeding out of the throne of God and of the Lamb"* (Revelation 22:1).

This river will bring life to the inhabitants of heaven. It will refresh and bring joy to everyone who sees it and drinks from it. It will water the landscape and the trees. It will make us feel at home. If heaven was all metalic we would remember the lush green days of spring on earth. But this place will be greater than anything we have ever seen. If this sounds too nostalgic, don't forget that after the resurrection when Jesus made an appointment to meet with His disciples He sent word. *"Go and tell my brothers to go to Galilee; there they will see me"* (Matthew 28:10). Jesus loved the Sea of Galilee and so did His disciples. There's something about a beautiful stream of clear running water or a placid lake that soothes and inspires. Heaven will have the greatest river that has ever flowed.

A Tree of Life

There will also be trees. *"In the midst of the street of it, and on either side of the river, was there the tree of life, which bare twelve manner of fruits, and yielded her fruit every month: and the leaves of the tree were for the healing of the nations"* (Revelation 22:2).

If trees and fruit, especially the Tree of Life with leaves for the healing of the nations, seem out of place in such a space age setting, remember God may be raising this Tree as a reminder to the world of what happened in the Garden of Eden when Adam and Eve sinned against God. How they were driven out of the garden and lost access to the Tree of Life and died. Each time someone eats the fruit from this Tree or uses the leaves for healing they will remember and probably retell the story. Jesus says, *"To him that overcometh will I give to eat of the tree of life, which is in the midst of the paradise of God"* (Revelation 2:7).

Death Is Abolished Forever

There will be no sorrow or death in this city. *"And God shall wipe away all tears from their eyes; and there shall be no more death, neither sorrow, nor crying, neither shall there be any more pain: for the former things are passed away"* (Revelation 21:4).

You will never hear the screaming of police and ambulance sirens in heaven. You will never see a hearse or a funeral procession. Hospitals and doctors will not exist. There will never be an ache or pain; tears will vanish in the presence of God. Everyone will experience health and happiness. There will be no condemnation or spiritual conflict in heaven either. *"And there shall be no more curse: but the throne of God and of* the Lamb shall be in it; and his servants shall serve him" (Revelaion 22:3).

All of our days on earth have been spent fighting the world, the flesh and the devil. Spiritual conflict has been part of our daily routine. This has toughened us into tried-and-tested saints, but the battle has been a long hard fight. The Bible says, *"Blessed are the dead which die in the Lord from henceforth"* (Revelation 14:13). Remember the dead are blessed because they inherit their new home. Death does not bankrupt Christians. It only brings us into our inheritance. It unites us with our fabulous fortune.

"Yea, saith the Spirit, THAT THEY MAY REST FROM THEIR LABORS; and their works do follow them" (Revelation 14:13).

"After this I beheld, and lo, a great multitude, which no man could number, of all nations, and kindreds, and people, and tongues, stood before the throne, and before the Lamb, clothed with white robes, and palms in their hands; And cried with a loud voice, saying, Salvation to our God which sitteth upon the throne, and unto the Lamb.

"And all the angels stood round about the throne, and about the elders, and the four [living creatures], and fell before the throne on their faces, and worshipped God, Saying, Amen: Blessing, and glory, and wisdom, and thanksgiving, and honor, and power, and might, be unto our God for ever and ever. Amen.

"And one of the elders answered, saying unto me,

What are these which are arrayed in white robes? [And where did they come from?] *And I said unto him, Sir,* [you know], *And he said to me, These are they which came out of great tribulation, and have washed their robes, and made them white in the blood of the Lamb.*

"Therefore are they before the throne of God, and serve him day and night in his temple [the holy city]: *and he that sitteth on the throne shall dwell among them.*

"They shall hunger no more, neither thirst any more; neither shall the sun light on them, nor any heat. For the Lamb which is in the midst of the throne shall feed them, and shall lead them unto living fountains of waters: and God shall wipe away all tears from their eyes" (Revelation 7:9-17).

We Shall Have New Bodies

If you have been struggling with a body that is worn out or broken down, you will be happy to hear what God has in store for you in heaven. You will have a new body in the world to come. Your new spiritual body will be free from pain and death. It will be incorruptible, glorious and powerful. Just as the caterpillar emerges from the chrysallis as a beautiful butterfly, free from the limitations of a worm, you will break away from the bondage of your earthly house.

The Bible says, *"Someone may ask, 'How are the dead raised? With what kind of body will they come?'*

How foolish! What you sow does not come to life unless it dies. When you sow, you do not plant the body that will be, but just the seed, perhaps of wheat or of something else.

"So it will be with the resurrection of the dead. The body that is sown is perishable, it is raised imperishable; it is sown in dishonor, it is raised in glory; it is sown in weakness, it is raised in power; it is sown a natural body, it is raised a spiritual body" (1 Corinthians 15:35-37 and 42-44, NIV).

What Happens When Death Comes

One of the most frequently asked questions about death is, "What happens to me when I die?"

If you are a Christian, your body is buried but your soul and spirit go to be with Jesus Christ in heaven. Jesus told the thief on the cross who repented at that late hour, *"Verily I say unto thee, Today shalt thou be with me in paradise"* (Luke 23:43).

Paul the apostle wrote to the Corinthian Christians saying, *"We are confident...and willing... to be absent from the body, and to be present with the Lord"* (2 Corinthians 5:8).

The New International Version renders Paul's words this way, *"We are confident, I say, and would prefer to be away from the body and at home with the Lord."*

Paul wrote to the Philippians saying, *"I am torn*

between the two: I desire to depart and be with Christ, which is better by far; but it is more necessary for you that I remain in the body" (Philippians 1:23, NIV).

Remember, Moses died and was buried, but he appeared with Jesus on the Mount of Transfiguration (see Matthew 17:3).

Today, some have falsely taught that your soul slumbers in the grave, that you experience "soul sleep" until the resurrection. But the Bible says you immediately join Jesus Christ in heaven after death.

The spiritual body you have in this interim period is not your resurrection body—that will come later. The great John Bunyan writes of his experience, "A shining form drew near. It was one of the redeemed. He told me that he had left his body below, resting in hope until the resurrection; *and that though he was still a substance, yet it was an immaterial one, not to be touched by mortals."*

So if the Lord tarries and you die, you will experience three different bodies in your existence. First, the physical body you have now. Second, the interim spiritual form you will have as you join the saints in paradise. Third, your new resurrection body that you will enjoy for all eternity.

You Will Be Known
Don't worry about your new body—everyone

will recognize you, but they will rejoice in the updated, glorified model. The Bible says, *"...then shall I know even as also I am known"* (1 Corinthians 13:12). You will recognize your loved ones immediately. There will be no mistaken identities in heaven. Today neurosurgeons and doctors who study the brain have discovered that each person has a "brain print" as unique as his fingerprints.

You will be able to communicate in a most unusual way in heaven. Betty Malz, the wife of my personal friend and associate, Carl Malz, had a life-after-death experience. She was clinically dead for 28 minutes. She said that as she stood among the multitude around the throne, there were people of many languages worshiping God. Even when they spoke in different languages, each fully understood what the others were saying. Communications will be perfect in heaven because everyone will have perfect understanding.

Daisy Dryden, a dying child whose brother often came to visit her while she lay on her deathbed, said, "We just talk with our think!" Imagine what an experience it will be to talk with your mind without saying a word.

Pleasures Beyond Comprehension

Whenever the afterlife is discussed the question often arises, "Why will God cancel

271

sex in heaven?" This is a good question that deserves a logical answer. To many, the cessation of sex may naturally appear to be limiting because sex is one of the most exciting experiences of the body.

Jesus said, "...*in the resurrection they neither marry, nor are given in marriage, but are as the angels of God in heaven*" (Matthew 22:30). Many who enjoy sex will naturally think this world offers more pleasure than heaven does. However, C. S. Lewis illustrates this misunderstanding by telling the story of a father who was trying to explain the pleasures of sexual intimacy to his boy.

The father said, "Son, when you grow older you will most likely find a girl you love, and you will want to hold her and know her in a physically intimate way." He continued to explain but the boy could not comprehend. He finally turned to his father and said, "Dad, can I eat chocolates at the same time?"

To this boy there wasn't anything better than Hershey's chocolate. It is easy for us to make the same mistake when it comes to sex. It is hard for us to comprehend spiritual pleasures beyond the physical delights we have known.

But let me assure you that you won't miss a single desire that is abandoned. God will bless you with spiritual joys beyond anything you have experienced in the flesh.

The new X-15 jet fighter plane is so powerful it can climb straight up at the speed of a bullet and gain speed while doing so. Can you imagine an X-15 fighter pilot walking by a tricycle saying, "Boy, do I miss my three-wheeler"? Never! He has found a rocket ride to the heavens; trikes and bikes are just childish toys.

Food and Fellowship

One nice feature of our new bodies is that we will be able to eat in heaven. *"Blessed are they which are called unto the marriage supper of the Lamb"* (Revelation 19:9).

Jesus told His disciples at the Last Supper, *"But I say unto you, I will not drink henceforth of this fruit of the vine, until that day when I drink it new with you in my Father's kingdom"* (Matthew 26:29).

He also said, *"I appoint unto you a kingdom, as my Father hath appointed unto me; That ye may eat and drink at my table in my kingdom"* (Luke 22:29-30).

After Jesus arose from the tomb and was clothed in His new resurrection body, He prepared a breakfast of fish for His disciples (see John 21:12). He also had supper with two of His disciples on the road to Emmaus (Luke 24:13-35).

In heaven, we won't be eating for the need of nourishment—we will be eating for the fun and fellowship. Imagine enjoying calorie-free feasts for eternity!

Our Appearance Will Change

Our Savior's encounter with the two disciples on the road to Emmaus teaches us something else about our new resurrected bodies; we will be able to change our appearance. As the two disciples walked along, discouraged because of the death and burial of Jesus, the Lord drew near and went with them. But the Bible says, *"Their eyes were holden that they should not know him"* (Luke 24:16) or as the New International Version says, *"But they were kept from recognizing him."*

Jesus was able to change His appearance and it wasn't until they ate supper that evening and He broke bread that their eyes were opened to recognize Him. *"And their eyes were opened, and they knew him; and he vanished out of their sight. And they said one to another, Did not our heart burn within us, while he talked with us by the way, and while he opened to us the scripture?"* (Luke 24:31,32).

(If *you* want *your* heart to burn with the reality of God, take time to study the scriptures and talk with Jesus.)

You may also remember that after the resurrection, Mary could not recognize Jesus (John 20:14). His own apostles did not recognize Him either (John 21:4), although in this case it might have been they were too far out on the lake to make out His features in the dim light of the early morning.

Your new, adaptable body will certainly come in handy when you rule the world with Christ. If rebels on earth plan an evil scheme during the Millennium, they will never be certain whether or not the stranger standing by is one of the Lord's or not. You have heard of plain-clothes policemen; with your new body you will be an effective deterrent to evil.

We Will Wear Crowns

We will also wear crowns in heaven. Now again, I must confess that the idea of wearing a heavenly victorian crown studded with jewels has never appealed to me until recently. Ralph Wilkerson in his interesting book *Beyond and Back* changed my mind about crowns.

There are reasons why a crown is important. First, it shows you have been given authority. A king or queen does not become official until coronation day.

Second, your crown will reveal your true attitude in your service to Christ our king. If you truly sacrificed out of love, the crown will show it.

Third, your crown is the only tangible gift you can offer the Lord. The Lord has everything He needs. The one symbol of all your achievements is your crown. When you cast it down at the Savior's feet in honor of Him, it will express your total loyalty to Him.

"The four and twenty elders [fell] *down before him that sat on the throne, and worshipped him that liveth for ever and ever, AND CAST THEIR CROWNS BEFORE THE THRONE SAYING,*

"Thou are worthy, O Lord, to receive glory and honor and power: for thou hast created all things, and for thy pleasure they are and were created" (Revelation 4:10,11).

Five Different Crowns Awarded

There are five crowns that will be awarded to the worthy.

1. *THE CROWN OF LIFE!* This crown is given to those who endure great tribulation or temptation and remain faithful unto the very end.

   "Blessed is the man that endureth temptation: for when he is tried, HE SHALL RE—CEIVE THE CROWN OF LIFE, which the Lord hath promised to them that love him" (James 1:12).

   "And ye shall have tribulation...be...faithful unto death, and I will give thee A CROWN OF LIFE" (Revelation 2:10).

2. *THE SOUL-WINNER'S CROWN.* This crown is given to those who help others find Jesus Christ as their personal Savior.

Paul considered his converts his crown.

He writes, *"For what is our hope, our joy, or the crown in which we will glory in the presence of our Lord Jesus when he comes? Is it not you? Indeed, you are our glory and joy"* (1 Thessalonians 2:19, NIV).

"Therefore, my brothers, you whom I love and long for, my joy and crown,....stand firm in the Lord, dear friends!" (Philippians 4:1).

"And they that be wise shall shine as the brightness of the firmament; and they that turn many to righteousness as the stars for ever and ever" (Daniel 12:3).

3. *THE INCORRUPTIBLE CROWN.* This crown is given to those who strive to be holy in all their ways.

Paul writes, *"Everyone who competes in the games goes into strict training. They do it to get a crown of laurel that will not last; but we do it to get a crown that will last forever. Therefore, I do not run like a man running aimlessly; I do not fight like a man [beating the air]. No, I beat my body and make it my slave so that after I have preached to others, I myself will not be disqualified for the prize"* (1 Corinthians 9:25-27, NIV).

4. *THE CROWN OF RIGHTEOUSNESS.* This crown is given to those who are especially faithful and looking for the appearing of Jesus Christ.

Paul writes, *"The time has come for my departure. I have fought the good fight, I have finished the race, I have kept the faith. Now there is in store for me the CROWN OF RIGHTEOUSNESS, which the Lord, the righteous Judge, will award to me on that day—and not only to me, but also to all who have longed for his appearing"* (2 Timothy 4:6-8, NIV).

5. *THE CROWN OF GLORY.* This crown is given to pastors and Christian leaders of the church who are faithful to feed God's word to those in their keeping.

"To the elders among you, I appeal as a fellow elder, a witness of Christ's sufferings and one who also will share in the glory to be revealed: Be shepherds of God's flock that is under your care, serving as overseers—not because you must, but because you are willing, as God wants you to be; not greedy for money, but eager to serve; not lording it over those entrusted to you, but being examples to the flock. And when the Chief Shepherd appears, you will receive THE CROWN OF GLORY that will never fade away" (1 Peter 5:1-4, NIV).

Sadhu Sundar Singh, a devout Christian from India, was given a vision of heaven and says, "The degree of goodness reached by the soul of a righteous man is known by the (degree) of brightness that radiates from his whole appearance. For character and virtue show themselves in the form of various glowing rainbows—like colors of great glory."

World Offers No Hope

You and I can thank God we have been given such a wonderful hope for the future. The world doesn't have it. This phrase expresses their despair:

"Man's a vapor and full of woes;
cuts a caper and away he goes."

Bertrand Russell, famed agnostic, wrote, "There is darkness without, and when I die there will be darkness within. There is no splendor, no vastness anywhere; only triviality for a moment and then nothing."

Gilbert Pyle said, "There is no ghost in the human machine."

Thank God these men are wrong! The Holy Spirit that dwells within us as Christians assures us that God is alive, that heaven is real and that we have eternal life.

You are greater than the grave! Job declared, *"I know that my redeemer liveth, and that he shall stand at the latter day upon the earth. And though after my skin worms destroy this body, yet in my flesh shall I see God"* (Job 19:25,26).

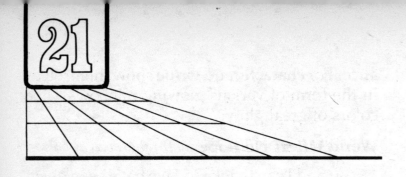

Superworld!

What is heaven like? I must confess that for many years it was difficult for me to get excited about heaven. I am an activist. I knew heaven would be wonderful, with the saints worshiping God and visiting with one another, but to spend eternity doing these things would seem to me like a family reunion that lasts too long.

Maybe you have had the same difficulty. The impression we are given of heaven is that it is a place where people float around on wet clouds, strumming harps, singing choruses and having endless church services without offerings.

I believe the next three chapters will revolutionize your concepts about the afterlife. You may believe in life after death—but it is another thing to know what heaven is like.

We Will Reign With Christ

The verse that changed my life was Revelation 3:21 where Jesus says, *"To him that overcometh will I grant to sit with me in my throne, even as I also overcame, and am set down with my Father in his throne."* The Holy Spirit illuminated this verse to my heart and suddenly I saw what heaven is all about.

It is true that we will worship God and commune with saints, but God has much more in mind. The Bible says if we overcome, Jesus Christ will allow us to be seated on His throne—the creative center of the universe.

Just imagine creating with Christ—building, planning, designing with God's eternal resources and knowledge! Suddenly I realized that heaven is not just a sleepy city. It is a place bustling with creative activity! Instead of spending forever worshiping and visiting, we are going to be assigned places of leadership and responsibility. If you are an overcomer, Jesus will allow you to be seated on His throne. Think of it! Our Lord is going to give you the opportunity of becoming more than you've ever dreamed. This is why I call heaven "Superworld."

If the idea of ruling with Christ is a new idea to you, here are some additional scriptures to support this glorious truth.

"And he that overcometh, and keepeth my works unto the end, to him will I give power over the nations: And he shall rule them with a rod of iron" (Revelation 2:26,27).

"And I saw thrones, and they sat upon them, and judgment was given unto them: and I saw the souls of them that were beheaded for the witness of Jesus, and for the word of God...and they lived and reigned with Christ a thousand years" (Revelation 20:4).

"And they shall reign forever and ever" (Revelation 22:5).

"Verily I say unto you, That ye which have followed me, in the regeneration when the Son of man shall sit in the throne of his glory, ye also shall sit upon twelve thrones, judging the twelve tribes of Israel" (Matthew 19:28).

"Well, thou good servant: because thou hast been faithful in a very little, have thou authority over ten cities" (Luke 19:17).

"Well done, thou good and faithful servant: thou hast been faithful over a few things, I will make thee ruler over many things" (Matthew 25:21).

So you can see, as an overcomer your future will be exciting. You won't be floating around heaven on a cloud. You will be directing part of the ever-growing kingdom of God. The Bible says, *"And his servants shall serve him"* (Revelation 22:3). You are going to be so busy that you will need eternity to complete everything that God has planned for you to accomplish.

The Wonders of Heaven

Once Paul the apostle was carried up into heaven. In 2 Corinthians 12:2 he described his experience, *"I know a man in Christ who fourteen years ago was caught up to the third heaven."* There are three heavens: FIRST, the atmospheric heaven above us with clouds; SECOND, the heavens with planets, sun, stars, moons, galaxies, etc.; THIRD, the spiritual heaven where God dwells.

"Whether it was in the body or out of the body I do not know—God knows" (2 Corinthians 12:2, NIV). In other words Paul is not certain if he was dead or alive. However, Paul is certain that he was caught up in the fifth dimension.

The five dimensions are:
1. Time
2. Space
3. Material
4. Mental
5. Spiritual

"[He] was caught up to Paradise. He heard inexpressible things, things that man is not permitted to tell" (2 Corinthians 12:4, NIV). Paul did not even feel at liberty to describe the wonders of heaven.

At another time he says, *"Eye hath not seen, nor ear heard, neither have entered into the heart of man, the things which God hath prepared for them that love him. But God hath revealed them unto us by his Spirit"* (1 Corinthians 2:9,10).

Paul says you cannot begin to imagine the spectacular wonders of heaven. He adds, *"But the natural man receiveth not the things of the Spirit of God: for they are foolishness unto him: neither can he know them, because they are spiritually discerned"* (1 Corinthians 2:14). Unless you are spiritually enlightened, the truths of heaven will seem foolishness to you.

Superworld is comprised of three parts: Supercity (the new Jerusalem), Superearth (the refurnished earth at the end of the millennium), and the Super-universe (the new heavens).

Look at Supercity

John the apostle gives us a dazzling description of the holy city. He says, *"I saw the Holy City, the new Jerusalem, coming down out of heaven from God, prepared as a bride beautifully dressed for her husband. And I heard a loud voice from the throne saying, 'Now the dwelling of God is with men, and he will live with them. They will be his people, and God himself...will be their God.'*

"And he carried me away in the Spirit to a mountain great and high, and showed me the Holy city, Jerusalem, coming down out of heaven from God. It shone with the glory of God, and its brilliance was like that of a very precious jewel, like a jasper, clear as crystal. It had a great, high wall with twelve gates, and with twelve angels [guarding] at the gates. On

the gates were written the names of the twelve tribes of Israel.

"There were three gates on the east, three on the north, three on the south and three on the west. The wall of the city had twelve foundations, and on them were the names of the twelve apostles of the Lamb.

"The angel who talked with me had a measuring rod of gold to measure the city, its gates and its wall. The city was laid out like a square, as long as it was wide. He measured the city with the rod and found it to be [around 1,500 miles] in length, and as wide and high as it is long. He measured its wall and it was [about 216 feet] thick, by man's measurement, which the angel was using. The wall was made of jasper, and the city of pure gold, as pure as glass.

"The foundations of the city walls were decorated with every kind of precious stone. The first foundation was jasper, the second sapphire, the third chalcedon, the fourth emerald, the fifth sardonyx, the sixth carnelian, the seventh chrysolite, the eighth beryl, the ninth topaz, the tenth chrysoprase, the eleventh jacinth, and the twelfth amethyst. The twelve gates were twelve pearls, each gate made of a single pearl. The street of the city was of pure gold, like transparent glass.

"I did not see a temple in the city, because the Lord God Almighty and the Lamb are its temple. The city does not need the sun or the moon to shine on it, for the glory of God gives it light, and the Lamb is its lamp. The nations will walk by its light, and the *kings of the earth will bring their splendor into it. On no day will its gates ever be shut, for there will be no night there. The glory and honor of the nations will be brought into it. Nothing impure will ever enter it, nor will anyone who does what is shameful or deceitful, but only those whose names are written in the Lamb's book of life"* (Revelation 21:2-3, 10-27, NIV).

Can you imagine a city made of pure gold, as clear as glass, gleaming with God's power? John makes special mention that the sun or moon does not shine on it, *"And there shall be no night there; and they need no candle...for the Lord God giveth them light"* (Revelation 22:5). This city does not need electricity or any illumination because it literally glows with God's glory!

And consider the size of our heavenly home— 1500 miles square. This city would cover more than the western half of the United States!

A mathematician put his pencil to these dimensions and this is what he discovered. "The thickness of the wall is 144 cubits (or about 216 feet thick). It is approximately 12,000 furlongs square or 1500 miles in each direction. It has 12 foundations or floors each separated by 125 miles. The second floor would be out of sight of the natural eye.

"If the city were divided into rooms, one mile in length, one mile wide and one mile high, it would contain 3 billion, 375 million rooms—each one cubit mile. If we began at the time of Adam and spent one hour in each room, at the end of 6,000 years we would have visited 52,570,560 rooms—leaving 3,322,529,440 rooms yet unvisited. This includes all leap years for 6,000 years, deducting the century year when there is no leap year."

Wow! When Jesus said, *"In my father's house are many mansions,"* He wasn't abusing the phrase. For nearly 2,000 years Jesus Christ has been preparing this Supercity for His saints! He said, *"I go to prepare a place for you"* (John 14:2). What an unbelievably glorious place this will be!

E. M. Bounds says, "The favorite Bible word for heaven is 'glory' which seems so especially suited to describe heaven. It means splendor, brightness, magnificence, excellence, preeminence, dignity, majesty in the sense of absolute perfection, a most glorious, a most exalted state, a glorious condition of blessedness."

The reason the Bible says, "Blessed is he that readeth, and they that hear the words of this prophecy" is because this book gives the only description of our eternal home. No wonder when D. L. Moody, the famous soulwinner and evangelist, lay dying he cried, "Earth is receding, heaven is opening and God is calling."

He was excited by what he saw.

Features of the Supercity

There are other spectacular features of this city.

1. *IT IS COMPLETELY SAFE.* Metropolitan areas have become jungles of corruption. Thieves, rapists, murderers, pimps, gamblers, and extortioners have frightened people until they no longer venture out at night.

The Bible says that heaven will be safe. Its gates will be guarded by angels, and the Bible says, *"Nothing impure will ever enter it, nor will anyone who does what is shameful or deceitful, but only those whose names are written in the Lamb's book of life"* (Revelation 21:27, NIV).

"Blessed are those who wash their robes, that they may have the right to the tree of life and may go through the gates into the city. Outside are the dogs, those who practice magic arts, the sexually immoral, the murderers, the idolaters and everyone who loves and practices falsehood" (Revelation 22:14,15, NIV).

2. *THE CITY HAS NO TEMPLE OR CHURCH.* John says, *"I saw no temple therein: for the Lord God Almighty and the Lamb are the temple of it"* (Revelation 21:22).

"Behold, a throne was set in heaven, and one sat on the throne" (Revelation 4:2).

"The throne of God and of the Lamb shall be in it...and they shall see his face" (Revelation 22:3,4).

When Moses was called to Mount Sinai to receive the Ten Commandments, he fasted 40 days and 40 nights and talked with God. Finally Moses said, *"Now show me your glory."* And the Lord said, *"...you cannot see my face, for no one may see me and live."*

Then the Lord said, *"There is a place near me where you may stand on a rock. When my glory passes by, I will put you in a cleft in the rock and cover you with my hand until I have passed by. Then I will remove my hand and you will see my back; but my face must not be seen"* (Exodus 33:18-23, NIV).

Then Moses was allowed to see the back of God's glory.

The Bible continues, *"When Moses came down from Mount Sinai with the two tablets of the Testimony in his hands, he was not aware that his face was radiant because he had spoken with the Lord. When Aaron and all the Israelites saw Moses, his face was radiant, and they were afraid to come near him....When Moses finished speaking to them, he put a veil over his face"* (Exodus 34:29,30,33, NIV).

The glory of God was so great, it so transfigured Moses that the people could not look upon his face. (May God transform us in the same way today.) Yet all of this happened as a result of Moses seeing only a part of God. Can you imagine the transformation that will take place in us when we see God face to face in His mighty majesty?

The Power of Energy

I read in the newspaper recently about a powerline worker who was awarded seven and a half million dollars because in an accident, an electrical cable he was working on was suddenly energized with 7,200 volts.

Here's what happened:

"Don't heat it up!" an electric company workman shouted.

But the first word was muffled and another worker threw a switch sending 7,200 volts down the powerline where Benjamin Styles was working—approximately 1,000 feet away.

"There was a ball of fire and a sound like an explosion" and then a safety device caused the line to go dead.

But in that instant the current shot through Styles' body, burning his hands and arms. Then it flowed through his blood vessels and nerves and severely burned his legs. When they found him he was unconscious, hanging upside down from his safety belt.

He was not expected to live when he arrived at the hospital. One leg had to be amputated above the knee and the other below. Miraculously, Styles lived. He has since learned to walk with the help of artificial legs and two canes.

Benjamin Styles says, "I just thank God I'm alive."

If Styles was disabled from one jolt of 7,200 volts, can you imagine what will happen to a man exposed to the total energy and glory of God? No wonder God said, "You cannot see me and live!"

However, Jesus says, *"Him that overcometh will I make a pillar in the temple of my God, and he shall go no more out"* (Revelation 3:12).

"And they shall see his face" (Revelation 22:4).

To earthlings who have experienced the pleasures of food, sex, liquor, drugs, etc., heaven may sound unexciting, but the opposite is true. Of all the exciting experiences, all of the thrills of passion, all of the great emotions of life, nothing will ever compare to one second in the presence of the living God. As you stand before God's throne, wave after wave of His glory will energize you until you are transfigured in His presence!

There Will be Angels in Heaven

"And I beheld, and I heard the voice of many angels round about the throne and the [living creatures] *and the elders: and the number of them was ten thousand times ten thousands, and thousands of thousands.* [This is at least one hundred million

or more. John is trying to say the host is innumerable.]

"Saying with a loud voice, Worthy is the Lamb that was slain to receive power, and riches, and wisdom, and strength, and honor, and glory, and blessing" (Revelation 5:11,12).

If you are not concerned about angels, you have forgotten that an angel has guarded you since childhood. Jesus said, *"Take heed that ye despise not one of these little ones; for I say unto you, That in heaven their angels do always behold the face of my Father which is in heaven"* (Matthew 18:10).

"Are [angels] *not...ministering spirits, sent forth to minister for them who shall be heirs of salvation?"* (Hebrews 1:14).

The Bible says that angels stand guard over the saints. You are given divine protection from Satan and the demonic enemies of your soul. Remember how Satan complained about Job? He accused God saying, *"Hast not thou made a hedge about him, and about his house, and about all that he hath on every side?"* (Job 1:10).

Friend, angelic security guards have been watching over you since the day you were born. I am certain you can recall many times when you have been miraculously spared from harm. You will meet your guardian angels in heaven. I am certain when God replays your life, you'll be thanking Him for the angelic protection He has given you.

Natural Minds Cannot Comprehend the Spiritual

Dr. Bernard Ramm has said, "The omission of a discussion of angels in almost every book on the philosophy of religion reveals the gulf between modern mentality and the biblical revelation. Philosophers of religion discuss God, the soul, and nature, but stop short of any serious discussion of angels. Skeptics will spend much time in refuting the proofs of the existence of God and the immortality of the soul, but will not even wet the pen to refute the existence of an angelic host. In contrast to this treatment of angels on behalf of philosophers (religious or skeptical) are the profuse references to angels in sacred scripture....in the universe of electrons and positrons, atomic energy and rocket power, Einsteinian astronomy and nuclear physics, angels seem out of place. They seem to intrude upon the scene like the unexpected visit of the country relatives to their rich city kinfolk. ATOMS SEEM AT HOME IN OUR CONTEMPORARY THINKING, BUT NOT ANGELS! The prospect of some interplanetary beagle cruising among the planets gathering scientific data surprises no educated man of today. But if such a man were called upon to comment upon angels, he would either act very nervous or else he would pompously deny that angels existed. He knows the principles whereby he can reasonably imagine a scientific cruise of the planets by a space-age Darwin, but he has no principles whereby he may discuss angels. So he prefers to dismiss the concept of angels as mythological."*

I have included the preceding statement to make a point—that to believe in God and then limit His workings to fit the rational mind is irrational. Once you say "God"—then nothing revealed by Him should come as a surprise. Remember as I said before, the Bible says,*"The natural man receiveth not the things of the Spirit of God: for they are foolishness unto him: neither can he know them, because they are spiritually discerned"* (1 Corinthians 2:14). Spiritual realities exist in the fifth dimension, invisible to the natural eye and unreasonable to the natural mind.

This reminds me of a doctor who took Peter Cartwright aside and expressed his frustration about evangelistic preachers. He said, "Reverend Cartwright, I notice that you are always talking about how people should 'feel they are saved.' Don't you realize that feeling is only one of the five senses? Tell me something, Reverend Cartwright, can you put your religion to the test

---

* Bernard Ramm, in *Basic Christian Doctrines*, ed. Carl F. H. Henry (New York: 1962), pp. 63, 65.

of the other four senses? Have you ever seen salvation?''

Cartwright answered, ''No, but I have seen the evidences of salvation.''

The doctor continued, ''Have you ever heard salvation?''

''No.''

''Have you ever tasted salvation?''

''No.''

''Have you ever smelled salvation?''

''No.''

''Then, I have come to the conclusion, by your own admission, that you can only experience salvation by one of your five senses. Therefore, our community would be a lot better off if we didn't have preachers like you running around stirring people up, talking about 'feeling saved.'''

But Cartwright was no fool. He looked at the doctor and said, ''Doc, you've been a physician around this town for many years, haven't you?''

''Yes.''

''Tell me something. Have you ever seen a pain?''

The doctor was flabbergasted but replied, ''Well no, but I have seen the evidences of pain.''

''Then tell me, have you ever heard a pain?''

''No.''

''Have you ever tasted a pain?''

''No.''

''Have you ever smelled a pain?''

"No."

"Well, I have come to the conclusion that you doctors are just a bunch of quacks, always talking about pain. Our community would be a lot better off without you."

Unseen Beauty

There are unseen realities of the spirit world. Guardian angels are part of it. When you get to heaven you will see the splendor of the Supercity glowing supernatural energy, inhabited by holy angels and the saints from all ages who served God.

A beautiful girl was born blind. As she grew up the only beauty she knew of this world came from her mother's lips. Then one day a famous surgeon performed a series of operations on her eyes, with excellent results.

Finally the day came when the last bandages were removed. The little girl ran to her mother's arms, then moved carefully to the open door and the open window. As the beauty of that soft summer day broke in upon her for the first time, she ran back to her mother and with eyes shining with excitement and wonder said, "Oh, Mother, why didn't you tell me it was so beautiful?" Wiping away her tears of joy, the mother said, "My precious child, I tried to tell you, but I just couldn't do it."

One of these days, when we walk into that

city of gold, gleaming with the glory of God, we'll say, "John, why didn't you tell us it was this beautiful?" Then the Apostle will say, "I tried to tell you by using every adjective I knew. I said it was like transparent gold, like pearls, jasper, sapphires, and emeralds. I just ran out of words. I just ran out of words."

We Are His Heirs

Praise God, your glorious new home is waiting for you in heaven! So don't be discouraged over your struggles here on earth because you and I are God's children. *"And if children, then heirs; heirs of God, and joint-heirs with Christ: if so be that we suffer with him, that we may be also glorified together.*

"For I reckon that the sufferings of this present time are not worthy to be compared with the glory which shall be revealed in us" (Revelation 8:17,18).

I will share with you even more amazing discoveries about this Supercity in the next chapter.

The Super-Universe!

Fasten your seatbelt, because we're going for a ride! We're taking a journey across the glittering galaxies of this universe. Someone has said that a mind stretched by a new idea never returns to its original dimension. Prepare yourself, because this chapter, if I can borrow a teenagers's phrase, "really blows my mind!"

Our earth is one of nine planets revolving around the sun. It is about 8,000 miles in diameter and weighs about 6,600,000,000,000,000,000,000 tons. At this moment we are cruising through space at 66,000 miles per hour.

The distance from the earth to the moon is 250,000 miles while it is 93,000,000 miles to the sun.

The sun has a diameter of 866,500 miles and a mass that is 330,000 times the size of the earth.

However, the sun is only one star in a galaxy of over 100 billion stars, a galaxy that has a mass 70 billion times greater than the sun.

When we begin to move out into space, it becomes too cumbersome to use miles to measure the vast distances, so astronomers use a more practical unit called a light year. Light travels at the speed of 186,000 miles per second or approximately six trillion miles in one year. If you traveled at the speed of light (six trillion miles per year), it would take you 100,000 years to make one journey around our galaxy.

But our galaxy is only one of over one billion galaxies. One of the closest galaxies, the Andromeda, is 1,500,000 light years away.

If the astronomers are correct in saying that each galaxy contains 100,000 million stars, then the entire universe has some 150 million million million (150,000,000,000,000,000,000) stars.

The Bible says that God telleth the number of the stars; He calleth them ALL by their names. The Bible also says, *"When I consider thy heavens, the work of thy fingers, the moon and the stars, which thou hast ordained; What is man, that thou art mindful of him? and the son of man, that thou visitest him?*

"For thou hast made him a little lower than the angels, and hast crowned him with glory and honor. Thou madest him to have dominion over the works

of thy hands; THOU HAST PUT ALL THINGS UNDER HIS FEET" (Psalm 8:3-6).

The Bible says that God created man to rule the entire universe! So that all things, including outer space, will eventually be put under His feet.

But hang on! With the help of the giant Mount Palomar telescope and its 200-inch lens and by using highly sensitive film exposed for four and five hours at a time, astronomers have discovered hot burning masses of stars shooting outward in space that are 40 billion light years away and still moving outward!

(At this point I feel as helpless as a man trying to explain color television to a parakeet. These figures are simply beyond our comprehension.)

Multiply 40 billion times 6 trillion and you will have an incomprehensible figure showing the size of this still-expanding universe.

What really "sinks" me is when I read in the book of Isaiah that God measures or holds the width and the breadth (the entire distance) of the heavens in the span of his hand (Isaiah 40:12). A span is the distance from your little finger to your thumb. God holds the ever-expanding universe in the span of His hand— like a giant holding a tiny pebble in his palm!

No wonder the songwriter wrote, "Then sings my soul, my Savior God, to Thee." We must sing it from our souls because we could never grasp it with our minds.

Pioneering Outer Space

Today the planets of outer space would be very difficult to inhabit. Space probes to Mars and Venus have shown the atmosphere to be 98 percent carbon monoxide with temperatures ranging from hundreds of degrees above centigrade to nearly as many below. The heat and freezing temperatures combined with an atmosphere without oxygen have made these planets desolate.

However, there is an amazing statement found in Revelation where John says, *"And I saw a new heaven...for the first heaven [was] passed away"* (Revelation 21:1). I believe God is going to remake the heavens just as He remade the earth. *"In the beginning God created the heaven and the earth. And the earth was without form, and void; and darkness was upon the face of the deep. And the Spirit of God moved upon the face of the waters"* (Genesis 1:1,2).

Right here I must point out an error in modern-day prophecy teaching. When John says, *"And I saw a new heaven and a new earth: for the first heaven and the first earth were passed away"* (Revelation 21:1) he is not saying the earth is going to be burned up at the end of the millennium. Many prophecy teachers connect this passage with 2 Peter 3 where it says, *"The heavens being*

301

on fire shall be dissolved, and the elements shall melt with fervent heat" (verse 12).

What John is saying is that after Jesus has ruled for 1,000 years in peace and prosperity, the earth will have turned into paradise. In this way it will have become a new earth. It surely wouldn't make sense for God to burn up what it has taken Christ and His saints a thousand years to build. I believe the passage in 2 Peter 3 takes place during the Tribulation judgments when the stars fall from heaven according to Revelation 6:12. Peter even speaks of the events taking place within Chapter 3 as happening during the day of the Lord (see 2 Peter 3:10).

Just as God remade the earth in the beginning, I believe He will remake the heavens into a habitable place at the end of the Millennium. This will enable outer space to become a super-world.

This will give you an idea of what God has in mind regarding your life and mine. God is allowing us to go through the testings here so He can prepare us for leadership positions in His new kingdom.

A Seed Becomes A Tree

There is another scripture that confirms my belief about pioneering outer space. The Bible says, *"Of the increase of his government and peace there shall be no end"* (Isaiah 9:7). There is no way the kingdom of God could grow eternally and still be bound within the borders of this planet. With perfect peace, health and provisions plus the proper direction, the population of the world will explode.

The parable of the mustard seed strengthens this truth. *"The kingdom of heaven is like to a grain of mustard seed, which a man took, and sowed in his field: Which indeed is the least* [or smallest] *of all seeds: but when it is grown, it is the greatest among herbs, and becometh a tree, so that the birds of the air come and lodge in the branches thereof"* (Matthew 13:31,32).

Arthur Bloomfield, in his excellent book *All Things New* published by Bethany Fellowship says, "The kingdom started with one man; nothing could start smaller than that. It grows now by the spread of the gospel, but there is a limit to this kind of growth. During the Millennium, the kingdom will expand until it covers the earth. The stone, cut out without hands (referring to Daniel's vision in Daniel 2:35), will become a great mountain and fill the whole world. When this is accomplished, the mustard seed has become a full-grown plant....

"But this mustard plant keeps on growing even after it has reached its full size. *It becomes a tree, a great* tree; the birds of the air lodge in its branches. This was noted to emphasize the great size of the tree or to show that it was a tree and no longer a plant.

"So when the kingdom has reached its full-grown size on earth, it does not need to stop growing; other worlds become available. It is becoming automatic that what men can conceive in time, man can do. Even in a sinful state, man is actually planning space travel. Given a few years of peace and plenty, space travel will become a reality. When we have Millennial conditions and the help of God, the spread of the kingdom to outer space will be only a matter of course. Then the planet will have become a tree."*

Our Supernatural Bodies

If you and I are going to negotiate the great distances of space, we will need to overcome several obstacles. Someone has said, "Man has reached out to the stars, but his feet are shackled to time and space."

First, God will give us supernatural bodies. After His resurrection from the dead, Jesus had a new supernatural body. He was able to escape His grave bindings without disturbing them and He was able to pass through unopened doors.

---

* Reprinted by permission
  from *All things New*
  by Arthur E. Bloomfield
  Published and copyrighted 1959
  Bethany House Publishers
  Minneapolis, MN 55438

Do you remember how the disciples feared for their lives after the crucifixion? They were afraid they would be captured and crucified too. As they spoke in whispers behind the locked door, suddenly Jesus materialized before their eyes!

Jesus said, *"Peace be with you!"* Then He turned to Thomas (who declared he would not believe unless he actually touched the prints of the wounds in Jesus' hands and side) and said, *"Put your finger here; see my hands. Reach out your hand and put it into my side. Stop doubting and believe.*

"Thomas said to him, 'My Lord and my God!'

"Then Jesus told him, 'Because you have seen me, you have believed; blessed are those who have not seen and yet have believed'" (John 20:26-29, NIV).

Jesus Christ had a supernatural body that could move in both the spirit and the material world. Albert Einstein said that if any material substance could reach the speed of light, it would be able to pass through another substance without disturbing its molecular structure. In other words, if you could throw a baseball fast enough to reach the speed of light, theoretically it could pass through a brick wall without disturbing either the brick or the ball!

Jesus said, *"I am the light of the world"* (John 8:12). When God raised Jesus from the dead He gave Jesus a glorified body that could pass through locked doors. This is the same supernatural body you and I will have in the super-world. In his letter to the Philippian Christians, Paul said that Jesus *"shall change our vile body, that it may be fashioned like unto his glorious body"* (Philippians 3:21).

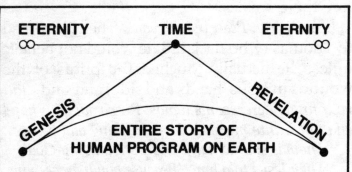

ETERNITY   TIME   ETERNITY

GENESIS   REVELATION

**ENTIRE STORY OF
HUMAN PROGRAM ON EARTH**

The drawings show the relationship between time and eternity. Try to grasp the difference between the LINE and the DOT. When you understand all of time is COMPRESSED INTO THAT DOT, you lay hold of the ingenious thing God has developed with His invention of time. In no way is eternity disturbed, and yet God is able to run out a complete program for man, using TIME as a separate medium. Time and eternity are two different ARENAS, where two different types of existence are experienced.*

Time Will Be Eliminated

The second change God will make is He will eliminate time. Einstein said, "If you travel at

---

* Reprinted by permission from
   Latest Word on the Last Days
   by C. S. Lovett
   © 1980

the speed of light, space shrinks to zero, time increases to infinity." When we begin to move in the Super-universe we will be moving at the speed of light and this will eliminate time. There won't be sundials, weather or calendars. You and I will live in the everlasting present!

Can you imagine the effects of timelessness? There will be no "then" because we will live in eternal "now." And there will be no "there" because all will be "here" in a universe filled with the glory of God.

Down through the years I have met many people who could have become great singers, artists, architects, teachers and leaders if they had only been given the time and opportunity to develop their talents. In the new world every child of God will be given the privilege of developing his abilities.

Henry Thomas, a great historian and writer, felt his need for more time. He had completed only two books of an intended six-volume work. At the time of his death, his last words were, "My books, my books." His plans were incomplete.

Victor Hugo said, "I feel in myself the future life. Winter is on my head, but eternal spring is in my heart. The nearer I approach the end, the plainer I hear around me the immortal symphonies of the world that invites me. For a half century I have been writing my thoughts in prose, verse, history, philosophy, drama, romance, tradition, satire, ode and song. I have tried all, but I feel that I have not said a thousandth part of what is in me. When I go down to the grave I can say like so many others, 'I have finished my day's work, but I cannot say I have finished my life's work.' My life's work will begin the next morning.

"The tomb is not a blind alley; it's a thoroughfare that closes on the twilight to open in the eternal dawn." Hugo had placed his faith in Jesus Christ and was ready to die, but he realized he needed more time! Can you imagine what men like Hugo, Michaelangelo, Raphael and others will accomplish in eternity?

If you need 10,000 years to become an architect, you've got it! You will have all the time and resources to make every one of your dreams come true.

A New Transportation System

Third, God will provide a new form of transportation. Even travel at the speed of light will be too slow for the needs of this expanding universe. We will probably travel at the speed of thought.

After Jesus arose from the dead He appeared to Mary. When she attempted to reach out to Him, Jesus said, *"Touch me not; for I am not yet ascended to my Father: but go to my brethren and say unto them, I ascend unto my Father, and your Father; and to my God and your God"* (John 20:17).

Let's not forget the distance Jesus would have to travel in just a few hours—the third heaven is beyond interstellar space—so that would be 40 billion light years multiplied by six trillion light years, a figure I cannot even total.

Yet Jesus traveled to the third heaven and back in just a few hours. Are you wondering how He did it? I believe He accomplished this by traveling at the speed of thought.

Think of it! Here on earth we began to travel by foot, then by horseback, then train, then aircraft, then spacecraft. With our new bodies we will move at the speed of light and finally at the speed of thought.

Sadhu Sundar Singh saw a vision of heaven and said, "In heaven, distance is never felt by anyone, for as soon as one forms the wish to go to a certain place he at once finds himself there. Distances are felt only in the material world. If one wishes to see a saint in another sphere, whether he is transported there in a moment of thought or at once, the distant saint arrives in his presence."

So with the heavens made new and with time and distance eliminated, you and I will enter a new frontier of existence.

Heaven Will Be A Learning Center

If you feel inadequate for what lies ahead, don't, because the Lord is going to teach you. The Bible says, *"And let us go up to the mountain of the Lord and He will teach us his ways"* (Micah 4:2). *"And all thy children shall be taught of the Lord"* (Isaiah 54:13).

You will have a chance to enroll in the Jesus university of heaven.

George Otis has written a great book entitled *The Millennium Man.* He suggests that in heaven we will study many interesting subjects:

Planet Management
Secrets of the Universe
Divine Principles
Celestial Music
Animal Management
Universal Laws
Cosmic Energy
Celestial Travel
Galaxy Pioneering*

Study is exciting when the subject is interesting and the teacher capable. Imagine attending class where Jesus Christ is our teacher. When the Lord begins to open to us the mysteries of this universe it will be so exciting you will be swept

---

* Reprinted by permission
from *Millennium Man*
by George Otis
© 1974

away with the joy of these new discoveries.

I also believe in heaven you will have an opportunity to develop in art, photography, true spiritual theatre, ice skating, opera, architecture and many more hundreds of subjects. Remember, God is preparing us to rule the universe.

A Doctor's View of Heaven

A medical doctor describes a life-after-life experience in which he visited heaven. (This experience is offered only as a glimpse of what might take place in heaven.) "I began to perceive the whole new realm. Enormous buildings stood in a beautiful sunny park and there was a relationship between the various structures, a pattern to the way they were arranged, that reminded me somewhat of a well-planned university.

"As we entered one of the buildings and started down a high-ceiling corridor lined with tall doorways, the air was so hushed I was actually startled to see people in the passageway. I could not tell if they were men or women, old or young, for all were covered from head to foot in loose-flowering hooded cloaks which made me think vaguely of monks. But the atmosphere of the place was not at all as like a monastery. It was more like some tremendous study center, humming with the excitement of great discovery.

Everyone we passed seemed caught up in some all-engrossing activity. Not many words were exchanged among them; and yet I sensed no unfriendliness between these beings, rather an aloofness of total concentration.

"Whatever else these people might be, they appeared utterly and supremely self-forgetful, absorbed in some vast purpose beyond themselves. Through open doors I glimpsed at enormous rooms filled with complex equipment. In several of the rooms hooded figures bent over intricate charts and diagrams, or sat at the controls of elaborate consoles flickering with lights.

"I prided myself a little on the beginnings of a scientific education; at the University I had majored in chemistry, minored in biology, studied physics, etc. But these were scientific activities of some kind. They were so far beyond anything I knew, that I couldn't even guess what field they were in. Somehow I felt that some vast experiment was being pursued— perhaps dozens and dozens of such experiments. I sensed that every activity on this mighty 'campus' had its source in God.

"And so I followed Him [Jesus Christ] into other buildings of this domain of thought. We entered a studio where music of a complexity I couldn't begin to follow was being composed and performed. There were complicated rhythms, tones not on any scale I knew. I found myself thinking, 'Why Bach is only the beginning!'

"Next we walked through a library the size of the whole University of Richmond, Virginia. I gazed into rooms lined from floor to ceiling with documents on parchment, clay, leather, metal and paper. The thought occurred to me, 'Here are assembled the important books of the universe.'

"Immediately I knew this was impossible. How could books be written somewhere beyond the earth? The thought persisted although my mind rejected it. The phrase 'The key works of the universe' kept recurring as we roamed the domed reading rooms crowded with silent scholars.

"Outside we moved again into the hushed park. Then into a building crowded with technological machinery.''*

As he continued his tour, the doctor became convinced that heaven is a place where people "have kept on growing."

So when you read on a tombstone "rest in peace," don't get the idea that heaven is some celestial rest home where they play spiritual

* *Return From Tomorrow*
  Copyright 1978
  George G. Ritchie, M.D.
  Published by Chosen Books Publishing Company
  Lincoln, VA 22078

Muzak while the residents slumber. Heaven is the Creative Center of the Universe where everything new and exciting happens first.

Athletics in Heaven

On the lighter side, I am convinced there will be sports in heaven. This was hard for me to handle at first because I had never thought of it. Remember Paul the apostle said, *"Eye hath not seen, nor ear heard, neither have entered into the heart of man the things which God hath prepared for them that love him. But God hath revealed them unto us by his Spirit"* (1 Corinthians 2:9,10).

I felt the Holy Spirit prompted me to include the mention of sports in this book. He reminded me of the time when Jesus was on earth, how He called the disciples apart for a time of rest and recreation. (See Mark 6:31,32.) As I thought of those 12 athletic men, fishermen, etc., I realized that they most certainly ran, played and laughed as they relaxed together with the Lord. Then the Holy Spirit reminded me that if we are going to eat in heaven (which is really an unnecessary function for people with supernatural bodies), why not run and play? Why not sports?

I began to share this illumination with my sister-in-law, Gloria Lundstrom, who once nearly died during a severe sickness. In a vision, she approached heaven. There she saw Jerry

Heinze, the son of Pastor B. C. Heinze who led so many of the Lundstroms and the Clair Brooks' family to the Lord. (Gloria is a Brooks.) Jerry Heinze had been a terrific athlete but died when he was a senior in high school, as his car was rammed from behind by a speeding driver.

When Gloria saw Jerry in the hallway of heaven, they greeted one another and then she asked, "What are you *doing* here? He looked at her with a "Don't-you-know?" look and said, "I'm coaching, of course."

This experience of Gloria's confirmed the illumination the Holy Spirit gave me about the reality of sports in heaven.

Visions May Be Telling Us Something

There are some Christians today who will deny the reality of any life-after-death experiences. They are quick to quote, *"It is appointed unto men once to die, but after this the judgment"* (Hebrews 9:27). But they never stop to realize this verse could never apply to someone who has returned from death because they never, in the truest sense, died in the first place.

I believe that God has allowed many Christians to reach heaven while clinically dead on an operating table or hospital bed, and return to encourage us to prepare. Why are doubters willing to accept Paul's life-after-life experience of 2 Corinthians 12, yet deny the realities of others who have been caught up to the third heaven?

Now, you don't have to accept every word of such an experience as "gospel"; for *"he that is spiritual judgeth all things"* (1 Corinthians 2:15)—but neither should you deny their experience. It could be God's way of giving you an exciting preview of what is ahead, provided the experience does not violate a basic Bible doctrine.

When Thomas Edison, the famous scientist and inventor, lay dying, he saw heaven and cried out, "It is very beautiful over there!" When D. L. Moody was dying, he said, "I have been within the gates and have seen the children, Dwight and Irene." (Dwight and Irene were two of his grandchildren whom he loved very much and had died years earlier.)

General Booth, founder of the Salvation Army had a vision of heaven and said he saw many angels and saints. He also described a celestial being as "human, yet angelic" in his beauty. He recognized this being as a friend who had died a number of years before.

Music Will be Great in Heaven!

Have you ever stopped to think of all the great musicians there are in heaven now? David, the Psalmist, Martin Luther, Handel and a host of others. *If* Beethoven, Bach and their creative contemporaries made it to heaven, it will surely be a musical experience.

The Bible says, *"I heard a voice from heaven as the voice of many waters, and as the voice of a great thunder: and I HEARD THE VOICE OF HARPERS HARPING WITH THEIR HARPS: And they sang...a new song before the throne"* (Revelation 14:2,3).

"And [the] *elders fell down before the Lamb, HAVING EVERY ONE OF THEM HARPS...and they sang a new song saying, 'Thou are worthy...for thou hast redeemed us to God...and hast made us kings and priests: and we shall reign on the earth"* (Revelation 8:8-10).

Now, I am certain the sounds we will hear in heaven will be more than that of harps and voices. John the apostle would never have understood the musical sounds of today because they would have been foreign to him. But one thing is certain—there will be a lot of music in the new world.

An Unexpected Visitor

Several years ago a minister in Montana had an unusual experience. One day as he was praying, the Holy Spirit impressed him that he was more concerned about his own church than he was about the kingdom of God in his city. He needed to begin praying for other churches to be blessed as much or more than his own. So for the next three months he began to cry out to God in prayer for the needs of the churches in his community.

This minister is a friend of mine and a great hunter. One morning, he was making his way up the Rockies to hunt elk when he noticed a man about a quarter of a mile away, making his way down the mountain toward him. In this remote area it was very unusual for any hunter to be going *down* at 10 o'clock in the morning. This is when the hunters are slowly working their way *up* to where the elk roam.

My friend stopped to watch the approaching stranger. He was impressed by how quickly the man moved across the terrain. There were six or eight inches of freshly fallen snow; yet the man moved at an amazing speed. He was also wearing a dress coat and hat—most unusual for anyone in this desolate area. But what made the chills run down the minister's spine was when he noticed the approaching man was not making any footprints in the snow.

When the stranger approached my friend, he said, "Do you know me?" My friend almost said, "No," but he noticed an unusual twinkle in the man's eye and a look he had never seen before. My friend answered, "Yes, I know you. You are a servant of the Lord."

The stranger said, "Yes, I am. The Lord sent me down today because He has been hearing your prayers and is very happy with the way you have been praying."

Then the angel looked around and surveyed the scene: The morning sun shining on the snow-covered Rockies is a breathtaking experience. He said, "It's really beautiful up here today, isn't it?"

"Yes," the minister replied.

The angel's eyes twinkled again as he smiled and said, "But you should have seen the place I came from this morning."

There was a large snow-covered rock a few yards away and the angel motioned toward it. Both of them walked over and sat down. Then the angel began to tell my friend things about the kingdom of God and ways in which he could expand the work of God to help more people to find God.

One truth stands out from their conversation. The angel remarked, "When you get to heaven and you've been with God for a million years and you think you know everything about Him, He will roll back the curtain and reveal Himself to you in a way that will take another million years to learn. This will go on forever and ever."

The minister doesn't know how long they visited, but finally the angel rose to leave. Then something very personal took place. From the days this pastor was a small boy, he had always prayed that the Lord would be proud of him. He would close each prayer with "Lord, I want You to be proud of me." As the angel was leaving, he added, "And one more thing, the Lord told me to tell you He's proud of you!"

In a few moments the angel was gone. As the minister stood at the edge of the mountain reflecting at what had happened, he looked back at the rock where they had been visiting. He noticed the snow on the rock was not disturbed, and the visitor had not left any footprints. Then he noticed something else: He had not left any footprints in the snow either!

My friend had been in the fifth dimension. The dimensions of time, space, mind and matter had not limited him in the supernatural realm. This is the way it will be in eternity. We won't be limited by time, space or matter. In our new home we will learn of God for millions and billions of years. We will build new worlds. We will create. We will grow and mature. We will be co-administrators of the universe. We will become one with God until the words of Jesus are fulfilled *"To him that overcometh will I grant to sit with me in my throne"* (Revelation 3:21).

Then the words of the Psalmist David will be complete, *"Thou madest him to have dominion over the works of thy hands; thou hast put all things under his feet"* (Psalm 8:6).

All things includes the universe—inner space, present space, outer space and eternal space.

This is why Jesus said, *"He that overcometh shall inherit all things"* (Revelation 21:7).

Pray that nothing will rob you of your great inheritance.

23

Living Now So It Counts Later — Part 1

Throughout this book I have shared with you the prophecies and promises of what's coming next. Because time is so short (this could be the last chapter I ever write and the last chapter you ever read), I'd like to challenge you with a question: How should we live now so it counts *later?*

Now you understand why God has placed you here on earth. This planet is just a training camp for the new world that is coming. God is allowing you to go through trials and testings to develop you into a leader suitable to reign upon the throne with Jesus Christ.

Just as God allowed His own son to go through the winepress of sorrow and suffering to prepare Him for the throne, so He is allowing you to suffer and be tempted so you will be ready to rule. The Bible says of Jesus, *"Who in the days of his flesh, when he had offered up prayers and supplications with strong crying and tears unto him that was able to save him from death, and was heard in that he feared;*

"Though he were a Son, yet learned he obedience by the things which he suffered; And being made perfect, he became the author of eternal salvation unto all them that obey him" (Hebrews 5:7-9).

So, just as the earthly sufferings of Jesus made Him perfect (by experience), your sufferings will perfect your life so you will be ready when God exalts you to the throne. This is why the Bible says to *"Count it all joy when ye fall into* [many different] *temptations; Knowing this, that the trying of your faith worketh patience. But let patience have her perfect work, that ye may be perfect...and wanting nothing"* (James 1:2-4).

The New International Version renders this passage, *"Consider it pure joy, my brothers, whenever you face trials of many kinds, because you know that the testing of your faith develops perseverance. Perseverance must finish its work so that you may be mature and complete, not lacking anything."*

An Unseen Lesson

Lead, South Dakota, is the home of one of the largest gold mines in America. But if you did not know what was happening there, you might think the operation was one noisy failure.

The heavy equipment, the deafening noise, the dust, the mud, the deaths of miners, the tension and strain upon the workers, the frustration, etc., don't seem to add up to anything worthwhile. But if you wait until the process is completed, you will see shiny bars of gold worth millions of dollars. This is what the entire operation is all about.

The same is true of planet earth. As you study history, you will see how it repeats its cycle of misery and woe. Wars and death, suffering, struggles, tears, fears, agony, etc., have caused the skeptics and unbelievers to dismiss life as a tragic blunder. Frederick Roleinson, dying at 32 said, "It is all a mystery; man is like a candle blown out by a puff of wind." Keats, the famous poet, dying at 22 wrote his epitaph, "Here lies one whose name is writ in water."

However, as a Christian you have an understanding of life that unbelievers don't have. YOU CAN SEE THE UNSEEN LESSON IN LIVING. You can see that God's purpose is to prepare you for the world to come. Therefore, as you are being prepared, you already get more out of life than nonchristians can ever imagine. Actually, this world is one giant mine where God is digging out "soul gold" for His kingdom.

This is why Peter the apostle declares, *"In this you greatly rejoice, though now for a little while*

you may have to suffer grief in all kinds of trials.
These have come so that your faith—of greater worth
than gold, which perishes even though refined by
fire—may be proved genuine and may result in praise,
glory and honor when Jesus Christ is revealed"
(1 Peter 1:6,7, NIV).

Learn to Rejoice

So, if you are a Christian, rejoice over every
event that takes place in your life—good or bad.
Pain is the process that perfects you for His
glory.

"I walked a mile with Pleasure
    She chattered all the way,
But left me none the wiser
    For all she had to say.

I walked a mile with Sorrow;
    And ne'er a word said she;
But, O, the things I learned from her
    When Sorrow walked with me."*

When you are going through a trial, don't
forget the glories that await you! Remember
the throne. Remember heaven. Remember the
superworld ahead of you.

---

* Author Unknown
  Reprinted by permission from
  Don't Waste Your Sorrows
  by Paul E. Billheimer
  © 1977
  Christian Literature Crusade, Inc.
  Fort Washington, PA

This is why Paul wrote, *"I consider that our present sufferings are not worth comparing with the glory that will be revealed in us. The creation waits in eager expectation for the sons of God to be revealed. For the creation was subject to frustration, not by its own choice, but by the will of the one who subjected it..."* (Romans 8:18-20, NIV).

In other words, Paul says that even nature itself is frustrated for the moment, anxious for the day when God completes His program of redemption and you and I are revealed in glory.

And don't worry that the strain of your trials are too much for you or that you are the victim of circumstances. The Bible says, *"And we know that in all things God works for the good of those who love him, who have been called according to his purpose. For those God foreknew he also predestined to be conformed to the likeness of his Son"* (Romans 8:28,29, NIV).

Everything that happens to you, even the evil things, God will work for good so that you can become like Jesus. This doesn't mean that *all* things *are* good, but God is great enough to *work* them for good. So when you cry and complain over a tough situation in your life, and even accuse God of being unfair for allowing you to get trapped in an unfair situation, you are actually resisting the process of suffering that will make you perfect.

If you are living in a hellish situation say,

"Hallelujah, I'm here! God is working something wonderful in my life." This attitude will deliver you from your self-imposed frustrations.

We Are Predestined

The word of God continues, *"And those he predestined, he also called; those he called, he also justified; those he justified, he also glorified.*

"What, then, shall we say in response to this? If God be for us, who can be against us? He who did not spare his own Son, but gave him up for us all— how will he not also, along with him, graciously give us all things?" (Romans 8:30-32, NIV).

Now, there is a life-changing truth in these scriptures. It reveals God's plan for your life even before He created the world. Throughout the Bible you can read about The Book of Life. When Moses interceded for the children of Israel, he pled with God saying, *"If thou wilt not forgive their sin...I pray thee, blot me out of thy book which thou hast written"* (Exodus 32:32,33).

Jesus said, *"He that overcometh, the same shall be clothed in white raiment; and I will not blot out his name out of the book of life, but I will confess his name before my Father, and before his angels"* (Revelation 3:5).

However, Revelation 17:8 reveals a mind-boggling truth. The Bible says that the wicked *"whose names were not written in the book of life from the foundation of the world,"* shall wonder after the beast, the antichrist. Here we see that before God created the earth He made up The Book of Life and wrote in it the names of the people He wanted in His kingdom. Then He created the world, and His kingdom has orchestrated events ever since to accomplish His goal of a completed company of believers. When God has mined enough "soul gold" here on planet earth, once the company of the committed is completed, God will shut things down and move unto the next phase of building the superworld.

Now, it blesses me to think that my name has been written down in The Book of Life even before the world was formed. How about you? If you are a Christian, God has had you in mind even before creation and He is carefully watching over events in your life, doing everything He can to accomplish His perfect purpose. So don't complain if God is allowing something difficult or painful. *Rejoice, for pain is the process to make you perfect!*

We Must Overcome

Now, don't let the doctrine of predestination bother you. In no way does it lead to a false security, for Jesus said in Revelation 3:5 that a man *must overcome* or He will blot his name out of The Book of Life. In Exodus 32:33 *"The Lord said unto Moses, Whosoever hath sinned against me, him will I blot out of my book."*

You cannot sit back as a Christian and say, "Well, I'm saved. Everything is all right now. I don't have anything to worry about." Jesus says that even though your *name is in The Book of Life it will be blotted out unless you overcome.* There is a popular lie today that says you can live in sin and still be saved. Nothing could be further from the truth. It was Satan who proposed that lie to Eve in the Garden of Eden. He said, *"You shall not surely die."* But Eve sinned and she died. Jesus said, "Overcome and I will not blot your name out of The Book of Life" (see Revelation 3:5).

We Must Bury Our Will

There is one basic concept of Christianity that must be pointed out here. That is the necessity of death to self-will. Jesus said, *"Except a corn of wheat fall into the ground and die, it abideth alone: but if it die, it bringeth forth much fruit"* (John 12:24).

Whenever the trials of life and the temptations of the flesh begin to close in on you, your flesh is sure to cry, "Help! This is going to kill me!" You're right! In one way it will kill you so that something greater can come forth.

Jesus said your life is like a living seed. Before you are converted you are just a shell, a husk, a dead seed without life. But when you are "born again" (see John 3:3), you receive the life of God. But this is not the final step in God's converting process. God wants you to plant your living seed in the soil of His perfect will so that you will die to yourself and come forth even greater than before.

So many times, after a man is born again, he will rise from his knees and say, "Now I can get on with living." Shortly afterward he is amazed to find that even though he has the living Christ abiding within him, even though he has now become a living seed, there are still habits of the flesh like temper, pride, lust, greed, jealousy, etc., that are pressing for position in his life.

He realizes in a sense he has become a spiritual "Jekyll and Hyde." He has Christ plus his self-nature struggling for first place in his heart. He becomes like the Indian man who went to the white missionary and said, "White preacher, I've got a dogfight inside of me. I have a big black dog that wants to do bad and a big white dog that wants to do good."

This missionary asked, "Which one wins?"

The Indian replied, "The one I feed the most."

Jesus goes one step further. He says you must *bury* your living seed or it will not multiply. *"Except a corn of wheat fall into the ground and die, it abideth alone: but if it die, it bringeth forth much fruit"* (John 12:24).

Chances are there are areas in your life that

must be buried. There are things that must die before you will ever become a fruitful Christian. This is the meaning of these verses:

"Don't you know that all of us who were baptized into Jesus Christ were baptized into his death? We were therefore buried with him through baptism into death in order that, just as Christ was raised from the dead through the glory of the Father, we too may live a new life.

"If we have been united with him in his death, we will certainly also be united with him in his resurrection. For we know that our old self was crucified with him so that the body of sin might be rendered powerless, that we should no longer be slaves to sin—because anyone who has died has been freed from sin.

"In the same way, count yourselves dead to sin but alive to God in Christ Jesus. Therefore do not let sin reign in your mortal body so that you obey its evil desires. Do not offer the parts of your body to sin, as instruments of wickedness, but rather offer yourselves to God, as those who have been brought from death to life; and offer the parts of your body to him as instruments of righteousness" (Romans 6:3-7, 11-13, NIV).

If you want to live *now* so it counts *later*, you MUST die to self. You must plant your living born-again seed in the soil of God's perfect will. This is the only way you will bring forth a great spiritual harvest.

A Modern Parable

Just imagine a little yellow kernel of corn happily surrounded by his corn buddies. They are laughing and having a great time rolling around in the sack. Then one day someone cries, "I hear the farmer coming!"

"Oh no, I'm afraid it's happening!" cries another.

"What?" asks the little yellow kernel.

"You mean you don't know?" says another. "The farmer is going to bury us."

All the kernels begin to weep and cry as they say goodby to one another.

Suddenly the farmer's rough hand plunges down into the sack and the little yellow kernel is first to go. After a brief trip he is plunged into a hole in the ground, alone.

He begins to wail, "I'm dying! I'm dying! I can't see a thing. It's dark and cold and I'm being smothered by all this black stuff!"

The days drag by and the grief overwhelms the seed. All he can think of is the "good old days" when he had so much fun in the sack with all of his buddies. But now he is plunged into a world of darkness against his will, smothered by yucky black stuff. Why, if there is a God in heaven, did this happen?

But one day he feels a strange sensation going through him. Something is moving. Something is gnawing in him. He has never felt this way before! He feels a supernatural swelling and suddenly—kerplunk! A sprout starts growing out of him.

"Amazing!" he says to himself. Then day after day the sprout reaches upward until at last it breaks through to the sunshine.

"Wow! I can see the sun again," the kernel cries. "But I don't look like I used to."

As the days and weeks continue, the shoot reaches for the sky. The kernel is ecstatic. "Hallelujah!" he shouts. He looks around at his buddies, and they are happy too. They are all there, growing next to him.

Then one day small ears of corn begin to grow on his stalk. He can hardly believe it. Within weeks there are 800 to 1,200 duplicates of himself on the ears. "Fantastic!" he cries. "And to think I was afraid to die."

Before long, harvest comes and the grown cornstalk bows before the farmer and sighs, "Thanks for putting me under. This is the greatest thing that could have happened to me."

God gave me this parable for you, friend. You are going to have to die if you want to multiply. But like the kernel of corn, you will rise and reproduce greater life as a result.

Avoid the Get-by Philosophy

How should you live now so that it counts

later?

Maintain your spiritual life. Don't become careless about your Bible reading and prayer. Remember, only one in ten Christians has as little as ten minutes with the Lord each day. You dare not gamble with your soul.

Jesus said, *"The kingdom of heaven will be like ten virgins who took their lamps and went out to meet the bridegroom. Five of them were foolish and five were wise. The foolish ones took their lamps but did not take any oil with them. The wise, however, took oil in jars along with their lamps. The bridegroom was a long time in coming, and they all became drowsy and fell asleep.*

"At midnight the cry rang out: 'Here's the bridegroom! Come out to meet him!'

"Then all the virgins woke up and trimmed their lamps. The foolish ones said to the wise, 'Give us some of your oil; our lamps are going out.'

"'No,' they replied, 'there may not be enough for both us and you. Instead, go to those who sell oil and buy some for yourselves.'

"But while they were on their way to buy the oil, the bridegroom arrived. The virgins who were ready went in with him to the wedding banquet. And the door was shut.

"Later the others also came. 'Sir! Sir!' they said. 'Open the door for us!'

"But he replied, 'I tell you the truth, I don't know you.'

"Therefore keep watch, because you do not know the day or the hour!" (Matthew 25:1-13, NIV).

The tragic mistake of the foolish virgins in this story is *they tried to get by!* They thought they didn't need the extra oil. But their get-by philosophy cost them dearly. They were shut out of the kingdom.

If you are trying to "get by" spiritually without regular Bible reading and prayer, you are a fool. There is NO WAY you will be prepared for death or the coming of Jesus Christ.

Even the beautiful and exciting truths I have shared about heaven and the superworld to come will not be real to you unless you have a fresh supply of the oil of the Spirit in your life.

Don't be like the foolish virgins. Seek God for an overflowing supply of the Holy Spirit in your life. This will help to keep your light burning as the world grows darker around us.

How to Prepare for Christ's Return

There are three areas of your life you must concentrate on if you are to be prepared for our Savior's return.

First, *you must seek to glorify God in everything you do.* The danger of living today is that you can become so comfortable that you are no longer effective in fulfilling God's will for your life. A large insurance company took a nationwide survey of thousands of Americans and discovered that 97 percent listed their #1 goal in life as comfort and security.

Christian, God did not place you here on earth to be comfortably secure. God placed you here to establish His kingdom on earth. John the apostle saw the elders in heaven worshiping the Lord saying, *"Thou are worthy, O Lord, to receive glory and honor and power! for thou hast created all things, and for thy pleasure they are and were created"* (Revelation 4:11).

Your life is not meant to be lived for your pleasure, but God's! It may sound cruel, but actually you should not be concerned whether you feel good, bad or in-between. The important thing is to glorify God and bring pleasure to Him. *"And when you seek His kingdom first, all the other things will be added to you"* (see Matthew 6:33).

Are you glorifying God in your body? Do your weight, your dress, your habits and mannerisms glorify the Lord? Do the things you say and the thoughts you think honor God? An unforgettable question is, "If you cannot rule your own body, how will you ever qualify to rule the world?"

No Pain—No Gain

If you are an average person you want comfort and security. But if you want to be a kingdom builder for God, you should desire pain and risk.

Because if there is no pain, there will be no gain.

You *can* lose weight if you are determined to endure pain. You *can* quit an ugly habit if you are willing to suffer. *You will become what God means you to be if you will be willing to hurt.*

The Bible says of Jesus, *"Who for the joy that was set before him endured the cross, despising the shame, and is set down at the right hand of the throne of God"* (Hebrews 12:2).

When you think you have it tough, think of heaven. Remind yourself that the prize is worth the suffering. Be willing to be *hard* on yourself. Paul wrote, *"Endure hardness, as a good soldier of Jesus Christ"* (2 Timothy 2:3).

Remember, if you cannot rule your own body you will never rule the world. And if you have no desire to rule, you have failed the purpose for which God created you. I know this sounds hard, but remember: NO PAIN—NO GAIN. If you hurt while doing God's will, shout hallelujah, for great will be your reward in heaven.

Glorify God by Learning

Paul wrote, *"I...cease not to give thanks for you, making mention of you in my prayers; That the God of our Lord Jesus Christ may give unto you the spirit of wisdom and revelation in the knowledge of him:*

"The eyes of your understanding being enlightened; that ye may know what is the hope of his calling...and what is the exceeding greatness of his

power to us who believe" (Ephesians 1:16-19).

You need to know, and you learn by study. The tragedy of today is that the average Christian only reads for 7½ minutes a day. This includes all newspapers, magazines, etc. Compare this with the five and one-half hours the TV is on in the average Christian home. You can easily see why the world has evangelized the Church instead of the Church evangelizing the world.

If you do not like to study, begin now. Make a pledge to God that you will use your brain for the glory of God. Paul said, *"Study to show thyself approved unto God, a workman that needeth not to be ashamed, rightly dividing the word of truth"* (2 Timothy 2:15).

Glorify God in Your Marriage

The reason why so many married couples live boring, useless lives is that they have failed to discover God's purpose in their marriage.

The reason God brings you together with someone else is so you can win more people to Christ. If you marry just for selfish reasons, to have security or to enjoy love and sex, you have missed what marriage is all about. You have only married for passion. However, if you marry to glorify God, to establish a Christian family, to support your church, conduct Bible studies, to raise children for God, then you will find your marriage to be an excellent one.

When was the last time you prayed together as a couple? When did you last conduct a Bible study in your home? When was the last time you prayed with your children? When did you last lead another couple to Jesus Christ?

Remember, if you cannot establish the kingdom of God in your own home, how will you ever qualify to rule on a throne?

Glorify God on Your Job

My heart literally aches as I write these words, because 90 percent of the Christian people I have surveyed across the United States and Canada do not enjoy their jobs. They are working just for the money to make a living. What a travesty upon the dignity of man!

Remember, as a child of God, the only job you want to have is one where you can glorify God. This doesn't mean it is a spiritual place. But it is a place where you can work without compromising your principles or ideals. If you are only working for money or the boss, you need to start working for God's glory. Ask yourself if you are really working where God wants you to work. If you cannot answer affirmatively, then pray until you know for certain where God wants you to be employed. Don't waste your years working just for money.

Now, there may be an interim period where you may have to work at a job you don't enjoy while you are training for one you do enjoy. But overall, don't waste your precious life doing something you don't enjoy.

Here is a suggestion: Do what you don't want to do while you are learning to do what you really want to do.

In other words, keep studying, learning, applying yourself and advancing. Don't get stuck on a dead end job. It doesn't matter how miserable your situation is, you can study books, listen to cassette tapes, listen to others, and even take a course by mail to learn a trade you really would love to perform.

Some time ago I was in Washington, D. C., and I took a yellow taxicab from the airport to my hotel. During the trip I asked the young driver how he liked his job and he said, "I hate it!" When I inquired why, he said he wanted to be a mechanical engineer, but was married, was the father of a baby and had to work to make a living. Then I suggested, "Why don't you get some books and tapes and apply at a nearby school for a home-study course to get started toward your goal. If you will use all of your spare time studying while you are waiting for customers, you will get a big start on your career. You can turn this cab into a 'MOBILE YELLOW UNIVERSITY.'"

He thanked me over and over again and drove

off with a smile because I had shown him the way out of his frustrating situation.

You will never be any good at a job unless you love it. If you don't love your work, pray until you find out what God's will is for your life. Then begin training for it as soon as you can. You can study books and listen to tapes until you are good enough to get a start in the area of your ability. Jesus said, *"The kingdom of God is like a man going on a journey, who called his servants and entrusted his property to them.* [Remember your life is God's property.]

"To one he gave five talents of money, to another two talents, and to another one talent, each according to his ability. Then he went on his journey.

"The man who had received the five talents went at once and put his money to work and gained five more. So also, the one with the two talents gained two more. But the man who had received the one talent went off, dug a hole in the ground and hid his master's money.

"After a long time the master of those servants returned and settled accounts with them. The man who had received the five talents brought the other five. 'Master,' he said, 'you entrusted me with five talents. See, I have gained five more.'

"His master replied, 'Well done, good and faithful servant! You have been faithful with a few things; I will put you in charge of many things. Come and

share your master's happiness!'

*"The man with the two talents also came. 'Master,'
he said, 'you entrusted me with two talents; see, I
have gained two more.'*

*"His master replied, 'Well done, good and faithful
servant! You have been faithful with a few things; I
will put you in charge of many things. Come and
share your master's happiness!'*

*"Then the man who had received the one talent
came. 'Master,' he said, 'I knew that you are a hard
man, harvesting where you have not sown and
gathering where you have not scattered seed. So I
was afraid and went out and hid your talent in the
ground. See, here is what belongs to you.'*

*"His master replied, 'You wicked, lazy servant! So
you knew that I harvest where I have not sown and
gather where I have not scattered seed? Well then,
you should have put my money on deposit with the
bankers, so that when I returned I would have received
it back with interest.'*

*"'Take the talent from him and give it to the one
who has the ten talents. For everyone who has will be
given more, and he will have an abundance. Whoever
does not have, even what he has, will be taken from
him. And throw that worthless servant outside, into
the darkness, where there will be weeping and
gnashing of teeth"* (Matthew 25:14-30, NIV).

Notice and never forget the tragedy of the
one-talent man. He was afraid to take a risk.
With 97 percent of the American people wanting

comfort and security, it is easy to fall into the rut of a job where you are financially secure, but you are not fulfilling God's will for your life.

God is trying to prepare you to rule the world. He wants you to rule your body, rule your marriage and family and rule your job to find life's work worthy of your calling.

Now let me tell you in the next chapter about two other areas you should concentrate on as you prepare for Jesus' return.

24

Living Now
So It Counts Later —
Part 2

The second way to prepare yourself for the Lord's appearing is to win others to Christ and minister unto them.

Surveys have shown that 95 out of 100 Christians have never led another person to Jesus Christ. Is it any wonder that attending church gets to be "old hat"? Jesus said, *"Go ye into all the world, and preach the gospel to every creature"* (Mark 16:15). Jesus has given you the divine commission to evangelize the world. This is why winning others to Christ should be your "magnificent obsession."

Sexual desire is natural for a healthy person because it results in the reproduction of the human race. However, when you are born again, God gives you a holy desire to reproduce Christ, to see others won to Him. If you lose this desire it reveals you are not living as close to God as you should.

344

There is a life-changing passage of scripture in Isaiah 6. The prophet describes here the experience that led him to help others become followers of God:

"In the year King Uzziah died, I saw the Lord seated on a throne, high and exalted, and the train of his robe filled the temple.

"'Woe to me!' I cried. 'I am ruined! For I am a man of unclean lips, and I live among a people of unclean lips, and my eyes have seen the King, the Lord Almighty.'

"Then one of the seraphs flew to me with a live coal in his hand...With it he touched my mouth and said, 'See, this has touched your lips; your guilt is taken away and your sin atoned for.'

"Then I heard the voice of the Lord saying, 'Whom shall I send? And who will go for us?'

"And I said, 'Here am I, Send me!'" (Isaiah 6:1, 5-8, NIV).

The lesson is obvious. When Isaiah saw God clearly, it prompted him to confess all of his sins and volunteer to help others. The reason many Christians feel so little compassion for the lost is that they have drifted away from God.

In one of the most shocking passages of scripture God warns that He will hold a believer accountable for failing to witness. *"Son of man, I have made you a watchman for the house of Israel; so hear the word I speak and give them warning from me. When I say to the wicked, 'O wicked man, you will surely die,' and you do not speak out to dissuade him from his ways, that wicked man will die for his sin, and I will hold you accountable for his blood"* (Ezekiel 33:7,8, NIV).

Think how grievous it will be to stand before God and give account for those you failed to reach! And imagine having those individuals blame you for their damnation!

You need to have the philosophy of a janitor in Minneapolis who said, "Lowell, I'm not a janitor. I'm a full-time soul winner. I'm just mopping this building to pay the bills."

Regardless of your occupation, when you become a Christian, you are called of God to win others to Jesus Christ on a full-time basis. Your secular job is your part-time employment.

Minister to the Unsaved

The second part of your obligation to others is to minister to them. Here is what Jesus said about ministering to others. Read this carefully:

"When the Son of Man comes in his glory, and all the angels with him, he will sit on his throne in heavenly glory. All the nations will be gathered before him....

"Then the King will say..., 'Come, you who are blessed by my Father; take your inheritance, the kingdom prepared for you since the creation of the world. For I was hungry and you gave me something to eat, I was thirsty and you gave me something to

drink, I was a stranger and you invited me in, I needed clothes and you clothed me, I was sick and you looked after me, I was in prison and you came to visit me.'

"Then the righteous will answer him, 'Lord, when did we see you hungry and feed you, or thirsty and give you something to drink? When did we see you a stranger and invite you in, or needing clothes and clothe you? When did we see you sick or in prison and go to visit you?'

"The King will reply, 'I tell you the truth, whatever you did for one of the least of these brothers of mine, you did for me.'

"Then he will say to those on his left, 'Depart from me, you who are cursed, into the eternal fire prepared for the devil and his angels. For I was hungry and you gave me nothing to eat, I was thirsty and you gave me nothing to drink, I was a stranger and you did not invite me in, I needed clothes and you did not clothe me, I was sick and in prison and you did not look after me.'

"They also will answer, 'Lord, when did we see you hungry or thirsty or a stranger or needing clothes or sick or in prison, and did not help you?'

"He will reply, 'I tell you the truth, whatever you did not do for one of the least of these, you did not do for me.'

"Then they will go away to eternal punishment, but the righteous to eternal life" (Matthew 25:31-46, NIV).

Jesus pointed out that on Judgment Day, you and I will give account for those we have ministered unto:
* For those we have fed
* For the strangers we have taken into our home
* For the people we have clothed
* For the sick we have visited
* For the prisoners we have ministered to in jail.

Record Your Service to Others

Now it is easy to skip over your obligation to others. So with your help and cooperation, I want to help penetrate an area in your life that you maybe have never faced as a Christian.

To how many poor people do you bring groceries each week?

☐ 5   ☐ 1   ☐ None

How many strangers do you bring into your home, or how much do you give towards providing a place where they are taken care of?

☐ 5   ☐ 1   ☐ None

How many people per week receive clothing because of your help?

☐ 5   ☐ 1   ☐ None

How many sick people do you visit each week?

☐ 5   ☐ 1   ☐ None

How many visits have you made to prisoners during the past month?

☐ 5   ☐ 1   ☐ None

Now, my point in asking you to record your activities is to reveal where you really are when it comes to serving your fellowman. Jesus said that on Judgment Day, the people who did not care for others will be cast into eternal punishment. If you faced judgment today and these criteria were applied to your life, would you make it?

Faith and Works Go Together

Many will say, "But I'm saved by grace." Yes, you are saved by grace, but a truly saved person gets involved in helping others. Good works do not save you from sin, but good works show you have had a change of heart. Others dismiss this scripture in Matthew 25 by saying that it refers to the judgment of the nations. It does, but remember that God will never expect from a nation something He does not expect from an individual, especially a professing Christian. James the apostle wrote, *"Faith without works is dead"* (James 2:20).

He also said, *"What good is it, my brothers, if a man claims to have faith but has no deeds? Can such faith save him? Suppose a brother or sister is without clothes and daily food. If one of you says to him, 'Go, I wish you well; keep warm and well fed,' but does nothing about his physical needs, what good is it? In the same way, faith by itself, if it is not accompanied by action, is dead"* (James 2:14-17, NIV).

349

This passage makes my heart tremble, because the Holy Spirit inspired the Apostle James to put his finger on the area of my life that is most convenient to ignore—my ministry to others. But Jesus and James agree. It we do not care for others our faith is phony and our punishment will be terrible.

Develop Your Character

The third way you can prepare for the Lord's return is by developing your character into what God intends it to be.

Your character is what you have made of yourself. Recently, one of America's most well-known entertainers was hospitalized for an overdose of heroin. As he lay in his hospital bed, he had a long talk with himself and concluded, "Self, I'm sorry for what I've done to you." If you are living in a way that lessens your dignity, you need to apologize to yourself. God created you to rule and reign upon the throne with Christ. If you are allowing anything in your life that makes you unfit for the throne, then stop it.

We have been given a way to build our character so it is like God's character. This way is through the precious Word of God.

The Apostle Peter declared, *"Whereby are given unto us exceeding great and precious promises: that by these ye might be partakers of the divine nature, having escaped the corruption that is in the world through lust"* (2 Peter 1:4).

If you want your inner nature to be similar to God's character, then you must study and meditate on God's Word. The reason is that God's Word is part of His own self. Jesus said, *"Except ye eat the flesh of the Son of man, and drink His blood, ye have no life in you"* (John 6:53). Just as Jesus Christ was God wrapped in skin, the Bible is God wrapped in print.

Think of it this way. The real essence of a man is not his body but his words and deeds. The same is true of God. The Bible says, *"In the beginning was the Word* [truth; thought or concept], *and the Word was with God, and the Word was God. And the Word was made flesh, and dwelt among us"* (John 1:1,14). When you read the Word of God you are actually partaking of His essence. This is why Jesus said, *"Man shall not live by bread alone, but by every word that proceedeth out of the mouth of God"* (Matthew 4:4). Just as your body consumes food calories, your spirit consumes the Word of God. If you want to weigh more, you eat more. If you desire to have the character of God, you spend more time in His Word.

Paul wrote, *"I beseech you therefore, brethren, by the mercies of God, that ye present your bodies a living sacrifice, holy, acceptable unto God, which is your reasonable service.*

"And be not conformed to this world [pressed into the world's mold], *but be ye transformed by the renewing of your mind, that ye may prove what is that good, and acceptable, and perfect, will of God"* (Romans 12:1,2).

Your character will be transformed as you fill your mind with holy truth. If you allow your schedule to get too busy for Bible reading and prayer, you will become like good seed choked by thorns: *"He that received* [the] *seed among the thorns is he that heareth the word; and the care of this world, and the deceitfulness of riches, choke the word, and he becometh unfruitful"* (Matthew 13:22).

However, our Savior encourages you saying, *"He that received seed into the good ground is he that heareth the word, and understandeth it; which also beareth fruit, and bringeth forth, some an hundredfold, some sixty, some thirty"* (Matthew 13:23).

If you want your character to become 30, 60 or 100 times more like God, His Word is the answer. This is why Paul said, *"Let the word of Christ dwell in you richly"* (Colossians 3:16).

Let the Holy Spirit Dwell in You

Another way you become like God is through the indwelling of the Holy Spirit.

Remember when James and John became angry at a village of ungrateful Samaritans and wanted to call down fire from heaven on it? Jesus rebuked them saying, *"Ye know not what manner of spirit ye are of. For the Son of man is not come to destroy men's lives, but to save them. And they went to another village"* (Luke 9:55,56).

When the villagers insulted Jesus, He was so humble that He simply went to another town.

Another glimpse of Christ's humility was shown at the Last Supper. *"Jesus knowing that the Father had given all things into his hands, and that he was come from God, and went to God; He riseth from supper, and laid aside his garments: and took a towel, and girded himself. After that he poureth water into the bason, and began to wash the disciples' feet..."* (John 13:3-5).

At the moment Jesus had the fullest revelation that He had come from God, when he realized that God had given and was to give all things into His hands, He knelt down and washed feet. He began to serve His disciples like a slave.

How different this is from the religious crowd of today who want "their rights" and seek to be exalted. Jesus revealed that when you are most filled with God, when you are most like your Creator, you serve. You wash dirty feet. If Christians could see this clearly and make it our lifestyle, we would convert the world to Jesus Christ in a few short years.

Needless to say, the disciples were transformed by walking with Jesus. However, there is an amazing statement in John 16 where Jesus told His disciples, *"I tell you the truth; It is expedient* [or better] *for you that I go away: for if I go not away, the Comforter will not come unto you; but if I depart, I will send him unto you...when he, the Spirit of truth, is come, he will guide you into all truth...he will* [show] *you things to come"* (John 16:7,13).

The great power that brought out the character of Jesus was the Holy Spirit. As Jesus neared the end of His ministry, He realized how important it was for you and me to have the same power dwelling in us. This is why He said it was better for Him to go away because He would then be able to send the Holy Spirit.

"I will pray the Father, and he shall give you another Comforter, that he may abide with you for ever; Even the Spirit of truth; whom the world cannot receive, because it seeth him not, neither knoweth him: but ye know him; for he dwelleth with you, and shall be in you. I will not leave you comfort-less" (John 14:16-18).

Each time the disciples had a problem or a question they would come to Jesus and have it solved. The thought of Jesus dying and returning to heaven shattered their dreams of a new kingdom.

But Jesus said, "It is better for you that I go away." Why? Because if Jesus had set up His kingdom in Jerusalem after His resurrection, anyone who ever wanted to know Him would have to travel to Israel and set up an appointment.

Just imagine under those conditions that a young man in Iowa wants to know Jesus. He must save his money to raise $1,000 for the air fare and accommodations. However, when he arrives in Tel Aviv, the airport is so jammed with people he can hardly move. He boards a crowded bus for Jerusalem and when he arrives, there is such a mob of people he has to fight his way to the temple.

There an old man greets him with the words, "It's no use, my boy. You'll never get to see Jesus. I came here 25 years ago to see Him but there are so many millions trying to get an audience with Him, that I haven't gotten in yet."

The young man is shocked at the thought that he cannot see Jesus. Finally, one of the temple attendants confirms his worst fears. If he wants to see Jesus, he must come back in 30 years.

Now do you see why Jesus said He must go away? The lesson is simply this: Jesus said He would pray the Father would send the same Holy Spirit upon us that was sent upon Him. In other words, Jesus would come into us by the Holy Spirit.

So now you don't have to travel to Jerusalem to know Jesus personally. You don't have to visit London, New York, Montreal, Chicago or

Minneapolis. You can know Jesus right where you are now. Through the Holy Spirit, Jesus is closer to you than this book in your hand.

If you will allow the Holy Spirit to have control of your life, He will accomplish the same purpose as if Jesus lived with you 24 hours a day. If you yield your body to the Holy Spirit, He will be your personal coach, your private tutor who will build your character so that you become exactly like Jesus.

Paul writes, *"You were taught with regard to your former way of life, to put off your old self, which is being corrupted by deceitful desires; to be made new in the attitude of your minds; and to put on the new self, created to be like God in true righteousness and holiness.*

"Therefore each of you must put off falsehood and speak truthfully to his neighbor, for we are all members of one body.

"In your anger do not sin: Do not let the sun go down while you are still angry, and do not give the devil a foothold. He who has been stealing must steal no longer, but must work, doing something useful with his own hands, that he may have something to share with those in need.

"Do not let any unwholesome talk come out of your mouths, but only what is helpful for building others up according to their needs, that it may benefit those who listen.

"And do not grieve the Holy Spirit of God, with

whom you were sealed for the day of redemption. Get rid of all bitterness, rage and anger, brawling and slander, along with every form of malice. Be kind and compassionate to one another, forgiving each other, just as in Christ God forgave you. Be imitators of God" (Ephesians 4:22-5:1, NIV).

As you fill your mind with God's Word and your spirit with the Holy Spirit, you will become truly Christian in your character.

Resist Evil

Finally, your character is built strong by your resistance to evil.

Character is saying "No" when the flesh and the devil say "Go." It is also saying "Go" when the flesh and the devil say "No." You must come under the command of Christ to become a world-changer.

In Arabia they train purebred Arabian horses to be ridden by the sheiks. The trainers work weeks and months with the finest horses, preparing them in every way.

The final test is an unusual one. Each day throughout the months of training, they water the horses from a trough approximately 100 yards away from the corral. Before the horses are chosen for the sheik, they are locked in their corral for days without drink. As the hot sun burns down upon them, they begin to stomp, snort and press against the corral, trying to get to the water.

Finally, the gate is opened and they stampede toward the water trough. But half way there, the trainer whistles the signal to return to his side. At that moment the decision is made about which horses the sheik will ride. Most of the horses continue racing toward the water trough; only one or two have the courage it takes to overcome their thirst and obey the trainer's command.

Do you want to carry the King? Do you desire the honor of becoming God's chosen instrument? Do you want to rule and reign with Christ? Then you *must* resist evil. You *must* deny your strongest lusts. You *must* command your body to obey God at all times. The costs are very high.

But the prize is worth it!

Years ago one of the pioneers of the Indianapolis 500, Andy Granitelli, brought a new race car to the track. It was powered by a turbine engine that made a "whooosh" sound when it went by. They nicknamed this strange new car "Silent Sam" because of the unusual noise it made.

The car was a great success during the time trials, and it led the big race on Memorial Day weekend until it was within a few laps of the checkered flag.

Then it stopped.

When the car was pulled into the pit, the crew was so disheartened they didn't even look at the engine. The driver told them it had blown up. The cloud of oil coming out the exhaust confirmed his report.

The next day the mechanics tore the engine apart and discovered a small $1.50 part had worked out of place and ruined the engine. Because of that one piece, they had lost the race.

God has lined up many spectacular events for the future—the Millennium when the saints rule the world; heaven where the saints will enjoy the city of God; eternity when the saints will rule the superworld, etc. Whatever you do, don't allow a small part of your life to get out of place so that it costs you the race.

Remember, *"Seeing we are compassed about with so great a cloud of witnesses* [the hosts of heaven, the departed saints and billions more than have ever watched the Indianapolis 500], *let us lay aside every weight, and the sin which doth so easily beset us* [the $1.50 part], *and let us run with patience the race that is set before us.*

"Looking unto Jesus the author and finisher of our faith; who for the joy that was set before him endured the cross, despising the shame, and is set down at the right hand of the throne of God" (Hebrews 12:1,2).

It Is Worth It

Remember, the throne of God is waiting for you. Jesus promises, *"To him that overcometh will I grant to sit with me in my throne, even as I also overcame, and am set down with my Father in his throne''* (Revelation 3:21).

And what's coming next? Jesus says, *"He that overcometh shall inherit everything!"* (see Revelation 21:7).

By God's grace and mercy, I will see you in the winner's circle!

We hope reading this book has been a meaningful experience for you.

Lowell Lundstrom has produced many other books, albums and cassette tapes for your personal growth and enjoyment. Please look over the following pages to see all the helpful material that is available to you.

LOWELL
LUNDSTROM
Ministries, Inc.
Sisseton, SD 57262

	PRICE	QTY	TOTAL PRICE
How To Pray With Power And Get Results	4.00	___	_____
How You Can Enjoy Supernatural Prosperity	3.50	___	_____
Heaven's Answer For The Home	3.50	___	_____
Lowell—The Story Of Lowell Lundstrom And His Ministry	3.50	___	_____
What's Coming Next? (Bible Prophecy)	4.95	___	_____
The Wind Whispers Warning (Bible Prophecy)	2.95	___	_____
The Muslims Are Coming (Bible Prophecy)	2.95	___	_____
How To Get Up When You're Down	2.00	___	_____
Our Favorite Recipes (contains over 400 special recipes)	9.95	___	_____
Rendezvous With Victory (Story about God's healing power over cancer)	.75	___	_____
How You Can Know You Are Saved For Sure	1.25	___	_____
Power For Living Tract Pack (16 life changing counseling aids)	1.95	___	_____
"Air Mail Storybook"—32 Boy's Devotionals	3.50	___	_____
"Air Mail Storybook"—32 Girl's Devotionals	3.50	___	_____
God's Promises For Your Every Need— (Contains the plan of salvation and 81 promises of God bound together in red leather. There are 3,400 scriptures, dealing with worry, depression, lust, etc., practical for today's living. Pocket size—made to carry in a lady's purse or a man's inside coat pocket)	19.95	___	_____

TOTAL COST_____

BONUS SPECIAL!! For your book order of $15.00 or more, you will receive FREE a personally selected ministry book.

Name _____

Address _____

City_____ State_____ Zip _____

Phone(_____)_____

Please return this coupon with your check or money order (in U.S. currency) made payable to:

FRESH RAIN PRODUCTIONS
P.O. Box 332, Sisseton, South Dakota 57262

LOWELL LUNDSTROM
MUSIC ORDER FORM

	QUANTITY			PRICE EACH	TOTAL PRICE
	8 TRACK	CASSETTE	L.P.		
Moving Ahead	_____	_____	_____	7.98	_____
The Great Gospel Classics	_____	_____	_____	7.98	_____
A Fresh Touch	_____	_____	_____	7.98	_____
Londa	_____	_____	_____	7.98	_____
Down Home Feeling		_____	_____	7.98	_____
Music, Music, Music		_____	_____	7.98	_____
The Very Best Of The Lundstroms		_____	_____	7.98	_____
Old Time Christmas Favorites		_____	_____	7.98	_____
Best Of Christmas (Double Album)			_____	11.98	_____
Just For Kids—Children's Album (Soon to be released—Nov. '82)		_____	_____	7.98	_____

SONGBOOKS

You Gave Me A Song	_____	4.00	_____
The Lundstrom Songbook #5, #6 or #8	_____	2.00	_____
Christmas Songbook	_____	2.00	_____

SOUNDTRACKS

All soundtracks are $7.00 each (list available on request)

TOTAL COST _____

SPECIAL: Buy 4 records—Get 1 FREE!
My "FREE" selection: _____
(except "Best of Christmas" double album)

Please Print

Name _____

Address _____

City_____ State_____ Zip _____

Phone(_____)_____

Please return this coupon with your check or money order (in U.S. currency) made payable to:

FRESH RAIN PRODUCTIONS
P.O. Box 332, Sisseton, South Dakota 57262

LOWELL LUNDSTROM
CASSETTE TAPE ORDER FORM

	PRICE EACH	QTY	TOTAL PRICE
The "**Family Life**" **Seminar**: 10 cassette series dealing with how to have a happier home. Lowell Lundstrom and his ministry staff give honest, down-to-earth answers for your home and marriage.	$39.95	___	_____
The "**Family Life**" **Seminar**: 4 cassette packet containing the most requested sessions from the 10 cassette series.	$15.95	___	_____
The "**Living to Win**" **Seminar**: 10 cassette series. Lowell and his ministry staff share exciting Biblical principles that will help you be a winner with God.	$39.95	___	_____
The "**Living to Win**" **Seminar**: 4 cassette packet containing the most requested sessions from the 10 cassette series.	$15.95	___	_____
The Lowell Lundstrom "**Pastor's**" **Seminar**: 6 cassette series. This series will be a tremendous help and encouragement to your pastor and will give him a spiritual lift.	$24.00	___	_____
The Lowell Lundstrom "**Crusade Cassette Library**": 8 cassette series. Contains Lowell's most requested crusade sermons to uplift, guide and strengthen your life.	$32.00	___	_____
The **New Testament Bible, King James Version**: 16 cassette series in a handsome vinyl case. The perfect way for you to listen to God's Word while driving, working or relaxing. Also effective for those who have difficulty reading.	$49.95	___	_____
All single ministry tapes (write for a complete listing).	$ 4.00	___	_____
	TOTAL COST		_____

BONUS!! Receive "FREE" with your tape order of $39.95 or more, the challenging 60-minute cassette, "Secrets That Will Help You Win Your Loved Ones To Christ."
_____ (check to receive)

Please Print

Name _____

Address _____

City_____ State_____ Zip _____

Phone(_____)_____

Please return this coupon with your check or money order (in U.S. currency) made payable to:

FRESH RAIN PRODUCTIONS
P.O. Box 332, Sisseton, South Dakota 57262

God has used Lowell Lundstrom to reach millions of people for over 25 years through books, seminars, area-wide crusades, radio and television. He is a noted evangelist, author, singer, husband and father of four children. Lowell has personally counseled thousands of people. The ministry books, albums and cassette tapes offered on the preceding pages reflect his understanding of people's needs and how to help them through their difficulties.

Millions of lives have been ministered to through these inspired items. They are being used in home Bible studies, Sunday school classrooms and for personal enjoyment. Because they are founded on Biblical principles, you will find inspiration and discover many answers to struggles in your life. You can also minister to friends and loved ones by giving these items as gifts.

As a special offer to you, we will send these ministry items to you at no charge for postage and handling.